INSTRUCTOR'S MANUAL AND TEST BANK

TO ACCOMPANY

BUILDING VOCABULARY SKILLS, Short Version, 4/e

IMPROVING VOCABULARY SKILLS, Short Version, 4/e

ADVANCING VOCABULARY SKILLS, Short Version, 4/e

JANET M. GOLDSTEIN

THE TOWNSEND PRESS VOCABULARY SERIES

Vocabulary Basics (reading level 4–6)
Groundwork for a Better Vocabulary (reading level 5–8)
Building Vocabulary Skills (reading level 7–9)
Improving Vocabulary Skills (reading level 9–11)
Advancing Vocabulary Skills (reading level 11–13)
*Building Vocabulary Skills, Short Version**
*Improving Vocabulary Skills, Short Version**
*Advancing Vocabulary Skills, Short Version**
Advanced Word Power (reading level 12–14)

*The short versions of the three books are limited to 200 words, in contrast to the 260 words and 40 word parts in each of the long versions. For some students and classes, the short versions of the books will provide an easier, more manageable approach to vocabulary development.

Printed in the United States of America
9 8 7 6 5 4 3 2 1

ISBN-13: 978-1-59194-206-1
ISBN-10: 1-59194-206-3

For book orders and requests for desk copies or supplements, contact us in any of the following ways:
By telephone: 1-800-772-6410
By fax: 1-800-225-8894
By e-mail: cs@townsendpress.com
Through our website: www.townsendpress.com

Contents

BUILDING VOCABULARY SKILLS, Short Version: Additional Unit Tests 61

IMPROVING VOCABULARY SKILLS, Short Version: Pretests and Posttests 69

IMPROVING VOCABULARY SKILLS, Short Version: Answers to the Activities in the Book 97

IMPROVING VOCABULARY SKILLS, Short Version: Additional Mastery Tests 101

IMPROVING VOCABULARY SKILLS, Short Version: Additional Unit Tests 123

ADVANCING VOCABULARY SKILLS, Short Version: Pretests and Posttests 131

ADVANCING VOCABULARY SKILLS, Short Version: Answers to the Activities in the Book 159

ADVANCING VOCABULARY SKILLS, Short Version: Additional Mastery Tests 163

ADVANCING VOCABULARY SKILLS, Short Version: Additional Unit Tests 185

APPENDIXES

The Townsend Press Vocabulary Placement Test 193

Introduction

BRIEF GUIDELINES FOR USING THE VOCABULARY BOOKS

1. As you probably know, each of the three vocabulary books has a recommended reading level:

Building Vocabulary Skills, Short Version: reading grade level 7–9
Improving Vocabulary Skills, Short Version: reading grade level 9–11
Advancing Vocabulary Skills, Short Version: reading grade level 11–13

Be careful not to choose a book on too high an instructional level. Ideally, most of your students should have a sense of *some* of the words in the book you choose. As they work through the chapters, they can then strengthen their knowledge of the words they already know, as well as master the words they're only half sure of, or don't know at all. To help you choose the appropriate book, you can give students the TP Vocabulary Placement Test, offered online or reprinted on pages 193–198 of this *Instructor's Manual.*

A given level is likely to be too difficult if students know almost none of the words. You run the risk of operating on a level of frustration rather than instruction. *To repeat, then: Please take very special care that you choose a book that will not be too difficult for the majority of your students.*

2. Don't feel you must cover every single chapter in a book. Each book is packed with activities—ones that will take a fair amount of time for students to work on at home, or for you to cover with them in class. The activities are necessary, for the simple truth is that the more students work with words, the better they will understand them. *It is better to cover fewer words more thoroughly than to try to cover too many too lightly.*

3. The "Final Check" passage in each chapter poses a more difficult challenge for students than the sentence-level activities that precede it. To handle the passages, students must have done their homework with the earlier activities. The passage will be an excellent final opportunity for them to deepen their knowledge of the words in the chapter.

Because the final check is such a challenge, as well as an opportunity to solidify learning, you should *not* use it as a mastery test. Instead, use the appropriate mastery test in this manual.

4. The pages in the student book (though not in the instructor's edition) are perforated and so can be easily torn out and removed. In particular, you may want students to hand in the unit tests, which are on the front and back sides of a page.

5. Pretests are available for each book as well as each vocabulary unit in each book. The pretests start on page 7 of this *Instructor's Manual.* You have permission to make as many copies as you want of these pretests (and the other materials in this book) if you are currently using one of the vocabulary texts in a course. The pretests can be used at the start of a unit, and the posttests at the end of a unit, as an accurate way to measure vocabulary progress and mastery.

A SUGGESTED INSTRUCTIONAL APPROACH

Here is a suggested classroom approach that will maintain interest and keep students active in learning the words. You may want to use all or part of it—or you may find that it helps you decide the special way you want to teach the words to your students.

First of all, have students work through the introduction to the book (on pages 1 to 6). Don't teach it; have them *read* it (they need the reading practice!), follow directions, and insert all the answers needed. Then spend a few minutes reviewing their answers and checking their understanding of the material.

Next, give students the pretest for the unit you will be covering. Explain that at the end of the unit, they will be given a posttest on the same words, so you and they will be able to measure what they have learned. Then proceed as follows:

1. Preview each of the ten words in a chapter by printing the words, one at a time, on the board. Ask students if they can pronounce each word. As needed, write some of the pronunciations on the board. You may also want to use, or ask students to use, some of the words in sentences. And it's OK to ask for or to give short meanings of some of the words. Don't go into a lot of detail, but make this a good general introduction to the words.

Then, based on the verbal preview, ask students to turn to the first page of the chapter. Explain that in each case the two sentences in "Ten Words in Context" will give clues to the meaning of the boldfaced word. You can say, "OK, take five minutes or so and read the sentences in "Ten Words in Context." Or you can proceed immediately to Step 2.

2. Put students in groups of two or three. (It is hard to overstate the value that small-group work can have: if managed successfully, it uses peer pressure to keep everyone involved in the work of the class.) Explain, "Here's what I want you to do. One of you read the first word and the two sentences that contain the word. Make sure the word is being pronounced correctly. Always help each other out with the pronunciation. Then think about the context very carefully. The context will give you very strong clues as to what the word means. Your ability to use the context surrounding an unfamiliar word is an excellent skill to have whenever you're reading something and you come upon a word you don't know. Then I'd like all of you to see if you can pick out the right meaning from the three answer choices that follow that first word.

"After you do that, have someone else in your group pronounce the second word and read the two sentences for that word. Then work together again and pick out the right answer choice. And so on, until you've done all ten words. Look up at me when you've done all the words."

3. Of course, not every group will finish the words at exactly the same time. Therefore, you should take a middle-ground approach to the challenging fact that every group will move at a different speed. When a couple of the groups are finished (and starting to get restless), and others are still working, say, "OK—even if you're not quite finished yet, we're going to go over the ten words as a class. Somebody please volunteer to pronounce the first word and give us its meaning."

4. After reviewing the pronunciations and meanings of the words, ask your students to complete the "Matching Words with Definitions" activity. They'll need these definitions to complete the remaining activities in the chapter, so be sure that students have the correct definition for each word.

5. Once you have checked their answers to the matching activity, say, "Now I want you to work as a group in adding the words needed in Sentence Check 1 and Sentence Check 2. Again, you want to practice *looking at context* very carefully. Context will give you clues you need to figure out the meanings of words."

6. When several groups are finished, say, "OK, not everyone is quite finished, but we're going to go over the sentences you've been working with. Will someone volunteer to read the first sentence and insert the word needed?"

7. Next, say, "The last activity here is the most challenging. Why don't you all work on this individually. Read over the passage once. Then go back and start reading more carefully and slowly, and try to put in some of the words. Then go back a third time to get the remaining words. You may not be able to get all the words at first. Try to get some of them. That will help you do the rest. Pay close attention to the context. Remember you're building up your skill at using context to figure out the meaning of a word."

8. When some people are finished, say, "All right—let's review the passage. Would someone read the first couple of sentences and insert the missing words?"

9. Finally, tell students to review and study the ten words at home. Then, at the beginning of the next class, say, "Spend about two minutes reviewing the words. I'll then pass out a mastery test for the ten words. I will grade this test, so you want to do your best to remember the words." (Knowing that a grade is going to be involved always provides students with an extra boost of incentive.)

An alternative instructional approach is to proceed as described above for steps 1 to 4. Then, instead of having students work in small groups, ask them to work individually on Sentence Check 1 and Sentence Check 2. After they are finished, have them come individually to your desk so that you can quickly check their answers, clarify any confusion, and move them on to the Final Check. In this individualized scenario, everyone is working at his or her own pace, and you are working at a *very* steady pace. When students finish the Final Check, you can either have them work with people who are not done, or get a head start on another chapter that you plan to assign for homework.

ADDITIONAL ACTIVITIES

To repeat a point stated earlier: *The more students work with words, the more they can learn.* Here are other activities you can use, in addition to the many in the book. Choose whichever combination of activities goes best with your teaching style and the learning styles of your students.

1. Word cards. Students can use 3 × 5 or 4 × 6 index cards to create a bank of words. Word cards can help students master words in the book; the cards are also a helpful tool for learning unknown words that students come across in reading. Students simply jot down an unfamiliar word on the front of the card. Then, when they have finished their reading, they can complete the front and back of a card. Here is a suggested format:

Front of Card

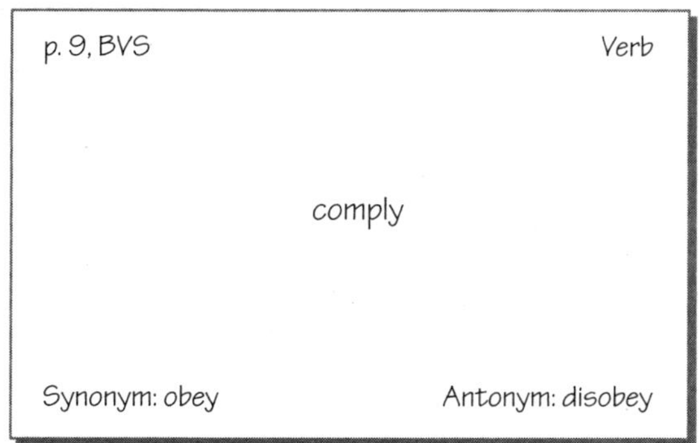

Back of Card

1) To do as commanded or asked.

2) "My wife is so used to being the boss at work," Ray said, "that she gets annoyed when I don't comply with every request she makes at home."

3) Our teacher expects us to comply with his instructions without asking any questions.

Note that the front of the card has the target word, the page number and source where the word can be located, the part of speech, a synonym, and an antonym. The back of the card has three entries: 1) the *definition*, based on the way the word is used in context; 2) a *phrase or sentence* showing the word in context (this can be taken from the source where the student has come upon the word); and 3) a *student-created sentence* which shows an understanding of the word. Students can use this same format when they encounter unfamiliar words in their textbooks and other reading.

2. Identifying words. Present lists of words written with diacritical marks and ask students to identify the words. For example:

tăk′tĭk ____________________
rĭ-kûr′ ____________________
ĭ-kwāt′ ____________________
mă-lĭsh′əs ____________________
rĭ-sĭp′rə-kāt ____________________

3. Analogies. Using analogies is another way to encourage students to think about words. Students should first be taught the format of analogies, and instructors should begin with the simpler types of analogies: synonyms and antonyms. For example:

Choose the italicized word needed to complete each analogy:
acknowledge : admit = avert : *cure, prevent, accept*
candid : dishonest = concise : *wordy, brief, funny*
precise : methodical = stop : *terminate, speculate, nurture*
modern : obsolete = pacify : *mediate, hamper, infuriate*

Keep in mind that analogies are difficult for students, especially at-risk students. But if instructor guidance is provided, analogies can help even at-risk students think about words conceptually.

Note that pages 5 and 6 in the introduction to the book explain how analogies work. Also, Unit Test 4 in each unit contains twenty word analogies.

4. Imaging. The use of imagery as a way of remembering vocabulary words has been researched rather extensively. Results typically indicate that students who are trained to use imagery techniques—or in simple terms, told to "form pictures in their minds"—remember the meanings of words better than those who do not employ such techniques.

Here's an example: Think of a mugger facing you, his hands clutching a long, heavy piece of gray pipe. On the pipe are written in dripping red paint the letters C-O-M-P-L-Y. You are handing over your wallet.

It's a good idea to take five or ten minutes every once in a while for students to get a piece of paper and write up their images—the more vivid the better—for remembering a given word in a chapter. Then ask students to hand in the paper (signing their names to the paper is optional). Quickly flip through the papers, reading the most effective ones aloud to the class.

5. Generating sentences. Have students generate their own sentences using the words, or as a more advanced activity, have them write a story using five of the words. (You may want to have a paraprofessional working with you for these activities, which require individual checking and detailed feedback.)

6. Group-Label. This more abstract activity is best used after students have a larger word bank from which to work. It might be used at the end of a unit of five vocabulary chapters. Students are asked to classify words into groups and to give each group a label that would be common somehow to all words in that group. Here are examples:

Words related to honesty (BVS, Unit One)	*Words relating to conflict (IVS, Unit One)*
acknowledge	animosity
candid	antagonist
impartial	assail
integrity	exploit
legitimate	malign

SUGGESTED SYLLABI

Suggested Syllabus for Using the Book as a Core Text

Since each book consists of 20 chapters packed with activities, it can easily serve as a core text for a vocabulary course—especially when supplemented by the test bank and the online exercises. In a 15-week class that meets three hours a week, you can cover slightly more than one chapter a week. The remaining time can be used for the unit tests that close each of the four units in each book, as well as for the pretests, posttests, mastery tests, and the additional material available online.

It is important that students be encouraged to do a lot of reading at the same time that they are learning vocabulary words. For students who need to develop vocabulary skills, widespread reading, in addition to continuing, intensive work on vocabulary, is the best way to achieve this purpose.

Suggested Syllabus for Using the Book as a Supplement in a Reading Course

In many courses, the vocabulary book will serve as a supplementary text. In such cases, and assuming a 15-week term with three hours of class a week, one hour a week can be devoted to vocabulary. In part of that hour, go over the first three pages in class, using a method similar to the one we have described on pages 2–3 of this manual. Assign the last part of the chapter (Sentence Check 2 and the Final Check) for homework. Then, as the first item of business in the next class, review that material. Follow up the review with the appropriate mastery test from this manual. In this manner, 14 or 15 chapters can be covered in class.

Assign as homework the remaining five or six chapters, one or two per unit. Then, at the end of each unit of five vocabulary chapters, give students one of the four vocabulary unit tests in the book. The unit test will enable you to hold students responsible for the outside-of-class vocabulary chapters as well.

You might want to tell students in advance that you will give them one of the unit tests. However, don't tell them *which* of the four tests you will give. Encourage them, in other words, to review all of the words in the unit test materials.

If there is not enough time in class to give the unit tests, you can ask students to do all four of the unit tests at home. Then, in class, collect and grade *one* of the four. (Again, students should not know which of the four you will collect. That way, they will have to assume responsibility for working with all of the words.)

ABOUT THE ONLINE EXERCISES

After students complete a vocabulary chapter in the book, they can deepen their learning by going to **www.townsendpress.com** and clicking on "Online Learning Center." Here, they will find two additional tests for each chapter in each Townsend Press vocabulary book: one testing *words in context*, the other (more advanced) testing the *meanings of the words without context.*

These online tests contain a number of user- and instructor friendly features, including actual, audible pronunciations of each word; brief explanations of the answers; a sound option; a running score at the bottom of the screen; and a record-keeping file. Students can access their scores at any time; instructors can access student scores and print score reports for individuals or entire classes. The advanced features of the Online Learning Center allow instructors to assign additional online tests based on exercises and tests in the books, drop students from and add students to a class roster, choose which explanations a student may view, and scramble the items in a particular test.

Here are more details about the features of this powerful online program:

- Frequent use is made of the user's first name—a highly motivational word to any student!
- Every answer is followed by a brief explanation of that answer. Such explanations help ensure learning. Thus the software *teaches* as well as tests.
- A running score appears at the bottom of each screen, so the user always knows how well he or she is doing.
- A score file, available to each student and to the instructor, shows or prints out the user's final scores.

POWERPOINT PRESENTATIONS

PowerPoint presentations are available for each book and may be downloaded from the "Supplements" area for instructors at **www.townsendpress.com**.

ABOUT THE WORD LISTS

As stated in the preface, word frequency lists were consulted in selecting the vocabulary words used in each book in the TP Vocabulary Series. Two sources in particular should be noted:

Word Frequency Book—John B. Carroll, Peter Davies, and Barry Richman
The American Heritage Publishing Company, Inc.

The Living Word Vocabulary—Edgar Dale and Joseph O'Rourke
World Book–Childcraft International, Inc.

Also consulted were lists in a wide number of vocabulary books as well as words in standardized reading tests. In addition, the authors and editors prepared their own lists. A computer was used to help in the consolidation of the many word lists. Group discussion then led to final decisions about the words that would be most appropriate for students on each reading level.

RESEARCH AND VOCABULARY INSTRUCTION

Sherrie Nist has prepared an article offering suggestions on vocabulary instruction in the context of current research on vocabulary development. Some of the article has been incorporated into this introduction. The article, which includes an extensive bibliography, is available at no charge by writing to Townsend Press.

A FINAL NOTE

The authors and editors invite you to share with us your experiences in using the Townsend Press vocabulary books. This series is not a static project; it will continue to be revised on a regular basis, and we welcome your suggestions as well as details about your ongoing classroom experiences with the texts. Send your comments to the Vocabulary Series Editor, Townsend Press, 439 Kelley Drive, West Berlin, NJ 08091; or email us at **cs@townsendpress.com**. By learning your reactions and your students' reactions, we can work at making what we feel are very good books even better.

BUILDING VOCABULARY SKILLS

Pretest

NAME: ____________________

SECTION: __________ DATE: __________

SCORE: ____________________

This test contains 100 items. In the space provided, write the letter of the choice that is closest in meaning to the **boldfaced** word.

Important: Keep in mind that this test is for diagnostic purposes only. **If you do not know a word, leave the space blank rather than guess at it.**

____ 1. **compel** **a)** avoid **b)** delight **c)** force **d)** finish

____ 2. **drastic** **a)** dirty **b)** suitable **c)** extreme **d)** sticky

____ 3. **comply** **a)** choose **b)** forget **c)** run into **d)** do as asked

____ 4. **acknowledge** **a)** prevent **b)** admit **c)** study **d)** deny

____ 5. **concise** **a)** peaceful **b)** clear and brief **c)** proper **d)** wordy

____ 6. **isolate** **a)** combine **b)** heat up **c)** separate **d)** freeze

____ 7. **fortify** **a)** suggest **b)** strengthen **c)** avoid **d)** approve of

____ 8. **extensive** **a)** bold **b)** separated **c)** outside **d)** large in space or amount

____ 9. **refuge** **a)** shelter **b)** rejection **c)** building **d)** garbage

____ 10. **erratic** **a)** inconsistent **b)** mistaken **c)** in a city **d)** noisy

____ 11. **morale** **a)** spirit **b)** principle **c)** threat **d)** majority

____ 12. **lenient** **a)** heavy **b)** not strict **c)** delayed **d)** not biased

____ 13. **undermine** **a)** weaken **b)** cross out **c)** reach **d)** dig up

____ 14. **menace** **a)** character **b)** threat **c)** assistance **d)** puzzle

____ 15. **impartial** **a)** without prejudice **b)** not whole **c)** hidden **d)** strict

____ 16. **endorse** **a)** suggest **b)** stop **c)** support **d)** start

____ 17. **imply** **a)** approve of **b)** interfere **c)** do mischief **d)** suggest

____ 18. **obstacle** **a)** barrier **b)** remedy **c)** list **d)** answer

____ 19. **novice** **a)** book **b)** false impression **c)** beginner **d)** servant

____ 20. **hypocrite** **a)** interference **b)** insincere person **c)** injection **d)** threat

____ 21. **superficial** **a)** lacking depth **b)** perfect **c)** very deep **d)** faulty

____ 22. **denounce** **a)** introduce **b)** condemn **c)** change **d)** compliment

____ 23. **transition** **a)** purchase **b)** invention **c)** repetition **d)** change

____ 24. **sustain** **a)** keep going **b)** approve of **c)** avoid **d)** wait for

____ 25. **conservative** **a)** not definite **b)** opinionated **c)** resisting change **d)** understanding

(Continues on next page)

____ 26. **compensate** **a)** change **b)** win out **c)** receive **d)** repay

____ 27. **verify** **a)** imagine **b)** prove **c)** keep going **d)** cancel

____ 28. **surpass** **a)** go beyond **b)** reverse **c)** take **d)** prove wrong

____ 29. **tentative** **a)** suitable **b)** not final **c)** outside **d)** definite

____ 30. **diversity** **a)** separation **b)** conclusion **c)** enthusiasm **d)** variety

____ 31. **prudent** **a)** rudely brief **b)** careful **c)** obvious **d)** delicate

____ 32. **apprehensive** **a)** uneasy **b)** thoughtful **c)** relaxed **d)** opinionated

____ 33. **acute** **a)** mild **b)** dull **c)** severe **d)** nervous

____ 34. **prominent** **a)** clean **b)** obvious **c)** dangerous **d)** reasonable

____ 35. **arrogant** **a)** wealthy **b)** ridiculous **c)** average **d)** overly proud

____ 36. **cite** **a)** repeat **b)** mention in support **c)** look for **d)** read

____ 37. **retort** **a)** great respect **b)** sharp reply **c)** false idea **d)** court order

____ 38. **exempt** **a)** needed badly **b)** attacked **c)** unconcerned **d)** free of a duty

____ 39. **accessible** **a)** easily reached **b)** itchy **c)** difficult **d)** folded

____ 40. **prevail** **a)** climb **b)** win out **c)** lose **d)** enroll early

____ 41. **evasive** **a)** talkative **b)** deliberately unclear **c)** friendly **d)** overly forceful

____ 42. **elapse** **a)** flow **b)** pass by **c)** measure **d)** record

____ 43. **lethal** **a)** sweet-smelling **b)** ancient **c)** deadly **d)** healthy

____ 44. **ordeal** **a)** change **b)** painful experience **c)** good time **d)** office

____ 45. **infer** **a)** offer **b)** conclude **c)** reject **d)** answer

____ 46. **unique** **a)** common **b)** pure **c)** one-of-a-kind **d)** well-known

____ 47. **subtle** **a)** early **b)** direct **c)** not obvious **d)** surprising

____ 48. **devise** **a)** steal **b)** escape **c)** think up **d)** redo

____ 49. **stimulate** **a)** arouse **b)** anger **c)** make tired **d)** confuse

____ 50. **convey** **a)** communicate **b)** allow **c)** invent **d)** approve

(Continues on next page)

____ 51. **inevitable** **a)** unavoidable **b)** dangerous **c)** spiteful **d)** doubtful

____ 52. **equate** **a)** adjust **b)** consider equal **c)** attack **d)** overcome

____ 53. **patron** **a)** father **b)** enemy **c)** steady customer **d)** one with a hopeless view

____ 54. **option** **a)** problem **b)** requirement **c)** attitude **d)** choice

____ 55. **endeavor** **a)** meet **b)** state **c)** try **d)** avoid

____ 56. **refute** **a)** prove wrong **b)** replay **c)** appeal **d)** walk

____ 57. **dismay** **a)** thrill **b)** lift **c)** return **d)** discourage

____ 58. **reciprocate** **a)** pay back **b)** frown **c)** slip **d)** step

____ 59. **retain** **a)** return **b)** keep **c)** redo **d)** come forth

____ 60. **adapt** **a)** stick to something **b)** adjust to a situation **c)** avoid **d)** strike

____ 61. **indifferent** **a)** similar **b)** calm **c)** well-adjusted **d)** unconcerned

____ 62. **elaborate** **a)** large **b)** complex **c)** expensive **d)** boring

____ 63. **liberal** **a)** generous **b)** thrifty **c)** famous **d)** short

____ 64. **mediocre** **a)** outstanding **b)** ordinary **c)** bad-tasting **d)** believable

____ 65. **emerge** **a)** go under water **b)** come forth **c)** lie **d)** draw back

____ 66. **elite** **a)** free **b)** underprivileged **c)** superior **d)** proud

____ 67. **essence** **a)** fundamental characteristic **b)** tiny part **c)** much later **d)** rule

____ 68. **allude** **a)** refer indirectly **b)** damage **c)** protest **d)** pay back

____ 69. **impair** **a)** fix **b)** write down **c)** employ **d)** damage

____ 70. **coerce** **a)** attract **b)** refuse **c)** remove **d)** force

____ 71. **plausible** **a)** boring **b)** unbearable **c)** believable **d)** misspelled

____ 72. **recur** **a)** prevent **b)** remember **c)** forget **d)** occur again

____ 73. **revoke** **a)** annoy **b)** protest **c)** cancel **d)** adjust

____ 74. **stereotype** **a)** oversimplified image **b)** two channels **c)** plan **d)** photograph

75. **reprimand** **a)** harsh criticism **b)** business deal **c)** ruling **d)** answer

(Continues on next page)

____ 76. **destiny** a) freedom b) fate c) generosity d) boredom

____ 77. **tedious** a) difficult b) heavy c) ridiculous d) boring

____ 78. **detain** a) care for b) attract c) delay d) describe

____ 79. **consequence** a) falsehood b) result c) method d) series

____ 80. **diminish** a) lessen b) make darker c) enlarge d) move upward

____ 81. **site** a) silence b) location c) time d) vision

____ 82. **discriminate** a) arrest b) delay c) distinguish d) discuss

____ 83. **profound** a) kind b) deeply felt c) cautious d) logical

____ 84. **vocation** a) hobby b) trip c) report d) profession

____ 85. **subside** a) calm down b) insult c) arouse d) tire easily

____ 86. **intervene** a) come between b) arrest c) resist d) send for

____ 87. **sedate** a) bold b) plain c) calm d) pure

____ 88. **perceptive** a) brave b) available c) aware d) careless

____ 89. **innate** a) learned b) underneath c) inborn d) clever

____ 90. **obstinate** a) friendly b) frightful c) stubborn d) cautious

____ 91. **susceptible** a) easily affected b) greedy c) lazy d) easily noticed

____ 92. **defy** a) send for b) approve c) improve d) resist

____ 93. **valid** a) logical b) pure c) clever d) gloomy

____ 94. **confirm** a) follow b) reject c) support the truth of something d) speed up

____ 95. **vigorous** a) harsh b) energetic c) kind d) rushed

____ 96. **adverse** a) strict b) profitable c) rhyming d) harmful

____ 97. **coherent** a) necessary b) lively c) wordy d) logical and orderly

____ 98. **deteriorate** a) worsen b) speed up c) age d) take advantage of

____ 99. **comparable** a) odd b) similar c) unavoidable d) lacking

____ 100. **audible** a) nearby b) believable c) willing d) able to be heard

STOP. This is the end of the test. If there is time remaining, you may go back and recheck your answers. When the time is up, hand in both your answer sheet and this test booklet to your instructor.

BUILDING VOCABULARY SKILLS

Posttest

NAME: ____________________

SECTION: __________ DATE: __________

SCORE: ____________________

This test contains 100 items. In the space provided, write the letter of the choice that is closest in meaning to the **boldfaced** word.

____ 1. **compel** a) finish b) delight c) force d) avoid

____ 2. **isolate** a) separate b) heat up c) combine d) freeze

____ 3. **endorse** a) suggest b) stop c) support d) start

____ 4. **refuge** a) garbage b) building c) rejection d) shelter

____ 5. **menace** a) character b) threat c) assistance d) puzzle

____ 6. **transition** a) invention b) purchase c) repetition d) change

____ 7. **acknowledge** a) prevent b) study c) admit d) deny

____ 8. **superficial** a) lacking depth b) perfect c) very deep d) faulty

____ 9. **extensive** a) outside b) large in space or amount c) bold d) separated

____ 10. **denounce** a) introduce b) condemn c) change d) compliment

____ 11. **morale** a) spirit b) majority c) threat d) principle

____ 12. **undermine** a) cross out b) weaken c) reach d) dig up

____ 13. **drastic** a) dirty b) extreme c) suitable d) sticky

____ 14. **impartial** a) strict b) not whole c) hidden d) without prejudice

____ 15. **imply** a) approve of b) interfere c) do mischief d) suggest

____ 16. **fortify** a) avoid b) strengthen c) approve of d) suggest

____ 17. **concise** a) wordy b) clear and brief c) peaceful d) proper

____ 18. **conservative** a) not definite b) opinionated c) resisting change d) understanding

____ 19. **novice** a) false impression b) book c) beginner d) servant

____ 20. **erratic** a) inconsistent b) mistaken c) in a city d) noisy

____ 21. **hypocrite** a) injection b) insincere person c) interference d) threat

____ 22. **lenient** a) not biased b) not strict c) delayed d) heavy

____ 23. **sustain** a) avoid b) approve of c) wait for d) keep going

____ 24. **obstacle** a) remedy b) list c) answer d) barrier

____ 25. **comply** a) choose b) run into c) forget d) do as asked

(Continues on next page)

___ 26. **arrogant** a) average b) wealthy c) ridiculous d) overly proud

___ 27. **infer** a) offer b) conclude c) reject d) answer

___ 28. **verify** a) cancel b) prove c) keep going d) improve

___ 29. **prudent** a) rudely brief b) careful c) obvious d) delicate

___ 30. **evasive** a) talkative b) deliberately unclear c) friendly d) overly forceful

___ 31. **apprehensive** a) relaxed b) thoughtful c) opinionated d) uneasy

___ 32. **accessible** a) easily reached b) folded c) difficult d) itchy

___ 33. **unique** a) pure b) common c) one-of-a-kind d) well-known

___ 34. **acute** a) dull b) mild c) nervous d) severe

___ 35. **subtle** a) surprising b) direct c) not obvious d) early

___ 36. **retort** a) great respect b) sharp reply c) false idea d) court order

___ 37. **diversity** a) variety b) enthusiasm c) conclusion d) separation

___ 38. **exempt** a) needed badly b) attacked c) unconcerned d) free of a duty

___ 39. **devise** a) escape b) think up c) steal d) redo

___ 40. **compensate** a) receive b) win out c) change d) repay

___ 41. **cite** a) read b) mention in support c) look for d) repeat

___ 42. **convey** a) invent b) allow c) communicate d) approve

___ 43. **lethal** a) sweet-smelling b) healthy c) ancient d) deadly

___ 44. **surpass** a) go beyond b) reverse c) take d) prove wrong

___ 45. **ordeal** a) office b) painful experience c) good time d) change

___ 46. **prevail** a) lose b) enroll early c) climb d) win out

___ 47. **stimulate** a) arouse b) anger c) make tired d) confuse

___ 48. **tentative** a) definite b) not final c) outside d) suitable

___ 49. **elapse** a) pass by b) record c) measure d) flow

___ 50. **prominent** a) dangerous b) clean c) obvious d) reasonable

(Continues on next page)

____ 51. **option** **a)** attitude **b)** requirement **c)** problem **d)** choice

____ 52. **reprimand** **a)** business deal **b)** harsh criticism **c)** answer **d)** ruling

____ 53. **adapt** **a)** adjust to a situation **b)** stick to something **c)** avoid **d)** strike

____ 54. **refute** **a)** prove wrong **b)** replay **c)** appeal **d)** walk

____ 55. **plausible** **a)** boring **b)** unbearable **c)** believable **d)** misspelled

____ 56. **reciprocate** **a)** pay back **b)** step **c)** frown **d)** slip

____ 57. **essence** **a)** rule **b)** tiny part **c)** much later **d)** fundamental characteristic

____ 58. **revoke** **a)** adjust **b)** annoy **c)** protect **d)** cancel

____ 59. **retain** **a)** redo **b)** keep **c)** return **d)** come forth

____ 60. **inevitable** **a)** unavoidable **b)** dangerous **c)** spiteful **d)** doubtful

____ 61. **emerge** **a)** draw back **b)** come forth **c)** lie **d)** go under water

____ 62. **impair** **a)** damage **b)** employ **c)** write down **d)** fix

____ 63. **equate** **a)** overcome **b)** consider equal **c)** attack **d)** adjust

____ 64. **coerce** **a)** attract **b)** refuse **c)** remove **d)** force

____ 65. **patron** **a)** steady customer **b)** enemy **c)** father **d)** one with a hopeless view

____ 66. **liberal** **a)** thrifty **b)** generous **c)** short **d)** famous

____ 67. **dismay** **a)** thrill **b)** lift **c)** return **d)** discourage

____ 68. **elite** **a)** underprivileged **b)** free **c)** proud **d)** superior

____ 69. **endeavor** **a)** state **b)** meet **c)** avoid **d)** try

____ 70. **allude** **a)** pay back **b)** damage **c)** protest **d)** refer indirectly

____ 71. **recur** **a)** occur again **b)** remember **c)** forget **d)** prevent

____ 72. **indifferent** **a)** similar **b)** calm **c)** well-adjusted **d)** unconcerned

____ 73. **mediocre** **a)** believable **b)** outstanding **c)** bad-tasting **d)** ordinary

____ 74. **stereotype** **a)** photograph **b)** oversimplified image **c)** plan **d)** two channels

____ 75. **elaborate** **a)** large **b)** complex **c)** expensive **d)** boring

(Continues on next page)

____ 76. **destiny** **a)** fate **b)** freedom **c)** generosity **d)** boredom

____ 77. **deteriorate** **a)** worsen **b)** speed up **c)** age **d)** take advantage of

____ 78. **perceptive** **a)** careless **b)** available **c)** aware **d)** brave

____ 79. **sedate** **a)** plain **b)** bold **c)** pure **d)** calm

____ 80. **vocation** **a)** profession **b)** hobby **c)** trip **d)** report

____ 81. **innate** **a)** learned **b)** underneath **c)** inborn **d)** clever

____ 82. **detain** **a)** care for **b)** delay **c)** describe **d)** attract

____ 83. **diminish** **a)** move upward **b)** make darker **c)** enlarge **d)** lessen

____ 84. **coherent** **a)** necessary **b)** lively **c)** wordy **d)** logical and orderly

____ 85. **intervene** **a)** send for **b)** come between **c)** arrest **d)** resist

____ 86. **profound** **a)** cautious **b)** deeply felt **c)** kind **d)** logical

____ 87. **obstinate** **a)** frightful **b)** stubborn **c)** friendly **d)** cautious

____ 88. **comparable** **a)** similar **b)** odd **c)** unavoidable **d)** lacking

____ 89. **susceptible** **a)** easily affected **b)** greedy **c)** lazy **d)** easily noticed

____ 90. **consequence** **a)** series **b)** falsehood **c)** result **d)** method

____ 91. **valid** **a)** clever **b)** pure **c)** logical **d)** gloomy

____ 92. **confirm** **a)** follow **b)** reject **c)** support the truth of something **d)** speed up

____ 93. **site** **a)** silence **b)** time **c)** location **d)** vision

____ 94. **vigorous** **a)** kind **b)** rushed **c)** harsh **d)** energetic

____ 95. **discriminate** **a)** arrest **b)** delay **c)** distinguish **d)** harm

____ 96. **tedious** **a)** difficult **b)** boring **c)** ridiculous **d)** heavy

____ 97. **adverse** **a)** harmful **b)** profitable **c)** rhyming **d)** strict

____ 98. **defy** **a)** send for **b)** approve **c)** improve **d)** resist

____ 99. **subside** **a)** tire easily **b)** arouse **c)** insult **d)** calm down

____ 100. **audible** **a)** willing **b)** believable **c)** nearby **d)** able to be heard

STOP. This is the end of the test. If there is time remaining, you may go back and recheck your answers. When the time is up, hand in both your answer sheet and this test booklet to your instructor.

Name: ______________________________

Unit One: *Pretest*

In the space provided, write the letter of the choice that is closest in meaning to the **boldfaced** word.

____ 1. **compel** a) avoid b) delight c) force d) finish
____ 2. **drastic** a) dirty b) suitable c) extreme d) sticky
____ 3. **comply** a) choose b) forget c) run into d) do as asked
____ 4. **alternative** a) command b) design c) assignment d) choice
____ 5. **acknowledge** a) prevent b) admit c) study d) deny
____ 6. **candid** a) honest b) intense c) long d) improper
____ 7. **concise** a) peaceful b) clear and brief c) proper d) wordy
____ 8. **appropriate** a) illegal b) proper c) extreme d) well-dressed
____ 9. **illuminate** a) lose b) become sick c) light up d) desire greatly
____ 10. **urban** a) of a city b) circular c) not allowed d) large
____ 11. **reminisce** a) gather b) remember c) travel d) strengthen
____ 12. **isolate** a) combine b) heat up c) separate d) freeze
____ 13. **fortify** a) suggest b) strengthen c) avoid d) approve of
____ 14. **extensive** a) bold b) separated c) outside d) large in space or amount
____ 15. **refuge** a) shelter b) rejection c) building d) garbage
____ 16. **erratic** a) inconsistent b) mistaken c) in a city d) noisy
____ 17. **legitimate** a) threatening b) profitable c) obvious d) lawful
____ 18. **overt** a) proper b) obvious c) completed d) fair
____ 19. **morale** a) spirit b) principle c) threat d) majority
____ 20. **lenient** a) heavy b) not strict c) delayed d) not biased
____ 21. **naive** a) clever b) fair c) unsuspecting d) merciful
____ 22. **undermine** a) weaken b) cross out c) reach d) dig up
____ 23. **menace** a) character b) threat c) assistance d) puzzle
____ 24. **impartial** a) without prejudice b) not whole c) hidden d) strict
____ 25. **endorse** a) suggest b) stop c) support d) start

(Continues on next page)

____ 26. **illusion** **a)** mistaken view **b)** bad health **c)** new idea **d)** power

____ 27. **imply** **a)** approve of **b)** interfere **c)** do mischief **d)** suggest

____ 28. **obstacle** **a)** barrier **b)** remedy **c)** list **d)** answer

____ 29. **novice** **a)** book **b)** false impression **c)** beginner **d)** servant

____ 30. **impact** **a)** force **b)** inside **c)** remedy **d)** agreement

____ 31. **hypocrite** **a)** interference **b)** insincere person **c)** injection **d)** threat

____ 32. **idealistic** **a)** full of ideas **b)** searching **c)** emphasizing ideals **d)** necessary

____ 33. **superficial** **a)** lacking depth **b)** perfect **c)** very deep **d)** faulty

____ 34. **concede** **a)** go beyond **b)** reveal **c)** dislike **d)** admit

____ 35. **deter** **a)** refuse **b)** make last longer **c)** prevent **d)** damage

____ 36. **denounce** **a)** introduce **b)** condemn **c)** change **d)** compliment

____ 37. **transition** **a)** purchase **b)** invention **c)** repetition **d)** change

____ 38. **sustain** **a)** keep going **b)** approve of **c)** avoid **d)** wait for

____ 39. **conservative** **a)** not definite **b)** opinionated **c)** resisting change **d)** understanding

____ 40. **scapegoat** **a)** example **b)** one blamed for another's mistake **c)** winner **d)** one who takes

____ 41. **avert** **a)** begin **b)** travel **c)** prevent **d)** do too late

____ 42. **anecdote** **a)** brief story **b)** reply **c)** cure **d)** confession

____ 43. **dialog** **a)** answer **b)** story **c)** a passage of conversation **d)** belief

____ 44. **forfeit** **a)** lose **b)** draw **c)** give **d)** recall

____ 45. **delete** **a)** obey **b)** go away **c)** erase **d)** damage

____ 46. **integrity** **a)** threat **b)** inside **c)** complication **d)** honesty

____ 47. **erode** **a)** drive **b)** wear away **c)** include **d)** express indirectly

____ 48. **gruesome** **a)** taller **b)** illegal **c)** frightful **d)** not practical

____ 49. **contrary** **a)** easily reached **b)** hard **c)** disrespectful **d)** opposite

____ 50. **disclose** **a)** reveal **b)** close **c)** hide **d)** continue

SCORE: (Number correct) ________ × 2 = __________ %

Name: ______________________________

Unit One: *Posttest*

In the space provided, write the letter of the choice that is closest in meaning to the **boldfaced** word.

____ 1. **compel** a) finish b) delight c) force d) avoid

____ 2. **concede** a) go beyond b) reveal c) dislike d) admit

____ 3. **isolate** a) separate b) heat up c) combine d) freeze

____ 4. **endorse** a) suggest b) stop c) support d) start

____ 5. **overt** a) proper b) fair c) completed d) obvious

____ 6. **deter** a) prevent b) make last longer c) refuse d) damage

____ 7. **reminisce** a) gather b) remember c) travel d) strengthen

____ 8. **comply** a) choose b) run into c) forget d) do as asked

____ 9. **alternative** a) command b) design c) assignment d) choice

____ 10. **refuge** a) garbage b) building c) rejection d) shelter

____ 11. **menace** a) character b) threat c) assistance d) puzzle

____ 12. **candid** a) improper b) long c) intense d) honest

____ 13. **transition** a) invention b) purchase c) repetition d) change

____ 14. **illuminate** a) lose b) desire greatly c) light up d) become sick

____ 15. **legitimate** a) threatening b) lawful c) obvious d) profitable

____ 16. **illusion** a) new idea b) bad health c) mistaken view d) power

____ 17. **acknowledge** a) prevent b) study c) admit d) deny

____ 18. **superficial** a) lacking depth b) perfect c) very deep d) faulty

____ 19. **extensive** a) outside b) large in space or amount c) bold d) separated

____ 20. **urban** a) not allowed b) circular c) of a city d) large

____ 21. **denounce** a) introduce b) condemn c) change d) compliment

____ 22. **morale** a) spirit b) majority c) threat d) principle

____ 23. **undermine** a) cross out b) weaken c) reach d) dig up

____ 24. **drastic** a) dirty b) extreme c) suitable d) sticky

____ 25. **impartial** a) strict b) not whole c) hidden d) without prejudice

(Continues on next page)

____ 26. **imply** a) approve of b) interfere c) do mischief d) suggest

____ 27. **fortify** a) avoid b) strengthen c) approve of d) suggest

____ 28. **concise** a) wordy b) clear and brief c) peaceful d) proper

____ 29. **conservative** a) not definite b) opinionated c) resisting change d) understanding

____ 30. **novice** a) false impression b) book c) beginner d) servant

____ 31. **scapegoat** a) example b) one who takes c) winner
d) one blamed for another's mistake

____ 32. **impact** a) force b) inside c) remedy d) agreement

____ 33. **erratic** a) inconsistent b) mistaken c) in a city d) noisy

____ 34. **naive** a) clever b) merciful c) unsuspecting d) fair

____ 35. **appropriate** a) illegal b) proper c) extreme d) well-dressed

____ 36. **hypocrite** a) injection b) insincere person c) interference d) threat

____ 37. **lenient** a) heavy b) not strict c) delayed d) not biased

____ 38. **sustain** a) avoid b) approve of c) wait for d) keep going

____ 39. **idealistic** a) full of ideas b) searching c) emphasizing ideals d) necessary

____ 40. **obstacle** a) remedy b) list c) answer d) barrier

____ 41. **forfeit** a) lose b) recall c) give d) draw

____ 42. **dialog** a) a passage of conversation b) short story c) answer d) belief

____ 43. **anecdote** a) cure b) brief story c) confession d) reply

____ 44. **integrity** a) honesty b) threat c) complication d) inside

____ 45. **contrary** a) hard b) disrespectful c) opposite d) easily reached

____ 46. **avert** a) prevent b) begin c) travel d) do too late

____ 47. **gruesome** a) frightful b) not practical c) taller d) illegal

____ 48. **erode** a) include b) drive c) express indirectly d) wear away

____ 49. **delete** a) go away b) obey c) damage d) erase

____ 50. **disclose** a) continue b) close c) reveal d) hide

SCORE: (Number correct) ________ × 2 = ___________ %

Name: ____________________

Unit Two: *Pretest*

In the space provided, write the letter of the choice that is closest in meaning to the **boldfaced** word.

____ 1. **derive** a) make known b) get c) hold back from d) give in

____ 2. **supplement** a) add to b) prevent c) support d) lower

____ 3. **compensate** a) change b) win out c) receive d) repay

____ 4. **verify** a) imagine b) prove c) keep going d) cancel

____ 5. **surpass** a) go beyond b) reverse c) take d) prove wrong

____ 6. **moderate** a) generous b) not final c) medium d) bright

____ 7. **tentative** a) suitable b) not final c) outside d) definite

____ 8. **diversity** a) separation b) conclusion c) enthusiasm d) variety

____ 9. **prudent** a) rudely brief b) careful c) obvious d) delicate

____ 10. **apprehensive** a) uneasy b) thoughtful c) relaxed d) opinionated

____ 11. **acute** a) mild b) dull c) severe d) nervous

____ 12. **prominent** a) clean b) obvious c) dangerous d) reasonable

____ 13. **donor** a) one who gives b) gift c) one who receives d) loan

____ 14. **recipient** a) one who receives b) steady customer c) contributor d) list

____ 15. **anonymous** a) famous b) common c) by an unknown author d) more than enough

____ 16. **arrogant** a) wealthy b) ridiculous c) average d) overly proud

____ 17. **cite** a) repeat b) mention in support c) look for d) read

____ 18. **rational** a) limited b) of poor quality c) logical d) patriotic

____ 19. **retort** a) great respect b) sharp reply c) false idea d) court order

____ 20. **exempt** a) needed badly b) attacked c) unconcerned d) free of a duty

____ 21. **accessible** a) easily reached b) itchy c) difficult d) folded

____ 22. **prevail** a) climb b) win out c) lose d) enroll early

____ 23. **awe** a) jealousy b) great respect c) pride d) great courage

____ 24. **retrieve** a) get back b) lose c) distribute d) announce

____ 25. **obsession** a) possession b) something pleasant c) something one is overly concerned about d) guilt

(Continues on next page)

____ 26. **evasive** **a)** talkative **b)** deliberately unclear **c)** friendly **d)** overly forceful

____ 27. **fluent** **a)** speaking smoothly **b)** full **c)** overflowing **d)** polluted

____ 28. **elapse** **a)** flow **b)** pass by **c)** measure **d)** record

____ 29. **lethal** **a)** sweet-smelling **b)** ancient **c)** deadly **d)** healthy

____ 30. **ordeal** **a)** change **b)** painful experience **c)** good time **d)** office

____ 31. **infer** **a)** offer **b)** conclude **c)** reject **d)** answer

____ 32. **persistent** **a)** not brave **b)** rude **c)** stubbornly continuing **d)** bad-smelling

____ 33. **unique** **a)** common **b)** pure **c)** one-of-a-kind **d)** well-known

____ 34. **savor** **a)** enjoy **b)** disapprove **c)** dread **d)** approve

____ 35. **vivid** **a)** brightly colored **b)** loud **c)** large **d)** very talkative

____ 36. **subtle** **a)** early **b)** direct **c)** not obvious **d)** surprising

____ 37. **devise** **a)** steal **b)** escape **c)** think up **d)** redo

____ 38. **stimulate** **a)** arouse **b)** anger **c)** make tired **d)** confuse

____ 39. **versatile** **a)** rich **b)** unclear **c)** lucky **d)** able to do many things well

____ 40. **convey** **a)** communicate **b)** allow **c)** invent **d)** approve

____ 41. **conceive** **a)** prevent **b)** make last longer **c)** enjoy **d)** think up

____ 42. **inhibit** **a)** forbid **b)** hold back **c)** live in **d)** provide

____ 43. **bestow** **a)** take advantage of **b)** try **c)** frighten **d)** give

____ 44. **phobia** **a)** difficult experience **b)** fear **c)** disease **d)** attraction

____ 45. **compatible** **a)** capable **b)** able to get along well **c)** proud **d)** friendly

____ 46. **propel** **a)** discourage **b)** attract **c)** push **d)** reject

____ 47. **futile** **a)** without prejudice **b)** useless **c)** old-fashioned **d)** kind

____ 48. **harass** **a)** compliment **b)** bother **c)** stock up **d)** encourage

____ 49. **delusion** **a)** escape **b)** announcement **c)** false belief **d)** example

____ 50. **universal** **a)** doubting **b)** easily understood **c)** including everyone **d)** local

SCORE: (Number correct) ________ × 2 = __________ %

Name: ______________________________

Unit Two: *Posttest*

In the space provided, write the letter of the choice that is closest in meaning to the **boldfaced** word.

____ 1. **arrogant** a) average b) wealthy c) ridiculous d) overly proud

____ 2. **persistent** a) not brave b) rude c) stubbornly continuing d) bad-smelling

____ 3. **awe** a) jealousy b) pride c) great respect d) great courage

____ 4. **infer** a) offer b) conclude c) reject d) answer

____ 5. **verify** a) cancel b) prove c) keep going d) improve

____ 6. **prudent** a) rudely brief b) careful c) obvious d) delicate

____ 7. **rational** a) logical b) of poor quality c) patriotic d) limited

____ 8. **evasive** a) talkative b) deliberately unclear c) friendly d) overly forceful

____ 9. **vivid** a) brightly colored b) large c) loud d) very talkative

____ 10. **apprehensive** a) relaxed b) thoughtful c) opinionated d) uneasy

____ 11. **derive** a) make known b) get c) hold back from d) give in

____ 12. **accessible** a) easily reached b) folded c) difficult d) itchy

____ 13. **prominent** a) dangerous b) clean c) obvious d) reasonable

____ 14. **donor** a) one who receives b) gift c) one who gives d) loan

____ 15. **unique** a) pure b) common c) one-of-a-kind d) well-known

____ 16. **acute** a) dull b) mild c) nervous d) severe

____ 17. **anonymous** a) famous b) common c) by an unknown author d) more than enough

____ 18. **subtle** a) surprising b) direct c) not obvious d) early

____ 19. **retort** a) great respect b) sharp reply c) false idea d) court order

____ 20. **diversity** a) variety b) enthusiasm c) conclusion d) separation

____ 21. **exempt** a) needed badly b) attacked c) unconcerned d) free of a duty

____ 22. **supplement** a) lower b) prevent c) support d) add to

____ 23. **devise** a) escape b) think up c) steal d) redo

____ 24. **retrieve** a) get back b) lose c) distribute d) announce

____ 25. **compensate** a) receive b) win out c) change d) repay

(Continues on next page)

____ 26. **cite** **a)** read **b)** mention in support **c)** look for **d)** repeat

____ 27. **obsession** **a)** guilt **b)** something pleasant **c)** something one is overly concerned about **d)** possession

____ 28. **recipient** **a)** list **b)** steady customer **c)** contributor **d)** one who receives

____ 29. **convey** **a)** invent **b)** allow **c)** communicate **d)** approve

____ 30. **fluent** **a)** speaking smoothly **b)** polluted **c)** overflowing **d)** full

____ 31. **savor** **a)** enjoy **b)** disapprove **c)** dread **d)** approve

____ 32. **lethal** **a)** sweet-smelling **b)** healthy **c)** ancient **d)** deadly

____ 33. **surpass** **a)** go beyond **b)** reverse **c)** take **d)** prove wrong

____ 34. **ordeal** **a)** office **b)** painful experience **c)** good time **d)** change

____ 35. **moderate** **a)** generous **b)** not final **c)** medium **d)** bright

____ 36. **prevail** **a)** lose **b)** enroll early **c)** climb **d)** win out

____ 37. **stimulate** **a)** arouse **b)** anger **c)** make tired **d)** confuse

____ 38. **tentative** **a)** definite **b)** not final **c)** outside **d)** suitable

____ 39. **versatile** **a)** lucky **b)** rich **c)** unclear **d)** able to do many things well

____ 40. **elapse** **a)** pass by **b)** record **c)** measure **d)** flow

____ 41. **propel** **a)** discourage **b)** attract **c)** reject **d)** push

____ 42. **universal** **a)** including everyone **b)** easily understood **c)** local **d)** doubting

____ 43. **futile** **a)** old-fashioned **b)** useless **c)** old **d)** without prejudice

____ 44. **delusion** **a)** announcement **b)** example **c)** false belief **d)** escape

____ 45. **bestow** **a)** try **b)** frighten **c)** give **d)** take advantage of

____ 46. **harass** **a)** bother **b)** stock up **c)** encourage **d)** compliment

____ 47. **inhibit** **a)** provide **b)** hold back **c)** live in **d)** forbid

____ 48. **phobia** **a)** attraction **b)** fear **c)** difficult experience **d)** disease

____ 49. **conceive** **a)** prevent **b)** think up **c)** enjoy **d)** make last longer

____ 50. **compatible** **a)** friendly **b)** proud **c)** able to get along well **d)** capable

SCORE: (Number correct) ________ × 2 = ____________ %

Name: ______________________________

Unit Three: *Pretest*

In the space provided, write the letter of the choice that is closest in meaning to the **boldfaced** word.

____ 1. **inevitable** **a)** unavoidable **b)** dangerous **c)** spiteful **d)** doubtful

____ 2. **equate** **a)** adjust **b)** consider equal **c)** attack **d)** overcome

____ 3. **passive** **a)** not active but acted upon **b)** joyful **c)** quiet **d)** moody

____ 4. **patron** **a)** father **b)** enemy **c)** steady customer **d)** one with a hopeless view

____ 5. **option** **a)** problem **b)** requirement **c)** attitude **d)** choice

____ 6. **indignant** **a)** impressed **b)** angry **c)** curious **d)** afraid

____ 7. **endeavor** **a)** meet **b)** state **c)** try **d)** avoid

____ 8. **impose on** **a)** arrest **b)** confuse **c)** disguise as **d)** take advantage of

____ 9. **refute** **a)** prove wrong **b)** replay **c)** appeal **d)** walk

____ 10. **dismay** **a)** thrill **b)** lift **c)** return **d)** discourage

____ 11. **gesture** **a)** guess **b)** thunder **c)** sign **d)** meal

____ 12. **reciprocate** **a)** pay back **b)** frown **c)** slip **d)** step

____ 13. **exile** **a)** formal criticism **b)** exit **c)** axe **d)** separation from native country

____ 14. **ritual** **a)** business deal **b)** war **c)** ceremony **d)** show

____ 15. **retain** **a)** return **b)** keep **c)** redo **d)** come forth

____ 16. **adapt** **a)** stick to something **b)** adjust to a situation **c)** avoid **d)** strike

____ 17. **indifferent** **a)** similar **b)** calm **c)** well-adjusted **d)** unconcerned

____ 18. **exotic** **a)** out **b)** infected **c)** local **d)** foreign

____ 19. **notable** **a)** well-known **b)** written **c)** unable **d)** odd

____ 20. **elaborate** **a)** large **b)** complex **c)** expensive **d)** boring

____ 21. **liberal** **a)** generous **b)** thrifty **c)** famous **d)** short

____ 22. **frugal** **a)** appealing **b)** illegal **c)** thrifty **d)** hasty

____ 23. **mediocre** **a)** outstanding **b)** ordinary **c)** bad-tasting **d)** believable

____ 24. **emerge** **a)** go under water **b)** come forth **c)** lie **d)** draw back

____ 25. **elite** **a)** free **b)** underprivileged **c)** superior **d)** proud

(Continues on next page)

____ 26. **query** **a)** answer **b)** argue **c)** question **d)** make strange

____ 27. **affirm** **a)** support **b)** reverse **c)** indicate to be true **d)** exercise

____ 28. **essence** **a)** fundamental characteristic **b)** tiny part **c)** much later **d)** rule

____ 29. **allude** **a)** refer indirectly **b)** damage **c)** protest **d)** pay back

____ 30. **impair** **a)** fix **b)** write down **c)** employ **d)** damage

____ 31. **sadistic** **a)** depressed **b)** infected **c)** taking pleasure in cruelty **d)** clever

____ 32. **coerce** **a)** attract **b)** refuse **c)** remove **d)** force

____ 33. **plausible** **a)** boring **b)** unbearable **c)** believable **d)** misspelled

____ 34. **recur** **a)** prevent **b)** remember **c)** forget **d)** occur again

____ 35. **shrewd** **a)** kind **b)** annoying **c)** tricky **d)** mad

____ 36. **tactic** **a)** result **b)** surrender **c)** method **d)** ceremony

____ 37. **revoke** **a)** annoy **b)** protest **c)** cancel **d)** adjust

____ 38. **stereotype** **a)** oversimplified image **b)** two channels **c)** plan **d)** photograph

____ 39. **reprimand** **a)** harsh criticism **b)** business deal **c)** ruling **d)** answer

____ 40. **skeptical** **a)** stubborn **b)** forceful **c)** generous **d)** doubting

____ 41. **defer** **a)** entertain **b)** intrude **c)** yield **d)** annoy

____ 42. **malicious** **a)** bright **b)** mean **c)** sweet **d)** clever

____ 43. **revert** **a)** claim **b)** return to former condition **c)** pay back **d)** answer

____ 44. **recede** **a)** remove **b)** move back **c)** hide **d)** flow over

____ 45. **indulgent** **a)** interesting **b)** giving in to someone's wishes **c)** poor **d)** uninteresting

____ 46. **impulsive** **a)** ugly **b)** prompt **c)** acting on sudden urges **d)** important

____ 47. **immunity** **a)** freedom from something required **b)** infection **c)** plenty **d)** thrift

____ 48. **alleged** **a)** supposed to be true **b)** factual **c)** trustworthy **d)** logical

____ 49. **provoke** **a)** make angry **b)** take back **c)** rise up **d)** prove wrong

____ 50. **ridicule** **a)** pay back **b)** compliment **c)** mock **d)** shrink

SCORE: (Number correct) ________ × 2 = __________ %

Name: ____________________

Unit Three: *Posttest*

In the space provided, write the letter of the choice that is closest in meaning to the **boldfaced** word.

____ 1. **option** a) attitude b) requirement c) problem d) choice

____ 2. **ritual** a) business deal b) ceremony c) war d) show

____ 3. **frugal** a) appealing b) illegal c) thrifty d) hasty

____ 4. **indignant** a) afraid b) curious c) angry d) impressed

____ 5. **reprimand** a) business deal b) harsh criticism c) answer d) ruling

____ 6. **impose on** a) confuse b) arrest c) disguise as d) take advantage of

____ 7. **query** a) answer b) argue c) question d) make strange

____ 8. **adapt** a) adjust to a situation b) stick to something c) avoid d) strike

____ 9. **sadistic** a) clever b) taking pleasure in cruelty c) infected d) depressed

____ 10. **refute** a) prove wrong b) replay c) appeal d) walk

____ 11. **gesture** a) sign b) meal c) guess d) thunder

____ 12. **plausible** a) boring b) unbearable c) believable d) misspelled

____ 13. **reciprocate** a) pay back b) step c) frown d) slip

____ 14. **exile** a) formal criticism b) exit c) axe d) separation from native country

____ 15. **essence** a) rule b) tiny part c) much later d) fundamental characteristic

____ 16. **revoke** a) adjust b) annoy c) protect d) cancel

____ 17. **retain** a) redo b) keep c) return d) come forth

____ 18. **inevitable** a) unavoidable b) dangerous c) spiteful d) doubtful

____ 19. **emerge** a) draw back b) come forth c) lie d) go under water

____ 20. **impair** a) damage b) employ c) write down d) fix

____ 21. **shrewd** a) kind b) annoying c) tricky d) mad

____ 22. **exotic** a) foreign b) out c) infected d) local

____ 23. **elaborate** a) large b) complex c) expensive d) boring

____ 24. **equate** a) overcome b) consider equal c) attack d) adjust

____ 25. **coerce** a) attract b) refuse c) remove d) force

(Continues on next page)

____ 26. **patron** **a)** steady customer **b)** enemy **c)** father **d)** one with a hopeless view

____ 27. **liberal** **a)** thrifty **b)** generous **c)** short **d)** famous

____ 28. **dismay** **a)** thrill **b)** lift **c)** return **d)** discourage

____ 29. **skeptical** **a)** doubting **b)** forceful **c)** generous **d)** stubborn

____ 30. **elite** **a)** underprivileged **b)** free **c)** proud **d)** superior

____ 31. **passive** **a)** not active but acted upon **b)** joyful **c)** quiet **d)** moody

____ 32. **notable** **a)** odd **b)** unable **c)** written **d)** well-known

____ 33. **endeavor** **a)** state **b)** meet **c)** avoid **d)** try

____ 34. **affirm** **a)** exercise **b)** reverse **c)** indicate to be true **d)** support

____ 35. **allude** **a)** pay back **b)** damage **c)** protest **d)** refer indirectly

____ 36. **recur** **a)** occur again **b)** remember **c)** forget **d)** prevent

____ 37. **tactic** **a)** surrender **b)** method **c)** result **d)** ceremony

____ 38. **indifferent** **a)** similar **b)** calm **c)** well-adjusted **d)** unconcerned

____ 39. **mediocre** **a)** believable **b)** outstanding **c)** bad-tasting **d)** ordinary

____ 40. **stereotype** **a)** photograph **b)** oversimplified image **c)** plan **d)** two channels

____ 41. **alleged** **a)** logical **b)** factual **c)** supposed to be true **d)** trustworthy

____ 42. **indulgent** **a)** interesting **b)** uninteresting **c)** poor **d)** giving in to someone's wishes

____ 43. **malicious** **a)** clever **b)** mean **c)** sweet **d)** bright

____ 44. **defer** **a)** annoy **b)** intrude **c)** yield **d)** entertain

____ 45. **impulsive** **a)** prompt **b)** important **c)** acting on sudden urges **d)** ugly

____ 46. **revert** **a)** claim **b)** answer **c)** pay back **d)** return to former condition

____ 47. **immunity** **a)** infection **b)** plenty **c)** freedom from something required **d)** thrift

____ 48. **recede** **a)** move back **b)** flow over **c)** hide **d)** remove

____ 49. **ridicule** **a)** shrink **b)** mock **c)** compliment **d)** pay back

____ 50. **provoke** **a)** take back **b)** prove wrong **c)** rise up **d)** make angry

SCORE: (Number correct) ________ × 2 = ___________ %

Name: ____________________

Unit Four: *Pretest*

In the space provided, write the letter of the choice that is closest in meaning to the **boldfaced** word.

____ 1. **vital** **a)** weak **b)** stiff **c)** necessary **d)** unimportant

____ 2. **destiny** **a)** freedom **b)** fate **c)** generosity **d)** boredom

____ 3. **tedious** **a)** difficult **b)** heavy **c)** ridiculous **d)** boring

____ 4. **detain** **a)** care for **b)** attract **c)** delay **d)** describe

____ 5. **transaction** **a)** trip **b)** business deal **c)** detour **d)** ceremony

____ 6. **procrastinate** **a)** remember **b)** put off doing something **c)** misbehave **d)** make angry

____ 7. **consequence** **a)** falsehood **b)** result **c)** method **d)** series

____ 8. **diminish** **a)** lessen **b)** make darker **c)** enlarge **d)** move upward

____ 9. **severity** **a)** rudeness **b)** generosity **c)** harshness **d)** calm

____ 10. **site** **a)** silence **b)** location **c)** time **d)** vision

____ 11. **discriminate** **a)** arrest **b)** delay **c)** distinguish **d)** discuss

____ 12. **profound** **a)** kind **b)** deeply felt **c)** cautious **d)** logical

____ 13. **vocation** **a)** hobby **b)** trip **c)** report **d)** profession

____ 14. **dispense** **a)** stop **b)** delay **c)** encourage **d)** distribute

____ 15. **dismal** **a)** unknown **b)** round **c)** tired **d)** gloomy

____ 16. **subside** **a)** calm down **b)** insult **c)** arouse **d)** tire easily

____ 17. **data** **a)** test **b)** information **c)** rumors **d)** conversation

____ 18. **intervene** **a)** come between **b)** arrest **c)** resist **d)** send for

____ 19. **sedate** **a)** bold **b)** plain **c)** calm **d)** pure

____ 20. **morbid** **a)** limited **b)** causing horror **c)** causing respect **d)** pleasurable

____ 21. **parallel** **a)** at a constant distance apart **b)** nearsighted **c)** farsighted **d)** far

____ 22. **perceptive** **a)** brave **b)** available **c)** aware **d)** careless

____ 23. **innate** **a)** learned **b)** underneath **c)** inborn **d)** clever

____ 24. **obstinate** **a)** friendly **b)** frightful **c)** stubborn **d)** cautious

____ 25. **susceptible** **a)** easily affected **b)** greedy **c)** lazy **d)** easily noticed

(Continues on next page)

____ 26. **defy** **a)** send for **b)** approve **c)** improve **d)** resist

____ 27. **valid** **a)** logical **b)** pure **c)** clever **d)** gloomy

____ 28. **deceptive** **a)** constant **b)** well-spoken **c)** misleading **d)** changing

____ 29. **confirm** **a)** follow **b)** reject **c)** support the truth of something **d)** speed up

____ 30. **vigorous** **a)** harsh **b)** energetic **c)** kind **d)** rushed

____ 31. **submit** **a)** make fun of **b)** arrest **c)** give in **d)** refuse

____ 32. **restrain** **a)** struggle **b)** hold back **c)** refuse **d)** order to come

____ 33. **adverse** **a)** strict **b)** profitable **c)** rhyming **d)** harmful

____ 34. **coherent** **a)** necessary **b)** lively **c)** wordy **d)** logical and orderly

____ 35. **competent** **a)** unavoidable **b)** able **c)** honest **d)** depressing

____ 36. **deteriorate** **a)** worsen **b)** speed up **c)** age **d)** take advantage of

____ 37. **consecutive** **a)** late **b)** following one after another **c)** able **d)** at the same time

____ 38. **comparable** **a)** odd **b)** similar **c)** unavoidable **d)** lacking

____ 39. **audible** **a)** nearby **b)** believable **c)** willing **d)** able to be heard

____ 40. **accelerate** **a)** quicken **b)** hold back **c)** distinguish **d)** calm down

____ 41. **simultaneous** **a)** done at the same time **b)** recorded **c)** very important **d)** fast

____ 42. **strategy** **a)** plan **b)** purpose **c)** discipline **d)** foundation

____ 43. **summon** **a)** add up **b)** send for **c)** delay **d)** insult

____ 44. **theoretical** **a)** gloomy **b)** based on theory **c)** practical **d)** pretty

____ 45. **inept** **a)** guilty **b)** tired **c)** clumsy **d)** stubborn

____ 46. **lament** **a)** delay **b)** rush **c)** struggle **d)** mourn

____ 47. **seclusion** **a)** punishment **b)** pride **c)** stubbornness **d)** separation

____ 48. **transmit** **a)** spread **b)** hold **c)** sleep **d)** grow

____ 49. **advocate** **a)** teacher **b)** supporter **c)** player **d)** business person

____ 50. **conspicuous** **a)** frightened **b)** stubborn **c)** obvious **d)** careful

SCORE: (Number correct) ________ × 2 = ___________ %

Name: ____________________

Unit Four: *Posttest*

In the space provided, write the letter of the choice that is closest in meaning to the **boldfaced** word.

____ 1. **destiny** a) fate b) freedom c) generosity d) boredom

____ 2. **dismal** a) unknown b) tired c) gloomy d) round

____ 3. **deteriorate** a) worsen b) speed up c) age d) take advantage of

____ 4. **perceptive** a) careless b) available c) aware d) brave

____ 5. **sedate** a) plain b) bold c) pure d) calm

____ 6. **transaction** a) trip b) business deal c) detour d) ceremony

____ 7. **consecutive** a) able b) following one after another c) late d) at the same time

____ 8. **vocation** a) profession b) hobby c) trip d) report

____ 9. **procrastinate** a) make angry b) put off doing something c) misbehave d) remember

____ 10. **innate** a) learned b) underneath c) inborn d) clever

____ 11. **competent** a) unavoidable b) depressing c) honest d) able

____ 12. **detain** a) care for b) delay c) describe d) attract

____ 13. **diminish** a) move upward b) make darker c) enlarge d) lessen

____ 14. **severity** a) rudeness b) generosity c) harshness d) calm

____ 15. **coherent** a) necessary b) lively c) wordy d) logical and orderly

____ 16. **intervene** a) send for b) come between c) arrest d) resist

____ 17. **profound** a) cautious b) deeply felt c) kind d) logical

____ 18. **vital** a) necessary b) stiff c) weak d) unimportant

____ 19. **obstinate** a) frightful b) stubborn c) friendly d) cautious

____ 20. **comparable** a) similar b) odd c) unavoidable d) lacking

____ 21. **dispense** a) list b) distribute c) encourage d) delay

____ 22. **parallel** a) nearsighted b) at a constant distance apart c) farsighted d) far

____ 23. **susceptible** a) easily affected b) greedy c) lazy d) easily noticed

____ 24. **consequence** a) series b) falsehood c) result d) method

____ 25. **valid** a) clever b) pure c) logical d) gloomy

(Continues on next page)

____ 26. **confirm** a) follow b) reject c) support the truth of something d) speed up

____ 27. **site** a) silence b) time c) location d) vision

____ 28. **vigorous** a) kind b) rushed c) harsh d) energetic

____ 29. **discriminate** a) arrest b) delay c) distinguish d) discuss

____ 30. **submit** a) make fun of b) arrest c) give in d) refuse

____ 31. **restrain** a) hold back b) struggle c) order to come d) refuse

____ 32. **tedious** a) difficult b) boring c) ridiculous d) heavy

____ 33. **adverse** a) harmful b) profitable c) rhyming d) strict

____ 34. **defy** a) send for b) approve c) improve d) resist

____ 35. **subside** a) tire easily b) arouse c) insult d) calm down

____ 36. **morbid** a) causing respect b) pleasurable c) limited d) causing horror

____ 37. **data** a) conversation b) rumors c) information d) test

____ 38. **audible** a) willing b) believable c) nearby d) able to be heard

____ 39. **accelerate** a) distinguish b) quicken c) hold back d) calm down

____ 40. **deceptive** a) changing b) well-spoken c) constant d) misleading

____ 41. **advocate** a) teacher b) business person c) player d) supporter

____ 42. **summon** a) delay b) send for c) insult d) add up

____ 43. **conspicuous** a) obvious b) stubborn c) frightened d) careful

____ 44. **simultaneous** a) recorded b) fast c) very important d) done at the same time

____ 45. **strategy** a) plan b) foundation c) purpose d) discipline

____ 46. **lament** a) rush b) mourn c) struggle d) delay

____ 47. **theoretical** a) gloomy b) pretty c) practical d) based on theory

____ 48. **inept** a) tired b) clumsy c) guilty d) stubborn

____ 49. **seclusion** a) pride b) separation c) stubbornness d) punishment

____ 50. **transmit** a) sleep b) hold c) grow d) spread

SCORE: (Number correct) ________ × 2 = __________ %

Pretest / Posttest

NAME: ______________________

SECTION: __________ DATE: __________

SCORE: ______________________

ANSWER SHEET

1. _____	26. _____	51. _____	76. _____
2. _____	27. _____	52. _____	77. _____
3. _____	28. _____	53. _____	78. _____
4. _____	29. _____	54. _____	79. _____
5. _____	30. _____	55. _____	80. _____
6. _____	31. _____	56. _____	81. _____
7. _____	32. _____	57. _____	82. _____
8. _____	33. _____	58. _____	83. _____
9. _____	34. _____	59. _____	84. _____
10. _____	35. _____	60. _____	85. _____
11. _____	36. _____	61. _____	86. _____
12. _____	37. _____	62. _____	87. _____
13. _____	38. _____	63. _____	88. _____
14. _____	39. _____	64. _____	89. _____
15. _____	40. _____	65. _____	90. _____
16. _____	41. _____	66. _____	91. _____
17. _____	42. _____	67. _____	92. _____
18. _____	43. _____	68. _____	93. _____
19. _____	44. _____	69. _____	94. _____
20. _____	45. _____	70. _____	95. _____
21. _____	46. _____	71. _____	96. _____
22. _____	47. _____	72. _____	97. _____
23. _____	48. _____	73. _____	98. _____
24. _____	49. _____	74. _____	99. _____
25. _____	50. _____	75. _____	100. _____

Pretest

ANSWER KEY

1. c
2. c
3. d
4. b
5. b
6. c
7. b
8. d
9. a
10. a
11. a
12. b
13. a
14. b
15. a
16. c
17. d
18. a
19. c
20. b
21. a
22. b
23. d
24. a
25. c
26. d
27. b
28. a
29. b
30. d
31. b
32. a
33. c
34. b
35. d
36. b
37. b
38. d
39. a
40. b
41. b
42. b
43. c
44. b
45. b
46. c
47. c
48. c
49. a
50. a
51. a
52. b
53. c
54. d
55. c
56. a
57. d
58. a
59. b
60. b
61. d
62. b
63. a
64. b
65. b
66. c
67. a
68. a
69. d
70. d
71. c
72. d
73. c
74. a
75. a
76. b
77. d
78. c
79. b
80. a
81. b
82. c
83. b
84. d
85. a
86. a
87. c
88. c
89. c
90. c
91. a
92. d
93. a
94. c
95. b
96. d
97. d
98. a
99. b
100. d

Posttest

ANSWER KEY

1. c	26. d	51. d	76. a
2. a	27. b	52. b	77. a
3. c	28. b	53. a	78. c
4. d	29. b	54. a	79. d
5. b	30. b	55. c	80. a
6. d	31. d	56. a	81. c
7. c	32. a	57. d	82. b
8. a	33. c	58. d	83. d
9. b	34. d	59. b	84. d
10. b	35. c	60. a	85. b
11. a	36. b	61. b	86. b
12. b	37. a	62. a	87. b
13. b	38. d	63. b	88. a
14. d	39. b	64. d	89. a
15. d	40. d	65. a	90. c
16. b	41. b	66. b	91. c
17. b	42. c	67. d	92. c
18. c	43. d	68. d	93. c
19. c	44. a	69. d	94. d
20. a	45. b	70. d	95. c
21. b	46. d	71. a	96. b
22. b	47. a	72. d	97. a
23. d	48. b	73. d	98. d
24. d	49. a	74. b	99. d
25. d	50. c	75. b	100. d

Answers to the Pretests and Posttests:
BUILDING VOCABULARY SKILLS, SHORT VERSION

Unit One		**Unit Two**		**Unit Three**		**Unit Four**	
Pretest	*Posttest*	*Pretest*	*Posttest*	*Pretest*	*Posttest*	*Pretest*	*Posttest*
1. c	1. c	1. b	1. d	1. a	1. d	1. c	1. a
2. c	2. d	2. a	2. c	2. b	2. b	2. b	2. c
3. d	3. a	3. d	3. c	3. a	3. c	3. d	3. a
4. d	4. c	4. b	4. b	4. c	4. c	4. c	4. c
5. b	5. d	5. a	5. b	5. d	5. b	5. b	5. d
6. a	6. a	6. c	6. b	6. b	6. d	6. b	6. b
7. b	7. b	7. b	7. a	7. c	7. c	7. b	7. b
8. b	8. d	8. d	8. b	8. d	8. a	8. a	8. a
9. c	9. d	9. b	9. a	9. a	9. b	9. c	9. b
10. a	10. d	10. a	10. d	10. d	10. a	10. b	10. c
11. b	11. b	11. c	11. b	11. c	11. a	11. c	11. d
12. c	12. d	12. b	12. a	12. a	12. c	12. b	12. b
13. b	13. d	13. a	13. c	13. d	13. a	13. d	13. d
14. d	14. c	14. a	14. c	14. c	14. d	14. d	14. c
15. a	15. b	15. c	15. c	15. b	15. d	15. d	15. d
16. a	16. c	16. d	16. d	16. b	16. d	16. a	16. b
17. d	17. c	17. b	17. c	17. d	17. b	17. b	17. b
18. b	18. a	18. c	18. c	18. d	18. a	18. a	18. a
19. a	19. b	19. b	19. b	19. a	19. b	19. c	19. b
20. b	20. c	20. d	20. a	20. b	20. a	20. b	20. a
21. c	21. b	21. a	21. d	21. a	21. c	21. a	21. b
22. a	22. a	22. b	22. d	22. c	22. a	22. c	22. b
23. b	23. b	23. b	23. b	23. b	23. b	23. c	23. a
24. a	24. b	24. a	24. a	24. b	24. b	24. c	24. c
25. c	25. d	25. c	25. d	25. c	25. d	25. a	25. c
26. a	26. d	26. b	26. b	26. c	26. a	26. d	26. c
27. d	27. b	27. a	27. c	27. c	27. b	27. a	27. c
28. a	28. b	28. b	28. d	28. a	28. d	28. c	28. d
29. c	29. c	29. c	29. c	29. a	29. a	29. c	29. c
30. a	30. c	30. b	30. a	30. d	30. d	30. b	30. c
31. b	31. d	31. b	31. a	31. c	31. a	31. c	31. a
32. c	32. a	32. c	32. d	32. d	32. d	32. b	32. b
33. a	33. a	33. c	33. a	33. c	33. d	33. d	33. a
34. d	34. c	34. a	34. b	34. d	34. c	34. d	34. d
35. c	35. b	35. a	35. c	35. c	35. d	35. b	35. d
36. b	36. b	36. c	36. d	36. c	36. a	36. a	36. d
37. d	37. b	37. c	37. a	37. c	37. b	37. b	37. c
38. a	38. d	38. a	38. b	38. a	38. d	38. b	38. d
39. c	39. c	39. d	39. d	39. a	39. d	39. d	39. b
40. b	40. d	40. a	40. a	40. d	40. b	40. a	40. d
41. c	41. a	41. d	41. d	41. c	41. c	41. a	41. d
42. a	42. a	42. b	42. a	42. b	42. d	42. a	42. b
43. c	43. b	43. d	43. b	43. b	43. b	43. b	43. a
44. a	44. a	44. b	44. c	44. b	44. c	44. b	44. d
45. c	45. c	45. b	45. c	45. b	45. c	45. c	45. a
46. d	46. a	46. c	46. a	46. c	46. d	46. d	46. b
47. b	47. a	47. b	47. b	47. a	47. c	47. d	47. d
48. c	48. d	48. b	48. b	48. a	48. a	48. a	48. b
49. d	49. d	49. c	49. b	49. a	49. b	49. b	49. b
50. a	50. c	50. c	50. c	50. c	50. d	50. c	50. d

Answers to the Chapter Activities:
BUILDING VOCABULARY SKILLS, SHORT VERSION

Chapter 1 (Taking Exams)

Ten Words in Context	*Matching Words/Defs*	*Sentence Check 1*	*Sentence Check 2*	*Final Check*
1. B 6. A	1. 8 6. 7	1. F 6. H	1–2. A, F	1. I 6. C
2. A 7. C	2. 4 7. 6	2. C 7. G	3–4. D, H	2. G 7. A
3. B 8. B	3. 2 8. 3	3. J 8. B	5–6. B, G	3. J 8. E
4. C 9. C	4. 10 9. 9	4. E 9. A	7–8. C, E	4. D 9. B
5. B 10. B	5. 1 10. 5	5. I 10. D	9–10. I, J	5. F 10. H

Chapter 2 (Nate the Woodsman)

Ten Words in Context	*Matching Words/Defs*	*Sentence Check 1*	*Sentence Check 2*	*Final Check*
1. B 6. C	1. 6 6. 7	1. B 6. I	1–2. C, H	1. J 6. B
2. C 7. B	2. 4 7. 3	2. H 7. F	3–4. I, B	2. G 7. I
3. C 8. A	3. 8 8. 5	3. E 8. A	5–6. J, F	3. H 8. C
4. A 9. A	4. 10 9. 9	4. D 9. C	7–8. G, E	4. D 9. A
5. B 10. B	5. 1 10. 2	5. G 10. J	9–10. A, D	5. F 10. E

Chapter 3 (Who's on Trial?)

Ten Words in Context	*Matching Words/Defs*	*Sentence Check 1*	*Sentence Check 2*	*Final Check*
1. C 6. C	1. 2 6. 10	1. B 6. H	1–2. I, H	1. B 6. F
2. B 7. A	2. 6 7. 9	2. J 7. A	3–4. G, D	2. H 7. G
3. A 8. A	3. 4 8. 5	3. F 8. I	5–6. C, A	3. D 8. I
4. B 9. A	4. 7 9. 8	4. G 9. E	7–8. F, J	4. C 9. E
5. B 10. C	5. 1 10. 3	5. D 10. C	9–10. B, E	5. J 10. A

Chapter 4 (Night Nurse)

Ten Words in Context	*Matching Words/Defs*	*Sentence Check 1*	*Sentence Check 2*	*Final Check*
1. B 6. C	1. 8 6. 3	1. C 6. D	1–2. H, A	1. D 6. H
2. A 7. A	2. 10 7. 9	2. B 7. A	3–4. F, G	2. A 7. I
3. C 8. C	3. 4 8. 7	3. H 8. G	5–6. E, J	3. F 8. B
4. A 9. B	4. 6 9. 2	4. I 9. J	7–8. I, D	4. J 9. C
5. B 10. C	5. 1 10. 5	5. E 10. F	9–10. B, C	5. E 10. G

Chapter 5 (Relating to Parents)

Ten Words in Context	*Matching Words/Defs*	*Sentence Check 1*	*Sentence Check 2*	*Final Check*
1. B 6. A	1. 8 6. 5	1. G 6. H	1–2. J, I	1. C 6. J
2. C 7. C	2. 3 7. 6	2. I 7. F	3–4. H, E	2. B 7. A
3. A 8. A	3. 10 8. 4	3. D 8. J	5–6. G, D	3. H 8. G
4. C 9. C	4. 7 9. 9	4. A 9. C	7–8. B, A	4. I 9. F
5. A 10. C	5. 1 10. 2	5. E 10. B	9–10. F, C	5. D 10. E

Chapter 6 (Job Choices)

Ten Words in Context	*Matching Words/Defs*	*Sentence Check 1*	*Sentence Check 2*	*Final Check*
1. B 6. B	1. 4 6. 3	1. C 6. G	1–2. B, E	1. I 6. G
2. A 7. B	2. 1 7. 9	2. J 7. E	3–4. I, J	2. J 7. E
3. B 8. A	3. 8 8. 6	3. F 8. B	5–6. A, H	3. D 8. H
4. C 9. B	4. 10 9. 2	4. I 9. D	7–8. C, G	4. A 9. B
5. A 10. C	5. 7 10. 5	5. H 10. A	9–10. D, F	5. F 10. C

Chapter 7 (Museum Pet)

Ten Words in Context	*Matching Words/Defs*	*Sentence Check 1*	*Sentence Check 2*	*Final Check*
1. A 6. B	1. 6 6. 4	1. G 6. E	1–2. D, F	1. E 6. H
2. B 7. B	2. 3 7. 8	2. B 7. I	3–4. I, A	2. B 7. J
3. A 8. C	3. 7 8. 10	3. A 8. C	5–6. C, H	3. C 8. A
4. C 9. C	4. 9 9. 2	4. D 9. F	7–8. J, B	4. F 9. I
5. C 10. B	5. 1 10. 5	5. J 10. H	9–10. E, G	5. G 10. D

Chapter 8 (Our Headstrong Baby)

Ten Words in Context	*Matching Words/Defs*	*Sentence Check 1*	*Sentence Check 2*	*Final Check*
1. B 6. A	1. 8 6. 10	1. F 6. B	1–2. B, F	1. E 6. G
2. B 7. B	2. 3 7. 4	2. G 7. D	3–4. C, E	2. D 7. C
3. B 8. C	3. 9 8. 6	3. J 8. C	5–6. D, G	3. H 8. A
4. C 9. B	4. 7 9. 2	4. E 9. H	7–8. H, J	4. B 9. J
5. A 10. C	5. 1 10. 5	5. A 10. I	9–10. A, I	5. F 10. I

Chapter 9 (A Narrow Escape)

Ten Words in Context	*Matching Words/Defs*	*Sentence Check 1*	*Sentence Check 2*	*Final Check*
1. C 6. A	1. 6 6. 7	1. C 6. G	1–2. H, G	1. H 6. B
2. B 7. B	2. 8 7. 10	2. E 7. I	3–4. B, F	2. C 7. D
3. C 8. C	3. 9 8. 1	3. H 8. D	5–6. A, I	3. F 8. G
4. A 9. C	4. 2 9. 3	4. B 9. J	7–8. J, C	4. A 9. E
5. B 10. A	5. 4 10. 5	5. A 10. F	9–10. E, D	5. J 10. I

Chapter 10 (The Power of Advertising)

Ten Words in Context	*Matching Words/Defs*	*Sentence Check 1*	*Sentence Check 2*	*Final Check*
1. C 6. C	1. 7 6. 5	1. C 6. E	1–2. A, I	1. J 6. I
2. B 7. C	2. 3 7. 8	2. H 7. A	3–4. D, G	2. F 7. H
3. A 8. B	3. 10 8. 4	3. D 8. B	5–6. C, E	3. E 8. B
4. B 9. A	4. 6 9. 2	4. F 9. G	7–8. J, F	4. D 9. G
5. A 10. B	5. 1 10. 9	5. J 10. I	9–10. H, B	5. A 10. C

Chapter 11 (Waiter)

Ten Words in Context	*Matching Words/Defs*	*Sentence Check 1*	*Sentence Check 2*	*Final Check*
1. B 6. C	1. 8 6. 2	1. F 6. G	1–2. E, C	1. E 6. C
2. A 7. A	2. 4 7. 5	2. H 7. D	3–4. J, B	2. I 7. F
3. B 8. C	3. 9 8. 10	3. C 8. E	5–6. I, D	3. J 8. H
4. A 9. B	4. 6 9. 7	4. I 9. A	7–8. F, H	4. B 9. G
5. A 10. C	5. 3 10. 1	5. J 10. B	9–10. G, A	5. D 10. A

Chapter 12 (Adjusting to a New Culture)

Ten Words in Context	*Matching Words/Defs*	*Sentence Check 1*	*Sentence Check 2*	*Final Check*
1. B 6. B	1. 9 6. 7	1. B 6. I	1–2. B, G	1. B 6. E
2. A 7. C	2. 4 7. 1	2. E 7. A	3–4. F, D	2. C 7. H
3. C 8. A	3. 6 8. 5	3. G 8. C	5–6. E, I	3. A 8. G
4. A 9. A	4. 3 9. 8	4. D 9. F	7–8. J, H	4. F 9. J
5. B 10. B	5. 10 10. 2	5. H 10. J	9–10. A, C	5. D 10. I

Chapter 13 (A Dream About Wealth)

Ten Words in Context	*Matching Words/Defs*	*Sentence Check 1*	*Sentence Check 2*	*Final Check*
1. B 6. B	1. 2 6. 9	1. I 6. A	1–2. J, I	1. J 6. G
2. A 7. B	2. 10 7. 5	2. G 7. F	3–4. B, D	2. C 7. H
3. B 8. C	3. 6 8. 3	3. B 8. D	5–6. C, A	3. A 8. F
4. C 9. A	4. 8 9. 4	4. J 9. E	7–8. F, H	4. I 9. B
5. C 10. B	5. 1 10. 7	5. H 10. C	9–10. E, G	5. E 10. D

Chapter 14 (Children and Drugs)

Ten Words in Context	*Matching Words/Defs*	*Sentence Check 1*	*Sentence Check 2*	*Final Check*
1. B 6. A	1. 8 6. 1	1. D 6. A	1–2. A, E	1. J 6. B
2. A 7. B	2. 3 7. 5	2. J 7. B	3–4. I, F	2. I 7. G
3. B 8. C	3. 10 8. 4	3. H 8. E	5–6. D, C	3. D 8. A
4. C 9. A	4. 6 9. 2	4. F 9. I	7–8. J, H	4. C 9. H
5. B 10. B	5. 7 10. 9	5. G 10. C	9–10. B, G	5. E 10. F

Chapter 15 (Party House)

Ten Words in Context	*Matching Words/Defs*	*Sentence Check 1*	*Sentence Check 2*	*Final Check*
1. B 6. C	1. 8 6. 10	1. F 6. J	1–2. G, J	1. B 6. H
2. C 7. C	2. 7 7. 4	2. I 7. H	3–4. I, C	2. G 7. I
3. C 8. B	3. 1 8. 6	3. A 8. D	5–6. H, A	3. A 8. J
4. B 9. A	4. 2 9. 3	4. G 9. B	7–8. D, E	4. C 9. F
5. A 10. A	5. 5 10. 9	5. C 10. E	9–10. F, B	5. D 10. E

Chapter 16 (Procrastinator)

Ten Words in Context	*Matching Words/Defs*	*Sentence Check 1*	*Sentence Check 2*	*Final Check*
1. A 6. B	1. 6 6. 10	1. I 6. G	1–2. G, F	1. E 6. A
2. B 7. C	2. 4 7. 8	2. D 7. B	3–4. C, I	2. C 7. D
3. A 8. A	3. 7 8. 3	3. E 8. J	5–6. A, J	3. G 8. I
4. C 9. B	4. 1 9. 5	4. A 9. C	7–8. E, D	4. J 9. F
5. C 10. B	5. 9 10. 2	5. F 10. H	9–10. H, B	5. H 10. B

Chapter 17 (A Change in View)

Ten Words in Context	*Matching Words/Defs*	*Sentence Check 1*	*Sentence Check 2*	*Final Check*
1. A 6. C	1. 4 6. 2	1. A 6. B	1–2. D, J	1. J 6. F
2. C 7. B	2. 1 7. 8	2. D 7. C	3–4. F, G	2. I 7. E
3. B 8. A	3. 6 8. 3	3. G 8. E	5–6. B, A	3. B 8. A
4. A 9. B	4. 10 9. 5	4. H 9. I	7–8. H, I	4. H 9. C
5. B 10. C	5. 9 10. 7	5. J 10. F	9–10. E, C	5. D 10. G

Chapter 18 (Family Differences)

Ten Words in Context	*Matching Words/Defs*	*Sentence Check 1*	*Sentence Check 2*	*Final Check*
1. B 6. A	1. 4 6. 3	1. A 6. I	1–2. J, G	1. B 6. I
2. B 7. C	2. 10 7. 5	2. B 7. D	3–4. F, A	2. D 7. F
3. A 8. B	3. 8 8. 6	3. F 8. G	5–6. C, H	3. J 8. E
4. C 9. B	4. 9 9. 2	4. J 9. E	7–8. E, B	4. G 9. H
5. A 10. C	5. 1 10. 7	5. H 10. C	9–10. I, D	5. C 10. A

Chapter 19 (Chicken Pox)

Ten Words in Context	*Matching Words/Defs*	*Sentence Check 1*	*Sentence Check 2*	*Final Check*
1. B 6. C	1. 5 6. 9	1. J 6. E	1–2. J, D	1. J 6. H
2. C 7. B	2. 7 7. 10	2. I 7. D	3–4. F, C	2. E 7. I
3. A 8. A	3. 2 8. 6	3. G 8. B	5–6. G, A	3. F 8. C
4. B 9. B	4. 3 9. 8	4. A 9. H	7–8. E, H	4. B 9. D
5. A 10. C	5. 1 10. 4	5. F 10. C	9–10. B, I	5. A 10. G

Chapter 20 (Walking)

Ten Words in Context	*Matching Words/Defs*	*Sentence Check 1*	*Sentence Check 2*	*Final Check*
1. B 6. B	1. 4 6. 9	1. I 6. D	1–2. J, G	1. C 6. H
2. B 7. C	2. 8 7. 5	2. G 7. J	3–4. H, D	2. F 7. I
3. C 8. C	3. 6 8. 3	3. B 8. F	5–6. B, A	3. B 8. A
4. C 9. A	4. 2 9. 10	4. C 9. E	7–8. E, F	4. G 9. E
5. A 10. C	5. 1 10. 7	5. A 10. H	9–10. C, I	5. J 10. D

Answers to the Unit Reviews:
BUILDING VOCABULARY SKILLS, SHORT VERSION

Unit One

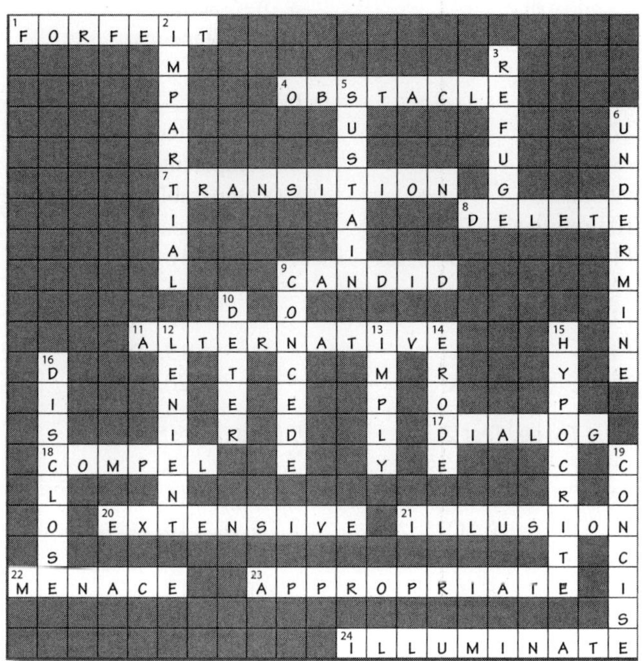

Unit Two

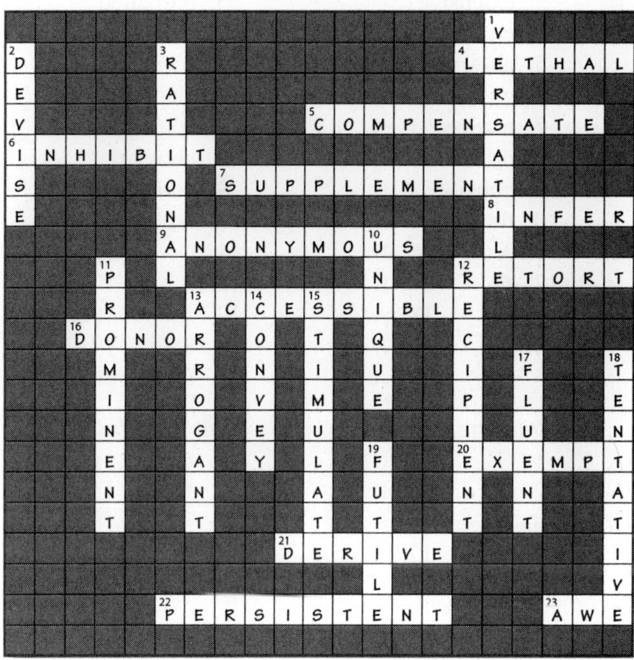

Unit Three

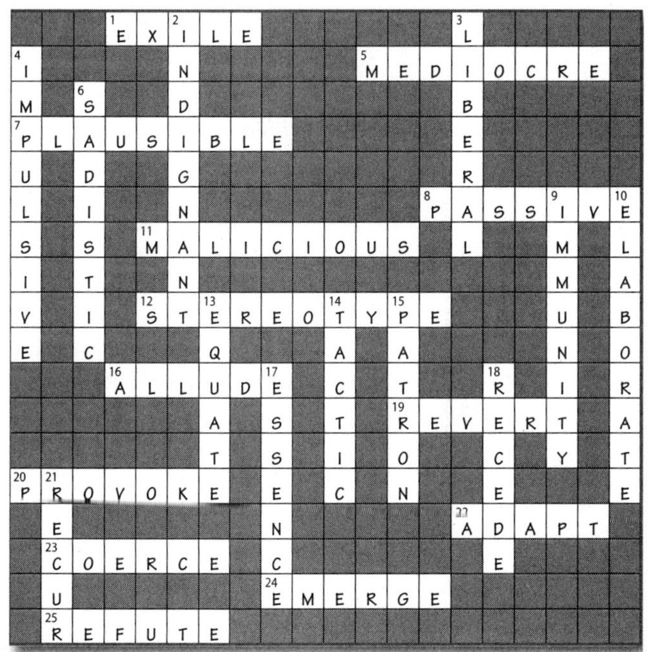

Unit Four

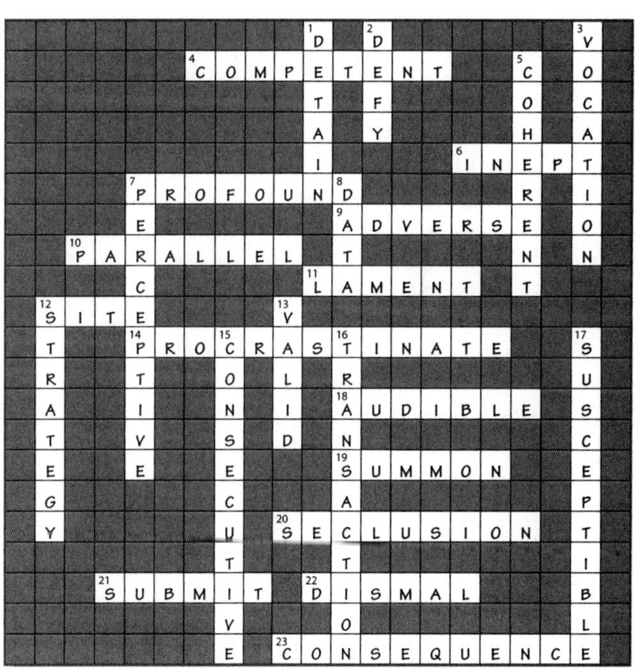

Answers to the Unit Tests: BUILDING VOCABULARY SKILLS, SHORT VERSION

Unit One

Unit One, Test 1

1. undermine
2. avert
3. extensive
4. endorse
5. alternative
6. gruesome
7. novice
8. urban
9. concise
10. transition

11. A 16. B
12. C 17. D
13. A 18. A
14. C 19. D
15. D 20. A

Unit One, Test 2

1. G 14. C
2. C 15. I
3. F 16. I
4. A 17. C
5. L 18. I
6. E 19. I
7. K 20. C
8. B 21. C
9. J 22. I
10. D 23. C
11. I 24. I
12. H 25. C
13. M

Unit One, Test 3

1. B 14. A 26. A 39. D
2. A 15. D 27. B 40. A
3. B 16. B 28. D 41. C
4. C 17. D 29. C 42. B
5. C 18. B 30. C 43. D
6. B 19. A 31. A 44. C
7. D 20. C 32. B 45. A
8. D 21. A 33. D 46. A
9. A 22. D 34. A 47. C
10. D 23. B 35. D 48. D
11. A 24. C 36. A 49. B
12. B 25. D 37. C 50. D
13. C 38. B

Unit One, Test 4

1. C 11. C
2. D 12. A
3. B 13. C
4. A 14. A
5. D 15. B
6. D 16. D
7. C 17. A
8. A 18. C
9. D 19. A
10. A 20. C

Unit Two

Unit Two, Test 1

1. retrieve
2. phobia
3. propelled
4. surpassed
5. accessible
6. elapse
7. convey
8. derived
9. verify
10. ordeal

11. C 16. C
12. C 17. D
13. A 18. C
14. B 19. A
15. D 20. B

Unit Two, Test 2

1. F 14. C
2. J 15. C
3. A 16. I
4. C 17. C
5. M 18. I
6. G 19. I
7. L 20. I
8. K 21. C
9. E 22. I
10. B 23. I
11. H 24. C
12. I 25. C
13. D

Unit Two, Test 3

1. A 14. B 26. D 39. C
2. C 15. A 27. A 40. D
3. B 16. D 28. B 41. B
4. D 17. A 29. C 42. A
5. A 18. C 30. D 43. B
6. C 19. B 31. C 44. C
7. B 20. A 32. B 45. C
8. D 21. A 33. A 46. A
9. A 22. B 34. C 47. B
10. C 23. C 35. A 48. D
11. D 24. D 36. B 49. C
12. D 25. A 37. D 50. B
13. C 38. B

Unit Two, Test 4

1. D 11. B
2. B 12. C
3. A 13. C
4. A 14. B
5. D 15. B
6. C 16. D
7. D 17. A
8. B 18. B
9. D 19. D
10. A 20. A

Unit Three

Unit Three, Test 1

1. reciprocated
2. plausible
3. provoke
4. frugal
5. mediocre
6. alleged
7. options
8. query
9. passive
10. refuted

11. A 16. B
12. C 17. D
13. B 18. A
14. B 19. C
15. A 20. A

Unit Three, Test 2

1. G 14. I
2. C 15. I
3. D 16. C
4. I 17. C
5. F 18. C
6. L 19. C
7. E 20. I
8. K 21. I
9. A 22. C
10. M 23. I
11. H 24. I
12. J 25. C
13. B

Unit Three, Test 3

1. C 14. C 26. D 39. A
2. A 15. B 27. A 40. C
3. A 16. D 28. C 41. B
4. C 17. A 29. D 42. D
5. B 18. D 30. A 43. A
6. D 19. C 31. B 44. C
7. C 20. B 32. B 45. C
8. A 21. A 33. D 46. A
9. C 22. B 34. B 47. D
10. B 23. D 35. D 48. D
11. D 24. C 36. C 49. D
12. A 25. D 37. A 50. A
13. B 38. C

Unit Three, Test 4

1. C 11. A
2. A 12. B
3. D 13. B
4. A 14. C
5. C 15. A
6. C 16. D
7. D 17. D
8. A 18. D
9. D 19. C
10. B 20. B

Unit Four

Unit Four, Test 1

1. site
2. susceptible
3. transaction
4. simultaneous
5. strategy
6. data
7. transmitted
8. competent
9. comparable
10. discriminate

11. B 16. A
12. C 17. C
13. C 18. A
14. D 19. D
15. B 20. D

Unit Four, Test 2

1. K 14. I
2. F 15. I
3. H 16. I
4. G 17. C
5. M 18. I
6. B 19. C
7. E 20. I
8. C 21. C
9. I 22. C
10. D 23. I
11. L 24. C
12. A 25. C
13. J

Unit Four, Test 3

1. C 14. A 26. A 39. A
2. B 15. B 27. D 40. B
3. D 16. D 28. B 41. A
4. D 17. D 29. A 42. B
5. A 18. A 30. C 43. B
6. C 19. C 31. D 44. C
7. B 20. B 32. B 45. D
8. D 21. A 33. A 46. A
9. D 22. B 34. D 47. D
10. A 23. C 35. B 48. C
11. B 24. A 36. C 49. C
12. C 25. D 37. C 50. D
13. B 38. B

Unit Four, Test 4

1. C 11. B
2. D 12. C
3. C 13. B
4. D 14. D
5. B 15. D
6. A 16. B
7. D 17. B
8. B 18. B
9. D 19. A
10. B 20. B

Mastery Test: *Chapter 1 (Taking Exams)*

In the space provided, write the word from the box needed to complete each sentence. Then put the **letter** of that word in the column at the left. Use each word once.

A. **acknowledge**	B. **alternative**	C. **anecdote**	D. **appropriate**	E. **avert**
F. **candid**	G. **compel**	H. **comply**	I. **concise**	J. **drastic**

____ 1. Fred thinks it's funny to do the opposite of what everyone else considers ____________________. For instance, he likes to send sympathy cards for weddings and birthdays.

____ 2. We keep a flashlight in every room to ____________________ being left in the dark in the event of a power failure.

____ 3. According to a(n) ____________________ a friend told me, someone once asked boxer Muhammed Ali if he were the "greatest" at golf. "Yes," Ali answered. "I just haven't played yet."

____ 4. A really successful commercial ____________________s viewers to leap from their chairs and rush out to buy the advertised item.

____ 5. All of the restaurant's desserts were fattening, so I chose another ____________________. I had a frozen fruit bar at home instead.

____ 6. To get me to ____________________ with her demands, my sister threatens to tell my boyfriend what I said after our first date: "Bo-ring!"

____ 7. Because they're not eager to ____________________ that cockroaches are among their residents, Germans refer to the "German cockroach" as the "Russian roach."

____ 8. Most newspapers have limited space for letters to the editor, so yours will have a better chance of being published if it's ____________________.

____ 9. Every day, polluters get away with dumping thousands of pounds of plastic into the sea. Clearly, we need more ____________________ penalties to make them stop.

____ 10. When Flora asked Rob to be really truthful in his opinion of her new dress, he told her, "To be perfectly ____________________, I don't like the color, style, or material, but it fits you really well."

SCORE: (Number correct) ________ × 10 = __________ %

Mastery Test: *Chapter 2 (Nate the Woodsman)*

In the space provided, write the word from the box needed to complete each sentence. Then put the **letter** of that word in the column at the left. Use each word once.

A. **dialog**	B. **erratic**	C. **extensive**	D. **forfeit**	E. **fortify**
F. **illuminate**	G. **isolate**	H. **refuge**	I. **reminisce**	J. **urban**

____ 1. Job opportunities are most numerous in ____________________ areas. Thus many people have no choice but to live surrounded by the concrete, metal, and glass of the city.

____ 2. In the movie, the characters' British accents were so thick that I had trouble understanding some of the ____________________.

____ 3. To ____________________ their stores against the coming hurricane, beachfront shopkeepers nailed boards over the windows.

____ 4. The zoo had to ____________________ one baboon who was attacking the others. He was put in his own cage in another building.

____ 5. At my class reunion, we ____________________(e)d about our years at school, including the time I broke my arm in gym and the day a piece of scenery fell during a play and hit the principal.

____ 6. Lately the weather has been wildly ____________________ . This morning, for example, it was raining and 90 degrees; by the late afternoon, it was dry and in the 50's, and it rained again at night.

____ 7. These days, candles are mainly used for decoration since most people have electric lights to ____________________ their homes.

____ 8. Many homeless people cannot find a place of ____________________ from wintry weather.

____ 9. The magazine printed only one paragraph on the "Save the Earth" meeting, but the local newspaper provided ____________________ coverage of the event—with photos and a full-page story.

____ 10. The Olympic swimmer had to ____________________ his gold medal when officials discovered that he had taken illegal muscle-building drugs.

SCORE: (Number correct) ________ × 10 = __________ %

Mastery Test: *Chapter 3 (Who's on Trial?)*

In the space provided, write the word from the box needed to complete each sentence. Then put the **letter** of that word in the column at the left. Use each word once.

A. **delete**	B. **impartial**	C. **integrity**	D. **legitimate**	E. **lenient**
F. **menace**	G. **morale**	H. **naive**	I. **overt**	J. **undermine**

____ 1. Abraham Lincoln is sometimes called "Honest Abe" because of his reputation for ______________________.

____ 2. The paperback version of the novel was a shortened one—two chapters had been ______________________(e)d.

____ 3. Violent crime is a(n) ______________________ to us all. In this century, nearly twice as many Americans have been murdered as have died in wars.

____ 4. The Smiths' pleasure in their son's engagement was certainly ______________________. They walked around with big smiles on their faces all night.

____ 5. When the cake collapsed, my ______________________ as a baker did too. I now don't even have enough confidence or desire to bake a cake from a mix.

____ 6. After Joe smashed the headlights of the family car, he hoped his parents would be ______________________. Instead, they grounded him until he paid for the damage.

____ 7. During the piano contest, the players were hidden behind a curtain so that the judges would cast ______________________ votes.

____ 8. For years, termites ______________________(e)d the house's wooden frame until it became dangerously damaged.

____ 9. When Lily started her job, she was ______________________ enough to think the other salespeople would be cooperative. However, she soon learned some people would stab her in the back for a sale.

____ 10. In most states, a marriage is not ______________________ unless the bride and groom applied for a license and got blood tests before the wedding.

SCORE: (Number correct) ________ × 10 = __________ %

Mastery Test: *Chapter 4 (Night Nurse)*

In the space provided, write the word from the box needed to complete each sentence. Then put the **letter** of that word in the column at the left. Use each word once.

A. **endorse**	B. **erode**	C. **gruesome**	D. **hypocrite**	E. **idealistic**
F. **illusion**	G. **impact**	H. **imply**	I. **novice**	J. **obstacle**

____ 1. The baseball struck the batter with such ____________________ that it broke his jaw.

____ 2. Although a majority of people in the state support the death penalty, the governor does not ____________________ it.

____ 3. If you blink two lights on and off in an otherwise dark room, you create the ____________________ that a single light is moving back and forth.

____ 4. Cliff's question to Judy—"Wouldn't you rather grab a hamburger than bother going to a fancy restaurant?"—was meant to ____________________ that he was low on cash.

____ 5. A(n) ____________________ at ice-skating, I can only manage to remain upright, while my experienced friends leap and twirl around me.

____ 6. The bodies taken out of the burned car were so ____________________ that even the medical examiner found the sight shocking.

____ 7. In the movie *Mr. Smith Goes to Washington*, Jimmy Stewart plays a(n) ____________________ senator who values honesty and public service more than riches.

____ 8. In the fairy tale "Rapunzel," there is one great ____________________ to the hero and heroine's happiness: she is locked in a tall tower with no door.

____ 9. The centuries had caused the Greek statue's colorful layer of paint to ____________________, leaving only the underlying white marble.

____ 10. Roy is such a(n) ____________________. He disapproves of handguns for other people, but he keeps one on his night table.

SCORE: (Number correct) ________ × 10 = ________ %

Mastery Test: *Chapter 5 (Relating to Parents)*

In the space provided, write the word from the box needed to complete each sentence. Then put the **letter** of that word in the column at the left. Use each word once.

A. **concede**	B. **conservative**	C. **contrary**	D. **denounce**	E. **deter**
F. **disclose**	G. **scapegoat**	H. **superficial**	I. **sustain**	J. **transition**

____ 1. There was too little time to make the ____________________ from bright sunlight to the dark movie theater. So I blindly felt my way down the aisle and then sat in the lap of a total stranger.

____ 2. Alex and Joe have ______________________ views of life. To Alex "life is a bowl of cherries," but to Joe "it's the pits."

____ 3. Gordon used to favor major changes in the company's treatment of workers. As soon as he became president, however, he turned ____________________.

____ 4. The car's patches of rust, lumpy seats, and moldy odor were enough to ____________________ me from buying it.

____ 5. When Max cheated on the test, the teacher ______________________(e)d him in front of the whole class and also expressed her disapproval of Max in a letter to his parents.

____ 6. Josie and Kate's friendship is deep, not ____________________. For example, they share their innermost thoughts and offer each other support in difficult times.

____ 7. Marilyn didn't intend to ______________________ the cost of the tie she gave Andy, but she revealed it down to the penny: when she wrapped the gift, she forgot to remove the price tag.

____ 8. After bragging about his skill as a carpenter, Tony was unwilling to __________________ that the crooked table was his own creation and not from a junk shop.

____ 9. Studies show that girls are more likely than boys to accept blame for their errors. Boys are more likely to look for ____________________s to blame instead.

____ 10. After the first ten minutes of weightlifting, I couldn't ____________________ the workout without risking muscle damage, so I stopped.

SCORE: (Number correct) ________ × 10 = __________ %

Mastery Test: *Chapter 6 (Job Choices)*

In the space provided, write the word from the box needed to complete each sentence. Then put the **letter** of that word in the column at the left. Use each word once.

A. **compensate**	B. **conceive**	C. **derive**	D. **diversity**	E. **inhibit**
F. **moderate**	G. **supplement**	H. **surpass**	I. **tentative**	J. **verify**

____ 1. No one in town could ______________________ of Gail as a drill instructor—she seemed too gentle and sweet to give orders.

____ 2. Bob had hoped to get a C in geometry, so the A he received certainly ____________________(e)d what he expected.

____ 3. Clint calls himself a ____________________ TV watcher, but I feel he watches much more than just a few programs a day.

____ 4. The ____________________ of products at outdoor markets is one of their attractions. Often they have baked goods, home decorations, fresh produce, and even clothing for sale.

____ 5. David ____________________s his income from several part-time jobs: word processing, waiting on tables, and yard work.

____ 6. Since mold grows most quickly in warm temperatures, refrigeration ____________________s its growth on food.

____ 7. When people apply for jobs at a company, the personnel director calls their previous employers to ____________________ that they have reported their job experience truthfully.

____ 8. Tyrone's supervisor gave him only ______________________ approval to take a day off. She had to check with her own boss to be sure.

____ 9. Because hay doesn't give our horses full nutrition, we ____________________ their diet with grains.

____ 10. Mrs. Brown promised to ______________________ Al for the gas he used driving her to the airport, but she hasn't paid him a penny yet.

SCORE: (Number correct) ________ × 10 = __________ %

 Name: ______________________________

Mastery Test: *Chapter 7 (Museum Pet)*

In the space provided, write the word from the box needed to complete each sentence. Then put the **letter** of that word in the column at the left. Use each word once.

A. **acute**	B. **anonymous**	C. **apprehensive**	D. **arrogant**	E. **bestow**
F. **donor**	G. **phobia**	H. **prominent**	I. **prudent**	J. **recipient**

____ 1. Some airlines offer classes to help people overcome their ________________s about air travel.

____ 2. Because the dentist had said the root canal would hurt "only a little," Doug wasn't prepared for the ________________ pain that followed.

____ 3. It isn't ________________ for a worker to insult the boss when quitting a job. The worker might need the boss later for a reference.

____ 4. The generous parents of the young man killed on the highway ________________(e)d his organs on transplant banks.

____ 5. The "No Smoking" sign was placed in a(n) ________________ spot near the restaurant's door so that customers would be sure to see it before entering.

____ 6. As the ________________ of an athletic scholarship, Brad has to keep up a B average or leave the team.

____ 7. The caller told police about a robbery going on at Fifth and Walnut, but she wouldn't give her name. For her own protection, she wanted her tip to remain ________________.

____ 8. Knowing he was wealthier than his classmates, the new boy was at first ________________, but his attitude changed when he realized he was one of the worst students in the class.

____ 9. The landscapers were ________________ about planting the bushes when the homeowner wasn't there, since he had strong opinions about the way his yard should look.

____ 10. Peggy volunteered to be a blood ________________ during the Red Cross drive, but a nurse said she weighed too little to give blood.

SCORE: (Number correct) ________ × 10 = __________ %

Mastery Test: *Chapter 8 (Our Headstrong Baby)*

In the space provided, write the word from the box needed to complete each sentence. Then put the **letter** of that word in the column at the left. Use each word once.

A. **accessible**	B. **awe**	C. **cite**	D. **compatible**	E. **exempt**
F. **prevail**	G. **propel**	H. **rational**	I. **retort**	J. **retrieve**

____ 1. I hate to say that Hank is a liar, but I could ____________________ many things he's told me that weren't true.

____ 2. The wheels that used to ____________________ Joshua's toy train are jammed with sand, so now it just sits there going "toot toot."

____ 3. The friendly way that Muffy and Ralph play together proves that a cat and dog can be ____________________.

____ 4. The sixth-graders looked up with ____________________ at the visiting professional baseball player.

____ 5. Because the prisoner had a weak heart, he was ____________________ from the hard physical labor required of the others.

____ 6. When my little nephew visited, I needed to move my supply of candy from a(n) ____________________ cupboard to one out of his reach.

____ 7. The paper boy threw the newspaper onto the Smiths' front porch and then went to ____________________ it when he remembered that the Smiths were out of town.

____ 8. When Lydia and Jeff discuss money, they always start out calm and ____________________ and end up yelling and unreasonable.

____ 9. If their best player is back in form tonight, the basketball team is sure to ____________________ over their opponents.

____ 10. When the rude customer tried to cut into the line, saying, "I don't like to be kept waiting," the clerk gave this ____________________: "Then I won't make you wait to hear just what I think of you."

SCORE: (Number correct) ________ × 10 = __________ %

Mastery Test: *Chapter 9 (A Narrow Escape)*

In the space provided, write the word from the box needed to complete each sentence. Then put the **letter** of that word in the column at the left. Use each word once.

A. **elapse**	B. **evasive**	C. **fluent**	D. **futile**	E. **harass**
F. **infer**	G. **lethal**	H. **obsession**	I. **ordeal**	J. **persistent**

____ 1. Grady's efforts to start his damaged car were ____________________, so he had to call a tow truck.

____ 2. The striking workers outside the factory ______________________(e)d people who crossed the picket line by yelling at them and calling them names.

____ 3. At first, the college counselor refused to let Chris retake the English entrance exam. But Chris was ____________________ in asking and was finally allowed to retake the test.

____ 4. When Yolanda discovered that Ben had been in prison for ten years, she understood why he had been so __________________ about his past.

____ 5. Being either extremely thin or very overweight indicates that food may be a(n) _______________.

____ 6. Tara is not speaking to her mother, so I ____________________ that they have had a fight.

____ 7. People who were abused as children often suffer an emotional _____________________ that goes on long after the physical pain is over.

____ 8. Dogs love chocolate, but the sweet stuff can be ____________________ for them. More than one family has seen its pet die after it ate chocolate candy.

____ 9. In order to control his temper, Ira let some time _______________________ before scolding his daughter about the broken lamp.

____ 10. You can learn a foreign language from books and records. But to become truly _______________ in the language, you must also converse with native speakers.

SCORE: (Number correct) ______ × 10 = ________ %

Mastery Test: *Chapter 10 (The Power of Advertising)*

In the space provided, write the word from the box needed to complete each sentence. Then put the **letter** of that word in the column at the left. Use each word once.

A. **convey**	B. **delusion**	C. **devise**	D. **savor**	E. **stimulate**
F. **subtle**	G. **unique**	H. **universal**	I. **versatile**	J. **vivid**

____ 1. We must ____________________ a way to keep Tia away from the house until we finish setting up her surprise party.

____ 2. Although Georgia dyed her hair, the color change was so ____________________ that few people noticed it.

____ 3. Because my brother's Volkswagen is ____________________, I would know it anywhere. It's painted in day-glo colors and has a bumper sticker that says, "Yo! I'm here!"

____ 4. As her Alzheimer's disease worsened, my grandmother held the ____________________ that people on TV could see her.

____ 5. Naomi's photo of hot-air balloons is ____________________—red, orange, and purple balloons are sailing through a bright blue sky.

____ 6. A talented actor can ____________________ emotions through gestures and postures, as well as through words.

____ 7. When we go to the movies, Sam fills his shirt pocket with M&Ms. Eating them one at a time, he____________________s them until the picture's end.

____ 8. "We're looking for someone really ____________________ for this position," said the interviewer, "someone who can write well, speak well in public, and demonstrate our new hang glider."

____ 9. The fruit cup served before the main course was supposed to ____________________ my appetite. Instead, it satisfied my hunger.

____ 10. Knowing that no movie can have ____________________ appeal, producers must decide what type of person they hope to reach.

SCORE: (Number correct) ________ × 10 = ___________ %

Mastery Test: *Chapter 11 (Waiter)*

In the space provided, write the word from the box needed to complete each sentence. Then put the **letter** of that word in the column at the left. Use each word once.

A. **defer**	B. **endeavor**	C. **equate**	D. **impose**	E. **indignant**
F. **inevitable**	G. **malicious**	H. **option**	I. **passive**	J. **patron**

____ 1. Donna wrote a letter of complaint to the publisher of a textbook. She was ____________ that the book always referred to doctors as "he" and nurses as "she."

____ 2. Some people believe any spanking of a child is wrong. They ____________ it with child abuse.

____ 3. If Vince continues to talk on his cell phone while he's driving, it's ____________ that he'll cause an accident.

____ 4. We've become loyal ____________s of the Lebanese restaurant because we enjoy its delicious Middle Eastern food.

____ 5. Devan's dog is the most ____________ animal I've ever seen. A mouse actually ran over its paw, and it didn't even bother to raise its head.

____ 6. I know you don't like Barry, but please ____________ to be polite to him when he's here as a guest.

____ 7. When you order a pizza here, you have the choice of usual toppings, like mushrooms and pepperoni, as well as unusual ____________s such as avocado, broccoli, or pineapple.

____ 8. My brother often ____________s on my mother's generosity by asking her for money.

____ 9. The children playing baseball broke a window by accident—it wasn't a(n) ____________ act.

____ 10. "When it comes to decorating our apartment," Jasmin said, "I ____________ to my husband's judgment. He has better taste than I do."

SCORE: (Number correct) ________ × 10 = ________ %

Mastery Test: *Chapter 12 (Adjusting to a New Culture)*

In the space provided, write the word from the box needed to complete each sentence. Then put the **letter** of that word in the column at the left. Use each word once.

A. **adapt**	B. **dismay**	C. **exile**	D. **gesture**	E. **recede**
F. **reciprocate**	G. **refute**	H. **retain**	I. **revert**	J. **ritual**

____ 1. The ____________________ of shaking one's head back and forth does not mean "no" in all cultures.

____ 2. The neatness of Bill's house ____________________s his claim that he is lazy and sloppy.

____ 3. Grandma sold most of her belongings when she moved to a retirement apartment, but she ____________________(e)d what had been Grandpa's favorite chair.

____ 4. After Alice Weston died, her dog would at first only lie quietly in his new owner's home. But after a few weeks, he ____________________(e)d to the situation and became livelier.

____ 5. The Bensons have had us over so often that we really should ____________________, but I don't know how we'll fit their large family into our small dining room.

____ 6. The long line outside the box office so ____________________(e)d Bryan that he didn't even attempt to buy a ticket.

____ 7. After he lost his throne, the Shah of Iran spent the rest of his life in ____________________, never returning to his native country.

____ 8. The hurricane victims had to wait until the flood waters ____________________(e)d before they could return to their homes.

____ 9. Mr. Byron is so fearful of germs that several times a day he goes through a(n) ____________________ of wiping his hands with alcohol and then rinsing them.

____ 10. Many teenagers speak politely in the presence of adults but ____________________ to rough slang when talking among themselves.

SCORE: (Number correct) ________ × 10 = __________ %

Mastery Test: *Chapter 13 (A Dream About Wealth)*

In the space provided, write the word from the box needed to complete each sentence. Then put the **letter** of that word in the column at the left. Use each word once.

A. **elaborate**	B. **emerge**	C. **exotic**	D. **frugal**	E. **impulsive**
F. **indifferent**	G. **indulgent**	H. **liberal**	I. **mediocre**	J. **notable**

____ 1. The Gilmans are ____________________ supporters of their local public TV station; they make a large donation every year.

____ 2. The crowd scene in the painting was so ____________________ that even the buttons on people's coats were carefully painted in.

____ 3. Aunt Mary shows how ____________________ she is when she carefully opens a gift so that the wrapping can be re-used.

____ 4. Maggie is ____________________, but she often regrets doing whatever she feels like, such as sliding down a muddy hill in her best pants.

____ 5. When the rock star ____________________(e)d from his car, screaming fans rushed forward to get his autograph.

____ 6. Before Ronald Reagan was President, he was ____________________ as a film star and TV actor.

____ 7. Kevin gets a haircut only to prevent hair from falling into his eyes. He's ____________________ about how stylish or well-groomed he looks.

____ 8. Phyllis loves to browse through shops with Indian brass work, African wood carvings, and other ____________________ arts and crafts.

____ 9. Eddy's ____________________ parents spoil him. They buy him lots of candy and toys and let his worst behavior go without even a scolding.

____ 10. The clothes at that shop are ____________________. They aren't as shabby as those in some of the cheapest stores, but they aren't as well-made as clothing in the best department stores.

SCORE: (Number correct) ________ × 10 = __________ %

Mastery Test: *Chapter 14 (Children and Drugs)*

In the space provided, write the word from the box needed to complete each sentence. Then put the **letter** of that word in the column at the left. Use each word once.

A. **affirm**	B. **alleged**	C. **allude**	D. **coerce**	E. **elite**
F. **essence**	G. **immunity**	H. **impair**	I. **query**	J. **sadistic**

____ 1. The Loch Ness Monster is ______________________ to live in a lake in Scotland, but there's no proof that the dinosaur-like creature even exists.

____ 2. Aging tends to ______________________ people's vision. They can't see as well as they used to.

____ 3. If a witness in a trial is uncomfortable with swearing on a Bible, he or she may simply ______________________ to tell the truth.

____ 4. The teacher promised ______________________ from punishment to whoever had broken the classroom window—if that person confessed immediately.

____ 5. Paul ______________________(e)d to his adoption when he said, "Not surprisingly, I don't look like either of my parents."

____ 6. Russell had several questions, but he was too shy to ______________________ the famous speaker.

____ 7. The ______________________ of Santa Claus is loving generosity.

____ 8. Some consider Columbian to be the ______________________ coffee—the best in aroma and flavor.

____ 9. When I was younger, my parents ______________________(e)d me into drinking eggnog every day. Not surprisingly, I still hate the taste of the stuff.

____ 10. Before being fired, the ______________________ teacher enjoyed embarrassing any student who displeased him in the slightest.

SCORE: (Number correct) ________ × 10 = ____________ %

Mastery Test: *Chapter 15 (Party House)*

In the space provided, write the word from the box needed to complete each sentence. Then put the **letter** of that word in the column at the left. Use each word once.

A. **plausible**	B. **provoke**	C. **recur**	D. **reprimand**	E. **revoke**
F. **ridicule**	G. **shrewd**	H. **skeptical**	I. **stereotype**	J. **tactic**

____ 1. It ____________________s me if someone tries to step in line in front of me. I feel like shoving the person away.

____ 2. Singer Dolly Parton laughs at the ________________________ of the "dumb blonde." "I know I'm not dumb," she says. "And I'm not really blonde, either."

____ 3. "Have some of this delicious wheat-and-bean-sprouts cake," I said to Tom, whose ____________ look showed he doubted it was wise to accept the offer.

____ 4. Since Chet was wearing a neck brace, the teacher found his excuse for missing the test—an auto accident—to be entirely ____________________.

____ 5. When Derrick was a teen, his parents' most effective weapon against him was the threat that they would ____________________ his driving privileges.

____ 6. In children's stories, the fox is often presented as a ____________________ individual who outsmarts all his enemies.

____ 7. The political cartoon ____________________(e)d the senator, but he found the mockery so clever that he couldn't help laughing.

____ 8. I have a frightening dream that ____________________s two or three times a year. I dream I'm in an elevator that gets stuck between floors, and I have no way to let anyone know where I am.

____ 9. My brother and I agreed on our ____________________ before asking to go to the fair. He would tell Mom that Dad said we could go, and I would tell Dad that Mom said we could go.

____ 10. People were angry when the police officer who had beaten an innocent bystander received only a ____________________. Community members felt he should have received a greater punishment.

SCORE: (Number correct) ________ × 10 = __________ %

Mastery Test: *Chapter 16 (Procrastinator)*

In the space provided, write the word from the box needed to complete each sentence. Then put the **letter** of that word in the column at the left. Use each word once.

A. **consequence**	B. **destiny**	C. **detain**	D. **diminish**	E. **procrastinate**
F. **simultaneous**	G. **strategy**	H. **tedious**	I. **transaction**	J. **vital**

____ 1. "If it is ______________ that you marry Roger, it will happen no matter what else happens," Aunt Blanche told my sister. "No one can escape fate."

____ 2. To celebrate the city's 200th birthday, there were several ______________ parties in city parks and streets. They were all scheduled to take place from 8 p.m. to midnight.

____ 3. When you buy something expensive, keep the receipt for a while. Then, if you return the purchase, you'll have proof the ______________ took place.

____ 4. "I need this delivered across town as quickly as possible," Will's boss told him. "Don't let anything ______________ you."

____ 5. Flo's ______________ for weight loss includes a three-mile walk every morning and absolutely no snacking at night.

____ 6. If the ivory trade is not stopped, the world's population of elephants will ______________ to such a low number that they could disappear from the wild.

____ 7. When you're involved in a ______________ task like window-washing, it helps to have someone to talk to—unless, of course, the person is as boring as the window-washing.

____ 8. Martin insulted several guests at Bea's party. As a ______________, Bea won't ever invite him over again.

____ 9. The restaurant failed because the owners overlooked one ______________ fact: There were already too many seafood restaurants in the area.

____ 10. When the brakes on Betsy's car began to make a strange sound, she took the car to a mechanic immediately. "I don't ______________ when my safety is involved," she said.

SCORE: (Number correct) ________ × 10 = __________ %

Mastery Test: *Chapter 17 (A Change in View)*

In the space provided, write the word from the box needed to complete each sentence. Then put the **letter** of that word in the column at the left. Use each word once.

A. **discriminate**	B. **dismal**	C. **dispense**	D. **profound**	E. **severity**
F. **site**	G. **subside**	H. **summon**	I. **theoretical**	J. **vocation**

____ 1. The relief workers ____________________(e)d bags of rice to the hungry refugees waiting in line.

____ 2. It's no use talking to Paul until his anger ________________s and he becomes more reasonable.

____ 3. Discussions about possible life on planets around other suns are ____________________ since no one has ever visited there.

____ 4. When Amy's uncle found her playing with his woodworking tools, he scolded her with such ____________________ that she started to cry.

____ 5. Randy feared a long lecture when he was ____________________(e)d to the principal's office.

____ 6. That rock band plays only on weekends. And you'd never guess the full-time ________________ of its lead singer—he's a lawyer.

____ 7. The ____________________ of the music festival had to be changed because local residents didn't want it nearby.

____ 8. The movie was so ____________________—with its sad story, cheerless characters, and gray skies—that afterwards we all felt low.

____ 9. Because he's color blind, Tom cannot ____________________ between blue and purple.

____ 10. After watching a man threaten to jump off a ledge, Maggie felt ____________________ relief when he was persuaded to climb back inside the building.

SCORE: (Number correct) ________ × 10 = __________ %

Mastery Test: *Chapter 18 (Family Differences)*

In the space provided, write the word from the box needed to complete each sentence. Then put the **letter** of that word in the column at the left. Use each word once.

A. **data**	B. **inept**	C. **innate**	D. **intervene**	E. **lament**
F. **morbid**	G. **obstinate**	H. **parallel**	I. **perceptive**	J. **sedate**

____ 1. Do most people have a(n)____________________ fear of spiders, or do they gain the fear after birth, through experience?

____ 2. The town council spent months studying ______________________ on the town recreation center before approving its construction.

____ 3. Some newspapers appeal to people's curiosity about horrible events by publishing every ______________________ detail of accidents and crimes.

____ 4. Rather than take a risk and ______________________ in the fight between two armed men, Ralph called the police to come and end the fight.

____ 5. The children shrieked as they splashed and dived, while I, remaining ______________________, swam calmly around the pool.

____ 6. Dad was such a(n) ______________________ handyman that when he tried to do home repairs, he usually made the problem worse.

____ 7. Train tracks are ______________________ and thus never meet, but when you look down the tracks at a distance, they appear to move closer and closer together.

____ 8. Diane, who ______________________s whenever she sees a dead animal on the road, keeps her own cats inside to protect them.

____ 9. The boss thinks he's ______________________ enough to know when there are problems at work, but the truth is that he's not aware of half of what goes on in the office.

____ 10. Sometimes it can be good to be ______________________. The author of the now-famous Dr. Seuss books stubbornly kept trying to get his first one published even though it was rejected 23 times.

SCORE: (Number correct) ________ × 10 = __________ %

Mastery Test: *Chapter 19 (Chicken Pox)*

In the space provided, write the word from the box needed to complete each sentence. Then put the **letter** of that word in the column at the left. Use each word once.

A. **confirm**	B. **deceptive**	C. **defy**	D. **restrain**	E. **seclusion**
F. **submit**	G. **susceptible**	H. **transmit**	I. **valid**	J. **vigorous**

____ 1. The little girl, very frightened of Santa Claus, was so determined to run out of the mall that her parents could hardly ______________________ her.

____ 2. Darryl recently went into ______________________ for an entire weekend. He needed to be alone in order to figure out his taxes.

____ 3. It's good Larry called to ______________________ our reservations because the motel had no record of our request for a room.

____ 4. Junk mail can be so ______________________. Often mail advertisements are designed to seem like announcements of wonderful prizes.

____ 5. Crystal loses one job after another because she won't ______________________ to anyone's orders. She argues with her supervisors constantly.

____ 6. It's no wonder Brad is out of shape. The most ______________________ exercise he gets is walking a block to the ice cream parlor.

____ 7. Because Carlos is so ______________________ to poison ivy, he wears long pants and long sleeves if he thinks he might get anywhere near the pesky plant.

____ 8. Since Mary's parents didn't approve of musicians, Mary had to ______________________ them if she wanted to go out with Buddy.

____ 9. If one child in a day care center gets measles, he or she is likely to ______________________ the catching illness to other children.

____ 10. Joan has a ______________________ reason for not trusting Paul: she's heard him lie many times.

SCORE: (Number correct) ________ × 10 = __________ %

Mastery Test: *Chapter 20 (Walking)*

In the space provided, write the word from the box needed to complete each sentence. Then put the **letter** of that word in the column at the left. Use each word once.

A. **accelerate**	B. **adverse**	C. **advocate**	D. **audible**	E. **coherent**
F. **comparable**	G. **competent**	H. **consecutive**	I. **conspicuous**	J. **deteriorate**

____ 1. Polly's family became frightened when she had a(n) ________________ reaction to penicillin.

____ 2. One lawyer's presentation was a model of logic and order, but the other's was far from ________________.

____ 3. Year after year, my grandfather's eyesight ________________s. Every time he goes to the eye doctor, he needs stronger lenses.

____ 4. The drugstore's own brand of lotion and shampoo seems ________________ to name brands in quality. There doesn't seem to be any difference.

____ 5. My mother opposed my sister's marrying Jim, but my father was a strong ________________ of their marriage.

____ 6. The teenagers thought that if they whispered, they would not be heard by others in the movie theater. However, their conversation was ________________ to many who sat nearby.

____ 7. Since both candidates for the job were equally ________________, the employer chose the one with the more pleasant personality.

____ 8. The test was designed to be taken in three ________________ parts: first, some multiple-choice questions; next, a matching exercise; and finally, an essay question.

____ 9. Not only is the cheetah the fastest mammal in the world; it takes this wild cat only two seconds to ________________ from a standing start to a speed of 45 miles an hour.

____ 10. To tease his wife, Vic pretended not to see the "Happy Birthday" sign strung along the living room wall, even though the sign was so big it was too ________________ to miss.

SCORE: (Number correct) ________ × 10 = __________ %

Answers to the Mastery Tests:
BUILDING VOCABULARY SKILLS, SHORT VERSION

Chapter 1 (Taking Exams)

1. D
2. E
3. C
4. G
5. B
6. H
7. A
8. I
9. J
10. F

Chapter 2 (Nate the Woodsman)

1. J
2. A
3. E
4. G
5. I
6. B
7. F
8. H
9. C
10. D

Chapter 3 (Who's on Trial?)

1. C
2. A
3. F
4. I
5. G
6. E
7. B
8. J
9. H
10. D

CHapter 4 (Night Nurse)

1. G
2. A
3. F
4. H
5. I
6. C
7. E
8. J
9. B
10. D

Chapter 5 (Relating to Parents)

1. J
2. C
3. B
4. E
5. D
6. H
7. F
8. A
9. G
10. I

Chapter 6 (Job Choices)

1. B
2. H
3. F
4. D
5. C
6. E
7. J
8. I
9. G
10. A

Chapter 7 (Museum Pet)

1. G
2. A
3. I
4. E
5. H
6. J
7. B
8. D
9. C
10. F

Chapter 8 (Our Headstrong Baby)

1. C
2. G
3. D
4. B
5. E
6. A
7. J
8. H
9. F
10. I

Chapter 9 (A Narrow Escape)

1. D
2. E
3. J
4. B
5. H
6. F
7. I
8. G
9. A
10. C

Chapter 10 (The Power of Advertising)

1. C
2. F
3. G
4. B
5. J
6. A
7. D
8. I
9. E
10. H

Chapter 11 (Waiter)

1. E
2. C
3. F
4. J
5. I
6. B
7. H
8. D
9. G
10. A

Chapter 12 (Adjusting to a New Culture)

1. D
2. G
3. H
4. A
5. F
6. B
7. C
8. E
9. J
10. I

Chapter 13 (A Dream About Wealth)

1. H	6. J
2. A	7. F
3. D	8. C
4. E	9. G
5. B	10. I

Chapter 14 (Children and Drugs)

1. B	6. I
2. H	7. F
3. A	8. E
4. G	9. D
5. C	10. J

Chapter 15 (Party House)

1. B	6. G
2. I	7. F
3. H	8. C
4. A	9. J
5. E	10. D

Chapter 16 (Procrastinator)

1. B	6. D
2. F	7. H
3. I	8. A
4. C	9. J
5. G	10. E

Chapter 17 (A Change in View)

1. C	6. J
2. G	7. F
3. I	8. B
4. E	9. A
5. H	10. D

Chapter 18 (Family Differences)

1. C	6. B
2. A	7. H
3. F	8. E
4. D	9. I
5. J	10. G

Chapter 19 (Chicken Pox)

1. D	6. J
2. E	7. G
3. A	8. C
4. B	9. H
5. F	10. I

Chapter 20 (Walking)

1. B	6. D
2. E	7. G
3. J	8. H
4. F	9. A
5. C	10. I

Mastery Test: *Unit One*

PART A

Complete each sentence in a way that clearly shows you understand the meaning of the **boldfaced** word. Take a minute to plan your answer before you write.

Example: If you receive a wedding invitation, it is **appropriate** to respond by the date requested.

1. One common **transition** that people make in life is ______________________________

______________________________.

2. Two things that can **illuminate** a room are ______________________________

______________________________.

3. One way I **compel** myself to study is by ______________________________

______________________________.

4. The driver **averted** a crash by ______________________________

______________________________.

5. A sign of high **morale** on a team is ______________________________

______________________________.

6. The judge was so **lenient** that ______________________________

______________________________.

7. Being a **novice** as a waiter, Artie ______________________________

______________________________.

8. Although the restaurant was attractive, its success was **undermined** by ______________________________

______________________________."

9. I decided to take **drastic** action to improve my social life, so I ______________________________

______________________________.

10. When Stephanie served roast goose and a delicious peanut-butter pie for Thanksgiving dinner, her **conservative** brother said, " ______________________________

______________________________."

(Continues on next page)

PART B

Use each of the following ten words in sentences of your own. Make it clear that you know the meaning of the word you use. Feel free to use the past tense or plural form of a word.

A. **alternative**	B. **candid**	C. **deter**	D. **erratic**	E. **idealistic**
F. **illusion**	G. **legitimate**	H. **menace**	I. **superficial**	J. **sustain**

11. ______________________________
____

12. ______________________________
____

13. ______________________________
____

14. ______________________________
____

15. ______________________________
____

16. ______________________________
____

17. ______________________________
____

18. ______________________________
____

19. ______________________________
____

20. ______________________________
____

SCORE: (Number correct) ________ × 5 = ___________ %

Mastery Test: *Unit Two*

PART A
Complete each sentence in a way that clearly shows you understand the meaning of the **boldfaced** word. Take a minute to plan your answer before you write.

Example: I wanted to **verify** the program's starting time, so I checked the listings in TV Guide.

1. Two ways a boat can be **propelled** are by ______________________________
______________________________."

2. People who write letters to advice columns like to be **anonymous** because ______________________________
______________________________.

3. My sister is so **versatile** that ______________________________
______________________________.

4. Fran decided to **supplement** her income by ______________________________
______________________________.

5. Wild teenagers on the street **harassed** passing cars by______________________________
______________________________."

6. A man who believes he and his date are **compatible** might say at the end of the evening," ______________________________
______________________________."

7. Pauline is so **arrogant** that when Greg told her she looked pretty, she replied, " ______________________________
______________________________."

8. While waiting for my turn for a haircut, I felt **apprehensive** because ______________________________
______________________________.

9. My friend Ted is very **prudent** about his money. For instance, ______________________________
______________________________.

10. When Joanne asked her husband why he hadn't washed the dinner dishes, his **retort** was, "______________________________
______________________________."

(Continues on next page)

PART B

Use each of the following ten words in sentences of your own. Make it clear that you know the meaning of the word you use. Feel free to use the past tense or plural form of a word.

A. **compensate**	B. **delusion**	C. **derive**	D. **elapse**	E. **infer**
F. **ordeal**	G. **persistent**	H. **prominent**	I. **retrieve**	J. **savor**

11. ______________________________

____

12. ______________________________

____

13. ______________________________

____

14. ______________________________

____

15. ______________________________

____

16. ______________________________

____

17. ______________________________

____

18. ______________________________

____

19. ______________________________

____

20. ______________________________

____

SCORE: (Number correct) ________ × 5 = __________ %

Mastery Test: *Unit Three*

PART A

Complete each sentence in a way that clearly shows you understand the meaning of the **boldfaced** word. Take a minute to plan your answer before you write.

Example: A **mediocre** essay is likely to ______ receive a grade of C ______.

1. Lonnie needs to get from New York to Florida. One of his **options** is to ______________________
______________________.

2. A cab driver might respond to a **liberal** tip by ______________________
______________________.

3. When the heater broke, we **adapted** to the sudden drop in temperature by ______________________
______________________.

4. One **tactic** for dieting is ______________________
______________________.

5. After Gina invited Daniel out for coffee, he **reciprocated** by ______________________
______________________.

6. An animal-lover would become **indignant** if ______________________
______________________.

7. A **shrewd** shopper will probably spend a lot of time ______________________
______________________.

8. When I was little, my mother always used to give me this **reprimand**: " ______________________
______________________."

9. One **exotic** place I'd like to visit some day is ______________________
______________________.

10. A **skeptical** response to "I love you" is " ______________________
______________________."

(Continues on next page)

PART B

Use each of the following ten words in sentences of your own. Make it clear that you know the meaning of the word you use. Feel free to use the past tense or plural form of a word.

A. **coerce**	B. **emerge**	C. **equate**	D. **gesture**	E. **indifferent**
F. **passive**	G. **recur**	H. **ritual**	I. **sadistic**	J. **stereotype**

11. ______________________________

12. ______________________________

13. ______________________________

14. ______________________________

15. ______________________________

16. ______________________________

17. ______________________________

18. ______________________________

19. ______________________________

20. ______________________________

SCORE: (Number correct) ________ × 5 = __________ %

Mastery Test: *Unit Four*

PART A

Complete each sentence in a way that clearly shows you understand the meaning of the **boldfaced** word. Take a minute to plan your answer before you write.

Example: A child might **defy** a parent by ______refusing to mow the lawn______.

1. A camper might experience such **adverse** conditions as ______________________ ______________________.

2. One **valid** reason for missing class is ______________________ ______________________.

3. Drivers usually **accelerate** their cars when ______________________ ______________________.

4. Ramon felt **dismal** because ______________________ ______________________.

5. One activity I find especially **tedious** is ______________________ ______________________.

6. I sometimes **procrastinate** when ______________________ ______________________.

7. Our teacher **confirmed** the rumor that the test was being postponed when she ______________________ ______________________.

8. Babies have an **innate** ability to ______________________ ______________________.

9. If you were to **submit** to someone's demand for a loan, you would ______________________ ______________________.

10. To stay healthy, it is **vital** that I ______________________ ______________________.

(Continues on next page)

PART B

Use each of the following ten words in sentences of your own. Make it clear that you know the meaning of the word you use. Feel free to use the past tense or plural form of a word.

A. **audible**	B. **comparable**	C. **consequence**	D. **deteriorate**	E. **intervene**
F. **perceptive**	G. **profound**	H. **severity**	I. **subside**	J. **vocation**

11. ______________________________

____

12. ______________________________

____

13. ______________________________

____

14. ______________________________

____

15. ______________________________

____

16. ______________________________

____

17. ______________________________

____

18. ______________________________

____

19. ______________________________

____

20. ______________________________

____

SCORE: (Number correct) ________ × 5 = __________ %

IMPROVING VOCABULARY SKILLS

Pretest

NAME: ______________________

SECTION: __________ DATE: __________

SCORE: ______________________

This test contains 100 items. In the space provided, write the letter of the choice that is closest in meaning to the **boldfaced** word.

Important: Keep in mind that this test is for diagnostic purposes only. **If you do not know a word, leave the space blank rather than guess at it.**

____ 1. **animosity** a) approval b) ill will c) fear d) shyness

____ 2. **encounter** a) meeting b) total c) departure d) attack

____ 3. **adamant** a) realistic b) stubborn c) weak d) flexible

____ 4. **eccentric** a) odd b) common c) active d) calm

____ 5. **malign** a) depend on b) speak evil of c) boast d) praise

____ 6. **tangible** a) more than normal b) touchable c) hidden d) orderly

____ 7. **acclaim** a) false name b) great approval c) disagreement d) sadness

____ 8. **escalate** a) remove b) lessen c) include d) intensify

____ 9. **elicit** a) draw forth b) approve c) praise d) disprove

____ 10. **obsolete** a) current b) difficult to believe c) out-of-date d) not sold

____ 11. **allusion** a) indirect reference b) physical weakness c) improvement d) short story

____ 12. **altruistic** a) honest b) lying c) proud d) unselfish

____ 13. **euphemism** a) false appearance b) degree c) substitute for offensive term d) title

____ 14. **arbitrary** a) wordy b) unreasonable c) demanding d) believable

____ 15. **assail** a) attack b) travel c) defend d) confuse

____ 16. **fluctuate** a) stand still b) vary irregularly c) float d) sink

____ 17. **calamity** a) disaster b) storm c) conference d) breeze

____ 18. **persevere** a) treat harshly b) mark c) continue d) delay

____ 19. **comprehensive** a) accidental b) including much c) delicate d) small

____ 20. **venture** a) turn aside b) urge c) risk d) misrepresent

____ 21. **enhance** a) reject b) get c) improve d) free

____ 22. **attribute** a) admiration b) program c) disease d) quality

____ 23. **discern** a) see clearly b) devise c) rule out d) consider

____ 24. **exemplify** a) construct b) represent c) plan d) test

____ 25. **attest** a) bear witness b) examine c) tear up d) dislike

(Continues on next page)

____ 26. **concurrent** **a)** apart **b)** happening together **c)** north **d)** off-and-on

____ 27. **constitute** **a)** make up **b)** eliminate **c)** separate **d)** remove

____ 28. **predominant** **a)** smallest **b)** most noticeable **c)** having a tendency **d)** hidden

____ 29. **nominal** **a)** open to harm **b)** large **c)** important **d)** slight

____ 30. **confiscate** **a)** deny **b)** make difficult **c)** desire **d)** seize with authority

____ 31. **suffice** **a)** think up **b)** be enough **c)** prevent **d)** pay back

____ 32. **degenerate** **a)** give up **b)** improve **c)** stay the same **d)** worsen

____ 33. **implausible** **a)** possible **b)** hard to believe **c)** imaginary **d)** historical

____ 34. **sinister** **a)** frightened **b)** lively **c)** generous **d)** evil

____ 35. **intricate** **a)** easy **b)** complex **c)** workable **d)** touching

____ 36. **qualm** **a)** pleasure **b)** dead end **c)** feeling of doubt **d)** place of safety

____ 37. **garble** **a)** refuse **b)** mix up **c)** claim **d)** speak clearly

____ 38. **immaculate** **a)** roomy **b)** clean **c)** empty **d)** complete

____ 39. **retaliate** **a)** repair **b)** repeat **c)** renew **d)** pay back

____ 40. **blatant** **a)** sudden **b)** immediate **c)** quiet **d)** obvious

____ 41. **intermittent** **a)** hesitant **b)** nervous **c)** off-and-on **d)** constant

____ 42. **digress** **a)** stray **b)** improve **c)** resist **d)** repeat

____ 43. **incentive** **a)** fear **b)** pride **c)** concern **d)** encouragement

____ 44. **succumb** **a)** approach **b)** repeat **c)** give in **d)** cut short

____ 45. **devastate** **a)** spread out **b)** begin again **c)** reassure **d)** upset greatly

____ 46. **speculate** **a)** search **b)** think about **c)** inspect **d)** state to be so

____ 47. **infamous** **a)** not known **b)** small **c)** having a bad reputation **d)** related

____ 48. **benefactor** **a)** landlord **b)** one who gives aid **c)** optimist **d)** kindness

____ 49. **intrinsic** **a)** belonging by its very nature **b)** on the surface **c)** not noticeable **d)** careful

____ 50. **alleviate** **a)** make anxious **b)** depart **c)** infect **d)** relieve

(Continues on next page)

____ 51. **mandatory** **a)** masculine **b)** sexist **c)** required **d)** threatening

____ 52. **lucrative** **a)** silly **b)** profitable **c)** causing disease **d)** attractive

____ 53. **aspire** **a)** dislike **b)** strongly desire **c)** impress **d)** deliver

____ 54. **benevolent** **a)** kind **b)** wealthy **c)** nasty **d)** poor

____ 55. **dissent** **a)** approval **b)** defeat **c)** winning **d)** disagreement

____ 56. **proponent** **a)** foe **b)** supporter **c)** examiner **d)** one part of the whole

____ 57. **quest** **a)** search **b)** request **c)** place **d)** memory

____ 58. **conversely** **a)** rudely **b)** uncooperative **c)** in an opposite manner **d)** unfriendly

____ 59. **prevalent** **a)** famous **b)** widespread **c)** escapable **d)** plain

____ 60. **traumatic** **a)** causing painful emotions **b)** reversed **c)** delicate **d)** harmless

____ 61. **flippant** **a)** cold **b)** formal **c)** disrespectful **d)** nervous

____ 62. **perception** **a)** meeting **b)** party **c)** dead end **d)** impression

____ 63. **prone** **a)** disliked **b)** tending **c)** active **d)** rested

____ 64. **rationale** **a)** research paper **b)** debate **c)** logical basis **d)** mood

____ 65. **impasse** **a)** exit **b)** central point **c)** gate **d)** dead end

____ 66. **divulge** **a)** reveal **b)** embarrass **c)** hide **d)** remove

____ 67. **nullify** **a)** harm **b)** allow **c)** examine **d)** cancel

____ 68. **elation** **a)** trade **b)** comparison **c)** joy **d)** majority opinion

____ 69. **ominous** **a)** happy **b)** threatening **c)** depressed **d)** friendly

____ 70. **averse** **a)** attracted **b)** fearful **c)** warm **d)** opposed

____ 71. **transcend** **a)** send **b)** travel **c)** show off **d)** rise above

____ 72. **deplete** **a)** encourage **b)** use up **c)** delay **d)** add to

____ 73. **complacent** **a)** workable **b)** easy **c)** self-satisfied **d)** healthy

____ 74. **empathy** **a)** fear **b)** encouragement **c)** ability to share someone's feelings **d)** avoidance

____ 75. **waive** **a)** sleep **b)** show off **c)** give up **d)** fly

(Continues on next page)

____ 76. **gape** **a)** stare **b)** repair **c)** beat **d)** hide from

____ 77. **punitive** **a)** inexpensive **b)** punishing **c)** ridiculously inadequate **d)** possible

____ 78. **condone** **a)** forgive **b)** represent **c)** arrest **d)** appoint

____ 79. **precedent** **a)** gift **b)** example **c)** fee **d)** later event

____ 80. **contemplate** **a)** think seriously about **b)** create **c)** add to **d)** reveal

____ 81. **detrimental** **a)** dirty **b)** nutritious **c)** harmful **d)** helpful

____ 82. **ironic** **a)** deeply felt **b)** meaning opposite of what is said **c)** simple **d)** great

____ 83. **vindictive** **a)** not easily understood **b)** gentle **c)** vengeful **d)** temporary

____ 84. **saturate** **a)** break apart **b)** put down **c)** fully soak **d)** describe

____ 85. **deficient** **a)** forgotten **b)** lacking **c)** complete **d)** well-known

____ 86. **fallible** **a)** capable of error **b)** complete **c)** incomplete **d)** simple

____ 87. **exhaustive** **a)** respected **b)** nervous **c)** complete **d)** tired

____ 88. **habitat** **a)** headache **b)** natural environment **c)** importance **d)** usual behavior

____ 89. **vile** **a)** offensive **b)** secretive **c)** nice **d)** tricky

____ 90. **pragmatic** **a)** ordinary **b)** slow **c)** wise **d)** practical

____ 91. **pacify** **a)** betray **b)** calm **c)** retreat **d)** remove

____ 92. **esteem** **a)** age **b)** doubt **c)** respect **d)** length of life

____ 93. **transient** **a)** stubborn **b)** temporary **c)** permanent **d)** easy-going

____ 94. **avid** **a)** bored **b)** disliked **c)** enthusiastic **d)** plentiful

____ 95. **nurture** **a)** harden **b)** thank **c)** nourish **d)** starve

____ 96. **augment** **a)** change **b)** cause to become **c)** increase **d)** describe

____ 97. **explicit** **a)** everyday **b)** distant **c)** permanent **d)** stated exactly

____ 98. **magnitude** **a)** large size **b)** attraction **c)** respect **d)** example

____ 99. **ambivalent** **a)** everyday **b)** having mixed feelings **c)** temporary **d)** able to be done

____ 100. **dispel** **a)** assist **b)** anger **c)** describe **d)** cause to vanish

STOP. This is the end of the test. If there is time remaining, you may go back and recheck your answers. When the time is up, hand in both your answer sheet and this test booklet to your instructor.

IMPROVING VOCABULARY SKILLS

Posttest

NAME: ______________________

SECTION: __________ DATE: __________

SCORE: ______________________

This test contains 100 items. In the space provided, write the letter of the choice that is closest in meaning to the **boldfaced** word.

____ 1. **enhance** a) free b) get c) improve d) reject

____ 2. **encounter** a) departure b) total c) meeting d) attack

____ 3. **obsolete** a) current b) out-of date c) difficult to believe d) not sold

____ 4. **eccentric** a) active b) common c) calm d) odd

____ 5. **escalate** a) remove b) include c) lessen d) intensify

____ 6. **euphemism** a) degree b) false appearance c) substitute for offensive term d) title

____ 7. **exemplify** a) test b) construct c) represent d) plan

____ 8. **adamant** a) flexible b) stubborn c) weak d) realistic

____ 9. **comprehensive** a) delicate b) including much c) accidental d) small

____ 10. **animosity** a) fear b) shyness c) approval d) ill will

____ 11. **discern** a) rule out b) devise c) see clearly d) consider

____ 12. **allusion** a) indirect reference b) physical weakness c) improvement d) short story

____ 13. **altruistic** a) unselfish b) honest c) lying d) proud

____ 14. **malign** a) praise b) boast c) speak evil of d) depend on

____ 15. **arbitrary** a) unreasonable b) wordy c) believable d) demanding

____ 16. **assail** a) defend b) travel c) attack d) confuse

____ 17. **fluctuate** a) sink b) vary irregularly c) float d) stand still

____ 18. **elicit** a) praise b) disprove c) draw forth d) approve

____ 19. **persevere** a) mark b) treat harshly c) continue d) delay

____ 20. **venture** a) misrepresent b) turn aside c) urge d) risk

____ 21. **attest** a) examine b) bear witness c) tear up d) dislike

____ 22. **acclaim** a) disagreement b) great approval c) false name d) sadness

____ 23. **calamity** a) conference b) breeze c) disaster d) storm

____ 24. **attribute** a) admiration b) quality c) disease d) program

____ 25. **tangible** a) more than normal b) touchable c) hidden d) orderly

(Continues on next page)

____ 26. **retaliate** **a)** repair **b)** pay back **c)** renew **d)** repeat

____ 27. **qualm** **a)** pleasure **b)** place of safety **c)** feeling of doubt **d)** dead end

____ 28. **intrinsic** **a)** belonging by its very nature **b)** not noticeable **c)** on the surface **d)** careful

____ 29. **confiscate** **a)** make difficult **b)** deny **c)** seize with authority **d)** desire

____ 30. **immaculate** **a)** roomy **b)** clean **c)** empty **d)** complete

____ 31. **degenerate** **a)** give up **b)** improve **c)** stay the same **d)** worsen

____ 32. **implausible** **a)** possible **b)** hard to believe **c)** imaginary **d)** historical

____ 33. **devastate** **a)** reassure **b)** upset greatly **c)** spread out **d)** begin again

____ 34. **sinister** **a)** frightened **b)** generous **c)** lively **d)** evil

____ 35. **nominal** **a)** slight **b)** large **c)** important **d)** open to harm

____ 36. **speculate** **a)** inspect **b)** think about **c)** search **d)** state to be so

____ 37. **succumb** **a)** cut short **b)** approach **c)** give in **d)** repeat

____ 38. **garble** **a)** claim **b)** mix up **c)** refuse **d)** speak clearly

____ 39. **constitute** **a)** make up **b)** remove **c)** eliminate **d)** separate

____ 40. **blatant** **a)** quiet **b)** sudden **c)** immediate **d)** obvious

____ 41. **intricate** **a)** complex **b)** easy **c)** workable **d)** touching

____ 42. **predominant** **a)** hidden **b)** having a tendency **c)** most noticeable **d)** smallest

____ 43. **incentive** **a)** fear **b)** concern **c)** pride **d)** encouragement

____ 44. **infamous** **a)** having a bad reputation **b)** not known **c)** small **d)** related

____ 45. **concurrent** **a)** apart **b)** north **c)** happening together **d)** off-and-on

____ 46. **benefactor** **a)** landlord **b)** one who gives aid **c)** optimist **d)** kindness

____ 47. **intermittent** **a)** hesitant **b)** nervous **c)** off-and-on **d)** constant

____ 48. **suffice** **a)** think up **b)** prevent **c)** be enough **d)** pay back

____ 49. **alleviate** **a)** infect **b)** relieve **c)** make anxious **d)** depart

____ 50. **digress** **a)** resist **b)** improve **c)** stray **d)** repeat

(Continues on next page)

____ 51. **averse** **a)** opposed **b)** fearful **c)** warm **d)** attracted

____ 52. **conversely** **a)** unfriendly **b)** rudely **c)** uncooperative **d)** in an opposite manner

____ 53. **aspire** **a)** dislike **b)** strongly desire **c)** impress **d)** deliver

____ 54. **elation** **a)** comparison **b)** trade **c)** joy **d)** majority opinion

____ 55. **quest** **a)** place **b)** memory **c)** search **d)** request

____ 56. **mandatory** **a)** sexist **b)** threatening **c)** required **d)** masculine

____ 57. **ominous** **a)** happy **b)** depressed **c)** threatening **d)** friendly

____ 58. **traumatic** **a)** harmless **b)** reversed **c)** delicate **d)** causing painful emotions

____ 59. **lucrative** **a)** causing disease **b)** profitable **c)** silly **d)** attractive

____ 60. **impasse** **a)** gate **b)** exit **c)** central point **d)** dead end

____ 61. **transcend** **a)** send **b)** travel **c)** show off **d)** rise above

____ 62. **complacent** **a)** workable **b)** self-satisfied **c)** healthy **d)** easy

____ 63. **divulge** **a)** remove **b)** reveal **c)** hide **d)** embarrass

____ 64. **benevolent** **a)** poor **b)** kind **c)** wealthy **d)** nasty

____ 65. **rationale** **a)** mood **b)** debate **c)** logical basis **d)** research paper

____ 66. **proponent** **a)** supporter **b)** examiner **c)** foe **d)** one part of the whole

____ 67. **nullify** **a)** cancel **b)** examine **c)** allow **d)** harm

____ 68. **flippant** **a)** cold **b)** disrespectful **c)** formal **d)** nervous

____ 69. **prone** **a)** active **b)** tending **c)** disliked **d)** rested

____ 70. **empathy** **a)** fear **b)** encouragement **c)** ability to share someone's feelings **d)** avoidance

____ 71. **waive** **a)** fly **b)** sleep **c)** show off **d)** give up

____ 72. **prevalent** **a)** plain **b)** widespread **c)** escapable **d)** famous

____ 73. **dissent** **a)** disagreement **b)** winning **c)** defeat **d)** approval

____ 74. **perception** **a)** impression **b)** meeting **c)** dead end **d)** party

____ 75. **deplete** **a)** add to **b)** delay **c)** use up **d)** encourage

(Continues on next page)

____ 76. **vindictive** a) not easily understood b) gentle c) vengeful d) temporary

____ 77. **precedent** a) gift b) fee c) example d) later event

____ 78. **vile** a) tricky b) nice c) secretive d) offensive

____ 79. **ironic** a) simple b) meaning opposite of what is said c) deeply felt d) great

____ 80. **saturate** a) fully soak b) put down c) break apart d) describe

____ 81. **pacify** a) betray b) remove c) retreat d) calm

____ 82. **detrimental** a) harmful b) nutritious c) dirty d) helpful

____ 83. **explicit** a) everyday b) permanent c) distant d) stated exactly

____ 84. **exhaustive** a) complete b) nervous c) respected d) tired

____ 85. **ambivalent** a) everyday b) temporary c) having mixed feelings d) able to be done

____ 86. **dispel** a) cause to vanish b) anger c) describe d) assist

____ 87. **pragmatic** a) practical b) slow c) wise d) ordinary

____ 88. **esteem** a) respect b) doubt c) age d) length of life

____ 89. **contemplate** a) think seriously about b) create c) add to d) reveal

____ 90. **transient** a) permanent b) easy-going c) stubborn d) temporary

____ 91. **augment** a) cause to become b) change c) describe d) increase

____ 92. **fallible** a) incomplete b) complete c) capable of error d) simple

____ 93. **punitive** a) punishing b) inexpensive c) ridiculously inadequate d) possible

____ 94. **avid** a) enthusiastic b) disliked c) bored d) plentiful

____ 95. **habitat** a) headache b) natural environment c) importance d) usual behavior

____ 96. **nurture** a) harden b) thank c) nourish d) starve

____ 97. **deficient** a) forgotten b) well-known c) complete d) lacking

____ 98. **gape** a) hide from b) beat c) stare d) repair

____ 99. **magnitude** a) large size b) attraction c) respect d) example

____ 100. **condone** a) arrest b) represent c) forgive d) appoint

STOP. This is the end of the test. If there is time remaining, you may go back and recheck your answers. When the time is up, hand in both your answer sheet and this test booklet to your instructor.

Name: ______________________________

Unit One: *Pretest*

In the space provided, write the letter of the choice that is closest in meaning to the **boldfaced** word.

____ 1. **animosity** a) approval b) ill will c) fear d) shyness

____ 2. **encounter** a) meeting b) total c) departure d) attack

____ 3. **absolve** a) make guilty b) reject c) clear from guilt d) approve

____ 4. **adamant** a) realistic b) stubborn c) weak d) flexible

____ 5. **eccentric** a) odd b) common c) active d) calm

____ 6. **amoral** a) honest b) poor c) without principles d) generous

____ 7. **malign** a) depend on b) speak evil of c) boast d) praise

____ 8. **antagonist** a) friend b) relative c) boss d) opponent

____ 9. **tangible** a) more than normal b) touchable c) hidden d) orderly

____ 10. **acclaim** a) false name b) great approval c) disagreement d) sadness

____ 11. **escalate** a) remove b) lessen c) include d) intensify

____ 12. **elicit** a) draw forth b) approve c) praise d) disprove

____ 13. **exploit** a) save b) throw away c) take advantage of d) sell overseas

____ 14. **obsolete** a) current b) difficult to believe c) out-of-date d) not sold

____ 15. **engross** a) destroy b) impress c) disgust d) hold the attention of

____ 16. **terminate** a) stop b) continue c) begin d) approach

____ 17. **banal** a) humid b) commonplace c) secret d) true

____ 18. **appease** a) make calm b) tell the truth c) attack d) approve

____ 19. **allusion** a) indirect reference b) physical weakness c) improvement d) short story

____ 20. **altruistic** a) honest b) lying c) proud d) unselfish

____ 21. **mercenary** a) clean b) mean c) calm d) greedy

____ 22. **euphemism** a) false appearance b) degree c) substitute for offensive term d) title

____ 23. **arbitrary** a) wordy b) unreasonable c) demanding d) believable

____ 24. **assail** a) attack b) travel c) defend d) confuse

____ 25. **fluctuate** a) stand still b) vary irregularly c) float d) sink

(Continues on next page)

____ 26. **rehabilitate** **a)** restore to normal life **b)** relax **c)** plan in meetings **d)** interpret

____ 27. **calamity** **a)** disaster **b)** storm **c)** conference **d)** breeze

____ 28. **persevere** **a)** treat harshly **b)** mark **c)** continue **d)** delay

____ 29. **comprehensive** **a)** accidental **b)** including much **c)** delicate **d)** small

____ 30. **venture** **a)** turn aside **b)** urge **c)** risk **d)** misrepresent

____ 31. **ponder** **a)** think deeply about **b)** allow **c)** reduce **d)** flatten

____ 32. **turmoil** **a)** workplace **b)** quiet setting **c)** fire **d)** uproar

____ 33. **enhance** **a)** reject **b)** get **c)** improve **d)** free

____ 34. **mobile** **a)** firm in opinion **b)** able to move **c)** stationary **d)** restricted

____ 35. **orient** **a)** determine the location of **b)** lose **c)** represent **d)** consist of

____ 36. **attribute** **a)** admiration **b)** program **c)** disease **d)** quality

____ 37. **discern** **a)** see clearly **b)** devise **c)** rule out **d)** consider

____ 38. **exemplify** **a)** construct **b)** represent **c)** plan **d)** test

____ 39. **nocturnal** **a)** supposed **b)** not logical **c)** complex **d)** active at night

____ 40. **attest** **a)** bear witness **b)** examine **c)** tear up **d)** dislike

____ 41. **amiable** **a)** stingy **b)** rude **c)** proud **d)** good-natured

____ 42. **epitome** **a)** perfect example **b)** large hole **c)** horrible sight **d)** tallest point

____ 43. **adjacent** **a)** above **b)** under **c)** next to **d)** within

____ 44. **methodical** **a)** religious **b)** systematic **c)** careless **d)** immoral

____ 45. **syndrome** **a)** attitude **b)** thought **c)** something required **d)** group of symptoms

____ 46. **taint** **a)** surprise **b)** dishonor **c)** annoy **d)** boast

____ 47. **flagrant** **a)** sweet-smelling **b)** outrageous **c)** hidden **d)** slight

____ 48. **conventional** **a)** large **b)** at a conference **c)** outstanding **d)** ordinary

____ 49. **enigma** **a)** rash **b)** puzzle **c)** tool **d)** cleanser

____ 50. **dispatch** **a)** recall **b)** remove **c)** send **d)** plant

SCORE: (Number correct) ________ × 2 = ___________ %

Name: ________________________________

Unit One: *Posttest*

In the space provided, write the letter of the choice that is closest in meaning to the **boldfaced** word.

____ 1. **enhance** **a)** free **b)** get **c)** improve **d)** reject

____ 2. **encounter** **a)** total **b)** attack **c)** departure **d)** meeting

____ 3. **mercenary** **a)** calm **b)** greedy **c)** clean **d)** mean

____ 4. **obsolete** **a)** current **b)** out-of date **c)** difficult to believe **d)** not sold

____ 5. **eccentric** **a)** active **b)** common **c)** calm **d)** odd

____ 6. **mobile** **a)** firm in opinion **b)** able to move **c)** stationary **d)** restricted

____ 7. **nocturnal** **a)** complex **b)** active at night **c)** supposed **d)** not logical

____ 8. **appease** **a)** attack **b)** tell the truth **c)** make calm **d)** approve

____ 9. **turmoil** **a)** fire **b)** uproar **c)** workplace **d)** quiet setting

____ 10. **antagonist** **a)** boss **b)** relative **c)** friend **d)** opponent

____ 11. **escalate** **a)** remove **b)** include **c)** lessen **d)** intensify

____ 12. **euphemism** **a)** degree **b)** false appearance **c)** substitute for offensive term **d)** title

____ 13. **engross** **a)** destroy **b)** impress **c)** disgust **d)** hold the attention of

____ 14. **exemplify** **a)** test **b)** construct **c)** represent **d)** plan

____ 15. **adamant** **a)** flexible **b)** stubborn **c)** weak **d)** realistic

____ 16. **terminate** **a)** begin **b)** stop **c)** continue **d)** approach

____ 17. **comprehensive** **a)** delicate **b)** including much **c)** accidental **d)** small

____ 18. **animosity** **a)** fear **b)** shyness **c)** approval **d)** ill will

____ 19. **banal** **a)** commonplace **b)** humid **c)** secret **d)** true

____ 20. **discern** **a)** rule out **b)** devise **c)** see clearly **d)** consider

____ 21. **allusion** **a)** indirect reference **b)** physical weakness **c)** improvement **d)** short story

____ 22. **altruistic** **a)** unselfish **b)** honest **c)** lying **d)** proud

____ 23. **malign** **a)** praise **b)** boast **c)** speak evil of **d)** depend on

____ 24. **orient** **a)** lose **b)** determine the location of **c)** consist of **d)** represent

____ 25. **arbitrary** **a)** unreasonable **b)** wordy **c)** believable **d)** demanding

(Continues on next page)

____ 26. **absolve** **a)** make guilty **b)** reject **c)** clear from guilt **d)** approve

____ 27. **assail** **a)** defend **b)** travel **c)** attack **d)** confuse

____ 28. **fluctuate** **a)** sink **b)** vary irregularly **c)** float **d)** stand still

____ 29. **elicit** **a)** praise **b)** disprove **c)** draw forth **d)** approve

____ 30. **exploit** **a)** take advantage of **b)** throw away **c)** save **d)** sell overseas

____ 31. **amoral** **a)** honest **b)** poor **c)** without principles **d)** generous

____ 32. **persevere** **a)** mark **b)** treat harshly **c)** continue **d)** delay

____ 33. **venture** **a)** misrepresent **b)** turn aside **c)** urge **d)** risk

____ 34. **attest** **a)** examine **b)** bear witness **c)** tear up **d)** dislike

____ 35. **acclaim** **a)** disagreement **b)** great approval **c)** false name **d)** sadness

____ 36. **ponder** **a)** think deeply about **b)** reduce **c)** allow **d)** flatten

____ 37. **calamity** **a)** conference **b)** breeze **c)** disaster **d)** storm

____ 38. **attribute** **a)** admiration **b)** quality **c)** disease **d)** program

____ 39. **rehabilitate** **a)** restore to normal life **b)** relax **c)** plan in meetings **d)** interpret

____ 40. **tangible** **a)** more than normal **b)** touchable **c)** hidden **d)** orderly

____ 41. **flagrant** **a)** slight **b)** hidden **c)** outrageous **d)** sweet-smelling

____ 42. **amiable** **a)** good-natured **b)** stingy **c)** proud **d)** rude

____ 43. **adjacent** **a)** under **b)** above **c)** next to **d)** within

____ 44. **taint** **a)** dishonor **b)** boast **c)** annoy **d)** surprise

____ 45. **dispatch** **a)** recall **b)** remove **c)** send **d)** plant

____ 46. **methodical** **a)** careless **b)** systematic **c)** immoral **d)** religious

____ 47. **epitome** **a)** horrible sight **b)** large hole **c)** tallest point **d)** perfect example

____ 48. **conventional** **a)** large **b)** outstanding **c)** at a conference **d)** ordinary

____ 49. **enigma** **a)** tool **b)** puzzle **c)** cleanser **d)** rash

____ 50. **syndrome** **a)** something required **b)** thought **c)** attitude **d)** group of symptoms

SCORE: (Number correct) ________ × 2 = __________ %

Name: ____________________

Unit Two: *Pretest*

In the space provided, write the letter of the choice that is closest in meaning to the **boldfaced** word.

____ 1. **concurrent** **a)** apart **b)** happening together **c)** north **d)** off-and-on

____ 2. **constitute** **a)** make up **b)** eliminate **c)** separate **d)** remove

____ 3. **predominant** **a)** smallest **b)** most noticeable **c)** having a tendency **d)** hidden

____ 4. **decipher** **a)** interpret **b)** study **c)** improve **d)** pay back

____ 5. **default** **a)** jump **b)** do automatically **c)** fail to do something required **d)** seize

____ 6. **nominal** **a)** open to harm **b)** large **c)** important **d)** slight

____ 7. **prerequisite** **a)** requirement beforehand **b)** test **c)** close inspection **d)** extra credit

____ 8. **confiscate** **a)** deny **b)** make difficult **c)** desire **d)** seize with authority

____ 9. **sanctuary** **a)** opinion **b)** hardship **c)** place of safety **d)** something complicated

____ 10. **suffice** **a)** think up **b)** be enough **c)** prevent **d)** pay back

____ 11. **degenerate** **a)** give up **b)** improve **c)** stay the same **d)** worsen

____ 12. **vulnerable** **a)** kind **b)** intelligent **c)** wicked **d)** sensitive

____ 13. **implausible** **a)** possible **b)** hard to believe **c)** imaginary **d)** historical

____ 14. **sinister** **a)** frightened **b)** lively **c)** generous **d)** evil

____ 15. **incoherent** **a)** not logical **b)** well-spoken **c)** quiet **d)** unable to read

____ 16. **intricate** **a)** easy **b)** complex **c)** workable **d)** touching

____ 17. **qualm** **a)** pleasure **b)** dead end **c)** feeling of doubt **d)** place of safety

____ 18. **blight** **a)** something that damages **b)** natural environment **c)** example **d)** storm

____ 19. **garble** **a)** refuse **b)** mix up **c)** claim **d)** speak clearly

____ 20. **immaculate** **a)** roomy **b)** clean **c)** empty **d)** complete

____ 21. **retaliate** **a)** repair **b)** repeat **c)** renew **d)** pay back

____ 22. **gloat** **a)** express spiteful pleasure **b)** give up **c)** eat **d)** deny

____ 23. **plagiarism** **a)** support **b)** contribution **c)** stealing someone's writings **d)** removal

____ 24. **blatant** **a)** sudden **b)** immediate **c)** quiet **d)** obvious

____ 25. **incorporate** **a)** anger **b)** separate **c)** combine **d)** calm

(Continues on next page)

____ 26. **intermittent** **a)** hesitant **b)** nervous **c)** off-and-on **d)** constant

____ 27. **digress** **a)** stray **b)** improve **c)** resist **d)** repeat

____ 28. **incentive** **a)** fear **b)** pride **c)** concern **d)** encouragement

____ 29. **succumb** **a)** approach **b)** repeat **c)** give in **d)** cut short

____ 30. **curtail** **a)** urge **b)** join **c)** cut short **d)** relieve

____ 31. **indispensable** **a)** necessary **b)** not important **c)** saved up **d)** wasted

____ 32. **devastate** **a)** spread out **b)** begin again **c)** reassure **d)** upset greatly

____ 33. **speculate** **a)** search **b)** think about **c)** inspect **d)** state to be so

____ 34. **infamous** **a)** not known **b)** small **c)** having a bad reputation **d)** related

____ 35. **benefactor** **a)** landlord **b)** one who gives aid **c)** optimist **d)** kindness

____ 36. **covert** **a)** distant **b)** hidden **c)** changed **d)** adjusted

____ 37. **virile** **a)** healthy **b)** manly **c)** wrinkled **d)** required

____ 38. **intrinsic** **a)** belonging by its very nature **b)** on the surface **c)** not noticeable **d)** careful

____ 39. **alleviate** **a)** make anxious **b)** depart **c)** infect **d)** relieve

____ 40. **revulsion** **a)** confession **b)** great disgust **c)** attraction **d)** compassion

____ 41. **hypothetical** **a)** moral **b)** factual **c)** avoidable **d)** supposed

____ 42. **recession** **a)** parade **b)** amusement **c)** giving in **d)** business decline

____ 43. **intercede** **a)** ask for a favor **b)** remove **c)** isolate **d)** come between to help solve

____ 44. **scrutiny** **a)** knowledge **b)** lack of interest **c)** close inspection **d)** ignorance

____ 45. **contrive** **a)** allow **b)** inspect **c)** think up **d)** prepare

____ 46. **gaunt** **a)** large **b)** complex **c)** well **d)** thin

____ 47. **rigor** **a)** ease **b)** hardship **c)** slowness **d)** meanness

____ 48. **squander** **a)** waste **b)** lose **c)** insult **d)** strongly desire

____ 49. **cynic** **a)** pessimist **b)** serious person **c)** single person **d)** clown

____ 50. **demise** **a)** trick **b)** death **c)** disguise **d)** departure

SCORE: (Number correct) ________ × 2 = ___________ %

Name: ______________________________

Unit Two: *Posttest*

In the space provided, write the letter of the choice that is closest in meaning to the **boldfaced** word.

____ 1. **decipher** a) interpret b) study c) improve d) pay back

____ 2. **retaliate** a) repair b) pay back c) renew d) repeat

____ 3. **qualm** a) pleasure b) place of safety c) feeling of doubt d) dead end

____ 4. **curtail** a) relieve b) join c) urge d) cut short

____ 5. **default** a) jump b) seize c) fail to do something required d) do automatically

____ 6. **plagiarism** a) removal b) stealing someone's writings c) contribution d) support

____ 7. **intrinsic** a) belonging by its very nature b) not noticeable c) on the surface d) careful

____ 8. **gloat** a) eat b) give up c) express spiteful pleasure d) deny

____ 9. **prerequisite** a) close inspection b) test c) requirement beforehand d) extra credit

____ 10. **confiscate** a) make difficult b) deny c) seize with authority d) desire

____ 11. **immaculate** a) roomy b) clean c) empty d) complete

____ 12. **degenerate** a) give up b) improve c) stay the same d) worsen

____ 13. **vulnerable** a) wicked b) sensitive c) kind d) intelligent

____ 14. **indispensable** a) necessary b) not important c) saved up d) wasted

____ 15. **implausible** a) possible b) hard to believe c) imaginary d) historical

____ 16. **devastate** a) reassure b) upset greatly c) spread out d) begin again

____ 17. **sinister** a) frightened b) generous c) lively d) evil

____ 18. **sanctuary** a) hardship b) opinion c) something complicated d) place of safety

____ 19. **nominal** a) slight b) large c) important d) open to harm

____ 20. **speculate** a) inspect b) think about c) search d) state to be so

____ 21. **blight** a) storm b) natural environment c) something that damages d) example

____ 22. **succumb** a) cut short b) approach c) give in d) repeat

____ 23. **garble** a) claim b) mix up c) refuse d) speak clearly

____ 24. **constitute** a) make up b) remove c) eliminate d) separate

____ 25. **virile** a) healthy b) wrinkled c) manly d) required

(Continues on next page)

____ 26. **blatant** **a)** quiet **b)** sudden **c)** immediate **d)** obvious

____ 27. **revulsion** **a)** great disgust **b)** confession **c)** attraction **d)** compassion

____ 28. **incorporate** **a)** calm **b)** separate **c)** combine **d)** anger

____ 29. **intricate** **a)** complex **b)** easy **c)** workable **d)** touching

____ 30. **predominant** **a)** hidden **b)** having a tendency **c)** most noticeable **d)** smallest

____ 31. **incentive** **a)** fear **b)** concern **c)** pride **d)** encouragement

____ 32. **infamous** **a)** having a bad reputation **b)** not known **c)** small **d)** related

____ 33. **concurrent** **a)** apart **b)** north **c)** happening together **d)** off-and-on

____ 34. **benefactor** **a)** landlord **b)** one who gives aid **c)** optimist **d)** kindness

____ 35. **intermittent** **a)** hesitant **b)** nervous **c)** off-and-on **d)** constant

____ 36. **incoherent** **a)** unable to read **b)** well-spoken **c)** not logical **d)** quiet

____ 37. **covert** **a)** changed **b)** adjusted **c)** distant **d)** hidden

____ 38. **suffice** **a)** think up **b)** prevent **c)** be enough **d)** pay back

____ 39. **alleviate** **a)** infect **b)** relieve **c)** make anxious **d)** depart

____ 40. **digress** **a)** resist **b)** improve **c)** stray **d)** repeat

____ 41. **intercede** **a)** remove **b)** come between to help solve **c)** isolate **d)** strike

____ 42. **demise** **a)** disguise **b)** death **c)** departure **d)** trick

____ 43. **rigor** **a)** meanness **b)** ease **c)** slowness **d)** hardship

____ 44. **contrive** **a)** inspect **b)** prepare **c)** allow **d)** think up

____ 45. **squander** **a)** insult **b)** lose **c)** strongly desire **d)** waste

____ 46. **cynic** **a)** serious person **b)** clown **c)** single person **d)** pessimist

____ 47. **hypothetical** **a)** factual **b)** avoidable **c)** moral **d)** supposed

____ 48. **gaunt** **a)** complex **b)** thin **c)** well **d)** large

____ 49. **recession** **a)** parade **b)** business decline **c)** giving in **d)** amusement

____ 50. **scrutiny** **a)** lack of interest **b)** ignorance **c)** close inspection **d)** knowledge

SCORE: (Number correct) ________ × 2 = ___________ %

Name: ______________________

Unit Three: *Pretest*

In the space provided, write the letter of the choice that is closest in meaning to the **boldfaced** word.

____ 1. **deficit** a) surplus b) remainder c) part of the whole d) shortage

____ 2. **mandatory** a) masculine b) sexist c) required d) threatening

____ 3. **abstain** a) do without b) disagree c) prepare d) approve of

____ 4. **lucrative** a) silly b) profitable c) causing disease d) attractive

____ 5. **agnostic** a) one who is unsure there's a God b) saint c) believer d) genius

____ 6. **aspire** a) dislike b) strongly desire c) impress d) deliver

____ 7. **benevolent** a) kind b) wealthy c) nasty d) poor

____ 8. **dissent** a) approval b) defeat c) winning d) disagreement

____ 9. **proponent** a) foe b) supporter c) examiner d) one part of the whole

____ 10. **charisma** a) friendship b) kindness c) obedience d) charm

____ 11. **quest** a) search b) request c) place d) memory

____ 12. **conversely** a) rudely b) uncooperative c) in an opposite manner d) unfriendly

____ 13. **contemporary** a) modern b) odd c) old-fashioned d) futuristic

____ 14. **extrovert** a) shy person b) magnetism c) main point d) outgoing person

____ 15. **prevalent** a) famous b) widespread c) escapable d) plain

____ 16. **traumatic** a) causing painful emotions b) reversed c) delicate d) harmless

____ 17. **rapport** a) support b) close relationship c) view d) report

____ 18. **flippant** a) cold b) formal c) disrespectful d) nervous

____ 19. **perception** a) meeting b) party c) dead end d) impression

____ 20. **congenial** a) pleasant b) intelligent c) mixed-up d) lacking

____ 21. **prone** a) disliked b) tending c) active d) rested

____ 22. **rationale** a) research paper b) debate c) logical basis d) mood

____ 23. **impasse** a) exit b) central point c) gate d) dead end

____ 24. **prompt** a) urge b) avoid c) waste d) lie

____ 25. **divulge** a) reveal b) embarrass c) hide d) remove

(Continues on next page)

____ 26. **endow** **a)** name **b)** tease **c)** give a quality to **d)** cancel

____ 27. **expulsion** **a)** promotion **b)** dismissal **c)** award **d)** attack

____ 28. **detract** **a)** provide **b)** compete **c)** lessen **d)** compliment

____ 29. **nullify** **a)** harm **b)** allow **c)** examine **d)** cancel

____ 30. **elation** **a)** trade **b)** comparison **c)** joy **d)** majority opinion

____ 31. **ominous** **a)** happy **b)** threatening **c)** depressed **d)** friendly

____ 32. **averse** **a)** attracted **b)** fearful **c)** warm **d)** opposed

____ 33. **transcend** **a)** send **b)** travel **c)** show off **d)** rise above

____ 34. **deplete** **a)** encourage **b)** use up **c)** delay **d)** add to

____ 35. **complacent** **a)** workable **b)** easy **c)** self-satisfied **d)** healthy

____ 36. **niche** **a)** memory **b)** wild outburst **c)** main idea **d)** one's place

____ 37. **diligent** **a)** careful in work **b)** odd **c)** obvious **d)** gentle

____ 38. **empathy** **a)** fear **b)** encouragement **c)** ability to share someone's feelings **d)** avoidance

____ 39. **consensus** **a)** majority opinion **b)** counting **c)** study **d)** approval

____ 40. **waive** **a)** sleep **b)** show off **c)** give up **d)** fly

____ 41. **affiliate** **a)** impress **b)** approve **c)** reject **d)** join

____ 42. **diversion** **a)** awareness **b)** practice **c)** amusement **d)** fate

____ 43. **contend** **a)** join **b)** claim **c)** arouse **d)** allow

____ 44. **poignant** **a)** annoying **b)** beautiful **c)** careless **d)** touching

____ 45. **reprisal** **a)** getting even **b)** defeat **c)** question **d)** search

____ 46. **relentless** **a)** angry **b)** persistent **c)** cruel **d)** kind

____ 47. **mortify** **a)** humiliate **b)** praise **c)** entertain **d)** remember

____ 48. **disdain** **a)** discouragement **b)** pain **c)** scorn **d)** approval

____ 49. **menial** **a)** important **b)** unkind **c)** lowly **d)** odd

____ 50. **commemorate** **a)** forget **b)** imitate **c)** add new members **d)** honor the memory of

SCORE: (Number correct) ________ × 2 = ___________ %

Name: ________________________________

Unit Three: *Posttest*

In the space provided, write the letter of the choice that is closest in meaning to the **boldfaced** word.

____ 1. **agnostic** **a)** believer **b)** saint **c)** one who is unsure there's a God **d)** genius

____ 2. **averse** **a)** opposed **b)** fearful **c)** warm **d)** attracted

____ 3. **conversely** **a)** unfriendly **b)** rudely **c)** uncooperative **d)** in an opposite manner

____ 4. **aspire** **a)** dislike **b)** strongly desire **c)** impress **d)** deliver

____ 5. **charisma** **a)** charm **b)** kindness **c)** obedience **d)** friendship

____ 6. **elation** **a)** comparison **b)** trade **c)** joy **d)** majority opinion

____ 7. **quest** **a)** place **b)** memory **c)** search **d)** request

____ 8. **contemporary** **a)** modern **b)** old-fashioned **c)** futuristic **d)** odd

____ 9. **mandatory** **a)** sexist **b)** threatening **c)** required **d)** masculine

____ 10. **niche** **a)** memory **b)** wild outburst **c)** main idea **d)** one's place

____ 11. **ominous** **a)** happy **b)** depressed **c)** threatening **d)** friendly

____ 12. **traumatic** **a)** harmless **b)** reversed **c)** delicate **d)** causing painful emotions

____ 13. **rapport** **a)** support **b)** view **c)** close relationship **d)** report

____ 14. **congenial** **a)** lacking **b)** pleasant **c)** intelligent **d)** mixed-up

____ 15. **lucrative** **a)** causing disease **b)** profitable **c)** silly **d)** attractive

____ 16. **impasse** **a)** gate **b)** exit **c)** central point **d)** dead end

____ 17. **transcend** **a)** send **b)** travel **c)** show off **d)** rise above

____ 18. **prompt** **a)** avoid **b)** urge **c)** lie **d)** waste

____ 19. **complacent** **a)** workable **b)** self-satisfied **c)** healthy **d)** easy

____ 20. **abstain** **a)** prepare **b)** disagree **c)** do without **d)** approve of

____ 21. **consensus** **a)** majority opinion **b)** counting **c)** study **d)** approval

____ 22. **divulge** **a)** remove **b)** reveal **c)** hide **d)** embarrass

____ 23. **extrovert** **a)** shy person **b)** magnetism **c)** main point **d)** outgoing person

____ 24. **endow** **a)** cancel **b)** name **c)** tease **d)** give a quality to

____ 25. **deficit** **a)** shortage **b)** remainder **c)** part of the whole **d)** surplus

(Continues on next page)

____ 26. **diligent** a) obvious b) odd c) careful in work d) gentle

____ 27. **perception** a) impression b) meeting c) dead end d) party

____ 28. **expulsion** a) promotion b) dismissal c) award d) attack

____ 29. **benevolent** a) poor b) kind c) wealthy d) nasty

____ 30. **rationale** a) mood b) debate c) logical basis d) research paper

____ 31. **proponent** a) supporter b) examiner c) foe d) one part of the whole

____ 32. **nullify** a) cancel b) examine c) allow d) harm

____ 33. **flippant** a) cold b) disrespectful c) formal d) nervous

____ 34. **prone** a) active b) tending c) disliked d) rested

____ 35. **empathy** a) fear b) encouragement c) ability to share someone's feelings d) avoidance

____ 36. **waive** a) fly b) sleep c) show off d) give up

____ 37. **prevalent** a) plain b) widespread c) escapable d) famous

____ 38. **dissent** a) disagreement b) winning c) defeat d) approval

____ 39. **detract** a) provide b) compete c) lessen d) compliment

____ 40. **deplete** a) add to b) delay c) use up d) encourage

____ 41. **mortify** a) humiliate b) remember c) entertain d) praise

____ 42. **affiliate** a) approve b) reject c) impress d) join

____ 43. **poignant** a) touching b) annoying c) careless d) beautiful

____ 44. **disdain** a) pain b) approval c) scorn d) discouragement

____ 45. **commemorate** a) imitate b) honor the memory of c) add new members d) forget

____ 46. **menial** a) unkind b) lowly c) important d) odd

____ 47. **relentless** a) kind b) persistent c) cruel d) angry

____ 48. **contend** a) arouse b) allow c) claim d) join

____ 49. **reprisal** a) defeat b) search c) question d) getting even

____ 50. **diversion** a) practice b) fate c) amusement d) awareness

SCORE: (Number correct) ________ × 2 = ___________ %

Name: ______________________

Unit Four: *Pretest*

In the space provided, write the letter of the choice that is closest in meaning to the **boldfaced** word.

____ 1. **feign** a) offend b) avoid c) overlook d) pretend

____ 2. **gape** a) stare b) repair c) beat d) hide from

____ 3. **punitive** a) inexpensive b) punishing c) ridiculously inadequate d) possible

____ 4. **condone** a) forgive b) represent c) arrest d) appoint

____ 5. **pathetic** a) rich b) puzzling c) wonderful d) pitifully lacking

____ 6. **precedent** a) gift b) example c) fee d) later event

____ 7. **contemplate** a) think seriously about b) create c) add to d) reveal

____ 8. **furtive** a) loud b) quiet c) public d) secretive

____ 9. **detrimental** a) dirty b) nutritious c) harmful d) helpful

____ 10. **ironic** a) deeply felt b) meaning opposite of what is said c) simple d) great

____ 11. **implicit** a) lacking b) attached c) above d) unstated but understood

____ 12. **vindictive** a) not easily understood b) gentle c) vengeful d) temporary

____ 13. **saturate** a) break apart b) put down c) fully soak d) describe

____ 14. **inhibition** a) attack b) delay c) holding back d) exhibit

____ 15. **deficient** a) forgotten b) lacking c) complete d) well-known

____ 16. **rupture** a) burst b) fill c) damage d) overlook

____ 17. **constrict** a) control b) prove c) make smaller d) regard

____ 18. **fallible** a) capable of error b) complete c) incomplete d) simple

____ 19. **exhaustive** a) respected b) nervous c) complete d) tired

____ 20. **formulate** a) allow b) move c) purchase d) develop

____ 21. **habitat** a) headache b) natural environment c) importance d) usual behavior

____ 22. **vile** a) offensive b) secretive c) nice d) tricky

____ 23. **reconcile** a) refine b) redo c) accept d) increase

____ 24. **pragmatic** a) ordinary b) slow c) wise d) practical

____ 25. **pacify** a) betray b) calm c) retreat d) remove

(Continues on next page)

____ 26. **esteem** **a)** age **b)** doubt **c)** respect **d)** length of life

____ 27. **transient** **a)** stubborn **b)** temporary **c)** permanent **d)** easy-going

____ 28. **legacy** **a)** size **b)** anything serving as an example for a later case **c)** inheritance **d)** length of life

____ 29. **muted** **a)** softened **b)** strangled **c)** bright **d)** puzzling

____ 30. **avid** **a)** bored **b)** disliked **c)** enthusiastic **d)** plentiful

____ 31. **dwindle** **a)** strip **b)** shrink **c)** weave **d)** cut

____ 32. **nurture** **a)** harden **b)** thank **c)** nourish **d)** starve

____ 33. **aloof** **a)** distant **b)** friendly **c)** not clearly expressed **d)** ordinary

____ 34. **augment** **a)** change **b)** cause to become **c)** increase **d)** describe

____ 35. **explicit** **a)** everyday **b)** distant **c)** permanent **d)** stated exactly

____ 36. **longevity** **a)** size **b)** holding back **c)** length of life **d)** health

____ 37. **magnitude** **a)** large size **b)** attraction **c)** respect **d)** example

____ 38. **ambivalent** **a)** everyday **b)** having mixed feelings **c)** temporary **d)** able to be done

____ 39. **dispel** **a)** assist **b)** anger **c)** describe **d)** cause to vanish

____ 40. **render** **a)** win out **b)** reveal **c)** cause to vanish **d)** cause to become

____ 41. **feasible** **a)** unbelievable **b)** possible **c)** amazing **d)** wild

____ 42. **fiscal** **a)** secretive **b)** about government **c)** financial **d)** personal

____ 43. **cryptic** **a)** harmful **b)** cruel **c)** puzzling **d)** loud

____ 44. **depict** **a)** describe **b)** settle **c)** accept **d)** control

____ 45. **genial** **a)** practical **b)** possible **c)** inherited **d)** pleasant

____ 46. **pretentious** **a)** pleasant **b)** showy **c)** required **d)** practical

____ 47. **evoke** **a)** pull back **b)** plant **c)** vote **d)** draw forth

____ 48. **mundane** **a)** odd **b)** ordinary **c)** softened **d)** loud

____ 49. **obscure** **a)** enthusiastic **b)** showy **c)** hard to understand **d)** bored

____ 50. **mediate** **a)** come between to settle **b)** measure **c)** explain in detail **d)** change

SCORE: (Number correct) ________ × 2 = __________ %

Name: ____________________

Unit Four: *Posttest*

In the space provided, write the letter of the choice that is closest in meaning to the **boldfaced** word.

____ 1. **feign** a) pretend b) offend c) overlook d) avoid

____ 2. **vindictive** a) not easily understood b) gentle c) vengeful d) temporary

____ 3. **dwindle** a) weave b) cut c) strip d) shrink

____ 4. **inhibition** a) attack b) holding back c) delay d) exhibit

____ 5. **aloof** a) friendly b) distant c) not clearly expressed d) ordinary

____ 6. **precedent** a) gift b) fee c) example d) later event

____ 7. **vile** a) tricky b) nice c) secretive d) offensive

____ 8. **detrimental** a) harmful b) nutritious c) dirty d) helpful

____ 9. **ironic** a) simple b) meaning opposite of what is said c) deeply felt d) great

____ 10. **saturate** a) fully soak b) put down c) break apart d) describe

____ 11. **pacify** a) betray b) remove c) retreat d) calm

____ 12. **constrict** a) control b) regard c) make smaller d) prove

____ 13. **explicit** a) everyday b) permanent c) distant d) stated exactly

____ 14. **reconcile** a) refine b) accept c) redo d) increase

____ 15. **exhaustive** a) complete b) nervous c) respected d) tired

____ 16. **formulate** a) move b) allow c) develop d) purchase

____ 17. **ambivalent** a) everyday b) temporary c) having mixed feelings d) able to be done

____ 18. **dispel** a) cause to vanish b) anger c) describe d) assist

____ 19. **pathetic** a) wonderful b) pitifully lacking c) rich d) puzzling

____ 20. **render** a) win out b) cause to become c) cause to vanish d) reveal

____ 21. **pragmatic** a) practical b) slow c) wise d) ordinary

____ 22. **implicit** a) unstated but understood b) above c) attached d) lacking

____ 23. **furtive** a) loud b) secretive c) public d) quiet

____ 24. **augment** a) cause to become b) change c) describe d) increase

____ 25. **esteem** a) respect b) doubt c) age d) length of life

(Continues on next page)

____ 26. **contemplate** **a)** think seriously about **b)** create **c)** add to **d)** reveal

____ 27. **transient** **a)** permanent **b)** easy-going **c)** stubborn **d)** temporary

____ 28. **fallible** **a)** incomplete **b)** complete **c)** capable of error **d)** simple

____ 29. **longevity** **a)** health **b)** size **c)** length of life **d)** holding back

____ 30. **legacy** **a)** size **b)** anything serving as an example for a later case **c)** inheritance **d)** length of life

____ 31. **punitive** **a)** punishing **b)** inexpensive **c)** ridiculously inadequate **d)** possible

____ 32. **muted** **a)** puzzling **b)** softened **c)** strangled **d)** bright

____ 33. **avid** **a)** enthusiastic **b)** disliked **c)** bored **d)** plentiful

____ 34. **habitat** **a)** headache **b)** natural environment **c)** importance **d)** usual behavior

____ 35. **nurture** **a)** harden **b)** thank **c)** nourish **d)** starve

____ 36. **deficient** **a)** forgotten **b)** well-known **c)** complete **d)** lacking

____ 37. **gape** **a)** hide from **b)** beat **c)** stare **d)** repair

____ 38. **rupture** **a)** overlook **b)** damage **c)** fill **d)** burst

____ 39. **magnitude** **a)** large size **b)** attraction **c)** respect **d)** example

____ 40. **condone** **a)** arrest **b)** represent **c)** forgive **d)** appoint

____ 41. **depict** **a)** control **b)** settle **c)** accept **d)** describe

____ 42. **pretentious** **a)** pleasant **b)** required **c)** showy **d)** practical

____ 43. **evoke** **a)** pull back **b)** draw forth **c)** vote **d)** plant

____ 44. **cryptic** **a)** puzzling **b)** cruel **c)** harmful **d)** loud

____ 45. **mundane** **a)** odd **b)** softened **c)** ordinary **d)** loud

____ 46. **fiscal** **a)** secretive **b)** personal **c)** financial **d)** about government

____ 47. **obscure** **a)** hard to understand **b)** showy **c)** enthusiastic **d)** bored

____ 48. **mediate** **a)** change **b)** measure **c)** explain in detail **d)** come between to settle

____ 49. **feasible** **a)** unbelievable **b)** wild **c)** amazing **d)** possible

____ 50. **genial** **a)** pleasant **b)** possible **c)** inherited **d)** practical

SCORE: (Number correct) ________ × 2 = ___________ %

IMPROVING VOCABULARY SKILLS

Pretest / Posttest

NAME: ____________________

SECTION: __________ DATE: __________

SCORE: ____________________

ANSWER SHEET

1. ____	26. ____	51. ____	76. ____
2. ____	27. ____	52. ____	77. ____
3. ____	28. ____	53. ____	78. ____
4. ____	29. ____	54. ____	79. ____
5. ____	30. ____	55. ____	80. ____
6. ____	31. ____	56. ____	81. ____
7. ____	32. ____	57. ____	82. ____
8. ____	33. ____	58. ____	83. ____
9. ____	34. ____	59. ____	84. ____
10. ____	35. ____	60. ____	85. ____
11. ____	36. ____	61. ____	86. ____
12. ____	37. ____	62. ____	87. ____
13. ____	38. ____	63. ____	88. ____
14. ____	39. ____	64. ____	89. ____
15. ____	40. ____	65. ____	90. ____
16. ____	41. ____	66. ____	91. ____
17. ____	42. ____	67. ____	92. ____
18. ____	43. ____	68. ____	93. ____
19. ____	44. ____	69. ____	94. ____
20. ____	45. ____	70. ____	95. ____
21. ____	46. ____	71. ____	96. ____
22. ____	47. ____	72. ____	97. ____
23. ____	48. ____	73. ____	98. ____
24. ____	49. ____	74. ____	99. ____
25. ____	50. ____	75. ____	100. ____

Pretest

ANSWER KEY

1. b
2. a
3. b
4. a
5. b
6. b
7. b
8. d
9. a
10. c
11. a
12. d
13. c
14. b
15. a
16. b
17. a
18. c
19. b
20. c
21. c
22. d
23. a
24. b
25. a
26. b
27. a
28. b
29. d
30. d
31. b
32. d
33. b
34. d
35. b
36. c
37. b
38. b
39. d
40. d
41. c
42. a
43. d
44. c
45. d
46. b
47. c
48. b
49. a
50. d
51. c
52. b
53. b
54. a
55. d
56. b
57. a
58. c
59. b
60. a
61. c
62. d
63. b
64. c
65. d
66. a
67. d
68. c
69. b
70. d
71. d
72. b
73. c
74. c
75. c
76. a
77. b
78. a
79. b
80. a
81. c
82. b
83. c
84. c
85. b
86. a
87. c
88. b
89. a
90. d
91. b
92. c
93. b
94. c
95. c
96. c
97. d
98. a
99. b
100. d

IMPROVING VOCABULARY SKILLS, SHORT VERSION

Posttest

ANSWER KEY

1. c
2. c
3. b
4. d
5. d
6. c
7. c
8. b
9. b
10. d
11. c
12. a
13. a
14. c
15. a
16. c
17. b
18. c
19. c
20. d
21. b
22. b
23. c
24. b
25. b
26. b
27. c
28. a
29. c
30. b
31. d
32. b
33. b
34. d
35. a
36. b
37. c
38. b
39. a
40. d
41. a
42. c
43. d
44. a
45. c
46. b
47. c
48. c
49. b
50. c
51. a
52. d
53. b
54. c
55. c
56. c
57. c
58. d
59. b
60. d
61. d
62. b
63. b
64. b
65. c
66. a
67. a
68. b
69. b
70. c
71. d
72. b
73. a
74. a
75. c
76. c
77. c
78. d
79. b
80. a
81. d
82. a
83. d
84. a
85. c
86. a
87. a
88. a
89. a
90. d
91. d
92. c
93. a
94. a
95. b
96. c
97. d
98. c
99. a
100. c

Answers to the Pretests and Posttests:
IMPROVING VOCABULARY SKILLS, SHORT VERSION

Unit One		Unit Two		Unit Three		Unit Four	
Pretest	*Posttest*	*Pretest*	*Posttest*	*Pretest*	*Posttest*	*Pretest*	*Posttest*
1. b	1. c	1. b	1. a	1. d	1. c	1. d	1. a
2. a	2. d	2. a	2. b	2. c	2. a	2. a	2. c
3. c	3. b	3. b	3. c	3. a	3. d	3. b	3. d
4. b	4. b	4. a	4. d	4. b	4. b	4. a	4. b
5. a	5. d	5. c	5. c	5. a	5. a	5. d	5. b
6. c	6. b	6. d	6. b	6. b	6. c	6. b	6. c
7. b	7. b	7. a	7. a	7. a	7. c	7. a	7. d
8. d	8. c	8. d	8. c	8. d	8. a	8. d	8. a
9. b	9. b	9. c	9. c	9. b	9. c	9. c	9. b
10. b	10. d	10. b	10. c	10. d	10. d	10. b	10. a
11. d	11. d	11. d	11. b	11. a	11. c	11. d	11. d
12. a	12. c	12. d	12. d	12. c	12. d	12. c	12. c
13. c	13. d	13. b	13. b	13. a	13. c	13. c	13. d
14. c	14. c	14. d	14. a	14. d	14. b	14. c	14. b
15. d	15. b	15. a	15. b	15. b	15. b	15. b	15. a
16. a	16. b	16. b	16. b	16. a	16. d	16. a	16. c
17. b	17. b	17. c	17. d	17. b	17. d	17. c	17. c
18. a	18. d	18. a	18. d	18. c	18. b	18. a	18. a
19. a	19. a	19. b	19. a	19. d	19. b	19. c	19. b
20. d	20. c	20. b	20. b	20. a	20. c	20. d	20. b
21. d	21. a	21. d	21. c	21. b	21. a	21. b	21. a
22. c	22. a	22. a	22. c	22. c	22. b	22. a	22. a
23. b	23. c	23. c	23. b	23. d	23. d	23. c	23. b
24. a	24. b	24. d	24. a	24. a	24. d	24. d	24. d
25. b	25. a	25. c	25. c	25. a	25. a	25. b	25. a
26. a	26. c	26. c	26. d	26. c	26. c	26. c	26. a
27. a	27. c	27. a	27. a	27. b	27. a	27. b	27. d
28. c	28. b	28. d	28. c	28. c	28. b	28. c	28. c
29. b	29. c	29. c	29. a	29. d	29. b	29. a	29. c
30. c	30. a	30. c	30. c	30. c	30. c	30. c	30. c
31. a	31. c	31. a	31. d	31. b	31. a	31. b	31. a
32. d	32. c	32. d	32. a	32. d	32. a	32. c	32. b
33. c	33. d	33. b	33. c	33. d	33. b	33. a	33. a
34. b	34. b	34. c	34. b	34. b	34. b	34. c	34. b
35. a	35. b	35. b	35. c	35. c	35. c	35. d	35. c
36. d	36. a	36. b	36. c	36. d	36. d	36. c	36. d
37. a	37. c	37. b	37. d	37. a	37. b	37. a	37. c
38. b	38. b	38. a	38. c	38. c	38. a	38. b	38. d
39. d	39. a	39. d	39. b	39. a	39. c	39. d	39. a
40. a	40. b	40. b	40. c	40. c	40. c	40. d	40. c
41. d	41. c	41. d	41. b	41. d	41. a	41. b	41. d
42. a	42. a	42. d	42. b	42. c	42. d	42. c	42. c
43. c	43. c	43. d	43. d	43. b	43. a	43. c	43. b
44. b	44. a	44. c	44. d	44. d	44. c	44. a	44. a
45. d	45. c	45. c	45. d	45. a	45. b	45. d	45. c
46. b	46. b	46. d	46. d	46. b	46. b	46. b	46. c
47. b	47. d	47. b	47. d	47. a	47. b	47. d	47. a
48. d	48. d	48. a	48. b	48. c	48. c	48. b	48. d
49. b	49. b	49. a	49. b	49. c	49. d	49. c	49. d
50. c	50. d	50. b	50. c	50. d	50. c	50. a	50. a

Answers to the Chapter Activities:
IMPROVING VOCABULARY SKILLS, SHORT VERSION

Chapter 1 (Joseph Palmer)

Ten Words in Context	*Matching Words/Defs*	*Sentence Check 1*	*Sentence Check 2*	*Final Check*
1. B 6. B	1. 2 6. 9	1. B 6. I	1–2. G, H	1. D 6. F
2. A 7. B	2. 4 7. 6	2. H 7. A	3–4. E, J	2. C 7. A
3. C 8. C	3. 7 8. 5	3. J 8. F	5–6. B, F	3. I 8. E
4. C 9. A	4. 1 9. 10	4. C 9. E	7–8. D, A	4. H 9. B
5. A 10. C	5. 8 10. 3	5. D 10. G	9–10. I, C	5. J 10. G

Chapter 2 (A Cruel Sport)

Ten Words in Context	*Matching Words/Defs*	*Sentence Check 1*	*Sentence Check 2*	*Final Check*
1. B 6. B	1. 3 6. 8	1. I 6. D	1–2. D, C	1. F 6. D
2. A 7. C	2. 10 7. 5	2. H 7. F	3–4. H, J	2. H 7. B
3. C 8. C	3. 7 8. 1	3. A 8. G	5–6. I, A	3. C 8. J
4. A 9. B	4. 2 9. 4	4. B 9. J	7–8. F, E	4. A 9. G
5. A 10. A	5. 9 10. 6	5. E 10. C	9–10. G, B	5. E 10. I

Chapter 3 (No Luck With Women)

Ten Words in Context	*Matching Words/Defs*	*Sentence Check 1*	*Sentence Check 2*	*Final Check*
1. B 6. B	1. 4 6. 3	1. H 6. J	1–2. B, H	1. E 6. C
2. A 7. B	2. 8 7. 6	2. A 7. C	3–4. E, C	2. F 7. D
3. C 8. C	3. 1 8. 10	3. B 8. I	5–6. I, J	3. H 8. I
4. C 9. A	4. 9 9. 5	4. E 9. D	7–8. D, G	4. A 9. B
5. A 10. B	5. 7 10. 2	5. G 10. F	9–10. F, A	5. J 10. G

Chapter 4 (Accident and Recovery)

Ten Words in Context	*Matching Words/Defs*	*Sentence Check 1*	*Sentence Check 2*	*Final Check*
1. B 6. C	1. 4 6. 9	1. A 6. F	1–2. J, A	1. D 6. H
2. A 7. C	2. 10 7. 1	2. G 7. H	3–4. H, F	2. A 7. J
3. C 8. B	3. 2 8. 5	3. D 8. I	5–6. C, D	3. E 8. G
4. A 9. B	4. 8 9. 7	4. B 9. E	7–8. G, B	4. I 9. F
5. B 10. A	5. 6 10. 3	5. C 10. J	9–10. E, I	5. B 10. C

Chapter 5 (Animal Senses)

Ten Words in Context	*Matching Words/Defs*	*Sentence Check 1*	*Sentence Check 2*	*Final Check*
1. A 6. B	1. 6 6. 3	1. E 6. I	1–2. E, C	1. D 6. B
2. C 7. A	2. 4 7. 5	2. A 7. C	3–4. H, J	2. J 7. I
3. A 8. C	3. 9 8. 8	3. D 8. J	5–6. B, G	3. F 8. G
4. B 9. C	4. 1 9. 2	4. G 9. H	7–8. D, F	4. E 9. H
5. A 10. A	5. 10 10. 7	5. F 10. B	9–10. A, I	5. C 10. A

Chapter 6 (Money Problems)

Ten Words in Context	*Matching Words/Defs*	*Sentence Check 1*	*Sentence Check 2*	*Final Check*
1. A 6. C	1. 3 6. 4	1. H 6. D	1–2. G, A	1. H 6. J
2. B 7. B	2. 5 7. 7	2. A 7. J	3–4. C, H	2. E 7. I
3. C 8. B	3. 8 8. 1	3. C 8. E	5–6. I, D	3. B 8. C
4. A 9. A	4. 9 9. 10	4. I 9. B	7–8. E, B	4. D 9. G
5. B 10. C	5. 2 10. 6	5. G 10. F	9–10. F, J	5. A 10. F

Chapter 7 (The New French Employee)

Ten Words in Context	*Matching Words/Defs*	*Sentence Check 1*	*Sentence Check 2*	*Final Check*
1. C 6. B	1. 5 6. 10	1. I 6. F	1–2. J, F	1. I 6. A
2. A 7. A	2. 9 7. 2	2. H 7. C	3–4. B, I	2. H 7. D
3. B 8. B	3. 1 8. 8	3. J 8. G	5–6. E, A	3. E 8. F
4. B 9. B	4. 6 9. 7	4. E 9. A	7–8. H, C	4. C 9. J
5. C 10. A	5. 4 10. 3	5. B 10. D	9–10. G, D	5. B 10. G

Chapter 8 (A Cruel Teacher)

Ten Words in Context	*Matching Words/Defs*	*Sentence Check 1*	*Sentence Check 2*	*Final Check*
1. A 6. B	1. 9 6. 3	1. G 6. D	1–2. G, A	1. E 6. G
2. C 7. B	2. 4 7. 10	2. B 7. J	3–4. J, I	2. A 7. H
3. A 8. B	3. 6 8. 1	3. F 8. E	5–6. E, C	3. D 8. I
4. C 9. A	4. 2 9. 7	4. A 9. I	7–8. H, D	4. F 9. J
5. A 10. B	5. 8 10. 5	5. C 10. H	9–10. B, F	5. C 10. B

Chapter 9 (Learning to Study)

Ten Words in Context	*Matching Words/Defs*	*Sentence Check 1*	*Sentence Check 2*	*Final Check*
1. B 6. B	1. 9 6. 2	1. G 6. H	1–2. I, H	1. H 6. A
2. C 7. A	2. 1 7. 10	2. B 7. I	3–4. A, E	2. I 7. F
3. B 8. C	3. 4 8. 6	3. E 8. A	5–6. G, J	3. B 8. J
4. A 9. B	4. 3 9. 5	4. F 9. C	7–8. B, C	4. D 9. G
5. B 10. A	5. 8 10. 7	5. D 10. J	9–10. D, F	5. C 10. E

Chapter 10 (The Mad Monk)

Ten Words in Context	*Matching Words/Defs*	*Sentence Check 1*	*Sentence Check 2*	*Final Check*
1. C 6. A	1. 3 6. 10	1. G 6. C	1–2. G, A	1. F 6. D
2. A 7. B	2. 4 7. 5	2. A 7. H	3–4. H, C	2. H 7. I
3. B 8. B	3. 7 8. 9	3. J 8. I	5–6. D, E	3. G 8. J
4. A 9. C	4. 6 9. 1	4. D 9. B	7–8. J, B	4. B 9. C
5. C 10. A	5. 2 10. 8	5. F 10. E	9–10. F, I	5. A 10. E

Chapter 11 (Conflict Over Holidays)

Ten Words in Context	*Matching Words/Defs*	*Sentence Check 1*	*Sentence Check 2*	*Final Check*
1. C 6. A	1. 4 6. 3	1. D 6. F	1–2. B, H	1. G 6. A
2. A 7. B	2. 9 7. 10	2. E 7. G	3–4. A, J	2. I 7. E
3. B 8. A	3. 6 8. 8	3. H 8. B	5–6. C, E	3. F 8. C
4. B 9. B	4. 1 9. 2	4. J 9. C	7–8. F, G	4. J 9. B
5. C 10. C	5. 5 10. 7	5. A 10. I	9–10. D, I	5. D 10. H

Chapter 12 (Dr. Martin Luther King, Jr.)

Ten Words in Context	*Matching Words/Defs*	*Sentence Check 1*	*Sentence Check 2*	*Final Check*
1. B 6. A	1. 4 6. 2	1. D 6. H	1–2. G, B	1. B 6. E
2. C 7. B	2. 1 7. 8	2. E 7. A	3–4. E, D	2. H 7. F
3. C 8. C	3. 9 8. 6	3. F 8. B	5–6. J, H	3. G 8. D
4. A 9. A	4. 7 9. 10	4. G 9. J	7–8. C, F	4. C 9. I
5. C 10. C	5. 3 10. 5	5. C 10. I	9–10. A, I	5. A 10. J

Chapter 13 (Relating to Parents)

Ten Words in Context	*Matching Words/Defs*	*Sentence Check 1*	*Sentence Check 2*	*Final Check*
1. C 6. A	1. 4 6. 1	1. F 6. C	1–2. A, G	1. J 6. I
2. A 7. B	2. 6 7. 5	2. A 7. I	3–4. H, E	2. H 7. A
3. A 8. B	3. 9 8. 10	3. B 8. D	5–6. F, B	3. C 8. G
4. B 9. C	4. 8 9. 3	4. E 9. J	7–8. D, C	4. B 9. F
5. C 10. B	5. 2 10. 7	5. G 10. H	9–10. I, J	5. D 10. E

Chapter 14 (The Nightmare of Gym)

Ten Words in Context	*Matching Words/Defs*	*Sentence Check 1*	*Sentence Check 2*	*Final Check*
1. A 6. A	1. 6 6. 1	1. B 6. F	1–2. A, I	1. F 6. C
2. C 7. B	2. 3 7. 8	2. J 7. G	3–4. F, B	2. G 7. A
3. B 8. A	3. 7 8. 2	3. A 8. C	5–6. D, G	3. B 8. E
4. C 9. C	4. 10 9. 5	4. E 9. D	7–8. H, C	4. H 9. D
5. C 10. B	5. 4 10. 9	5. I 10. H	9–10. J, E	5. J 10. I

Chapter 15 (A Model Teacher)

Ten Words in Context	*Matching Words/Defs*	*Sentence Check 1*	*Sentence Check 2*	*Final Check*
1. B 6. B	1. 7 6. 3	1. J 6. H	1–2. J, D	1. C 6. E
2. C 7. A	2. 6 7. 2	2. A 7. G	3–4. C, F	2. H 7. F
3. A 8. B	3. 9 8. 5	3. D 8. E	5–6. H, I	3. I 8. J
4. A 9. B	4. 1 9. 8	4. I 9. C	7–8. A, G	4. D 9. G
5. C 10. C	5. 10 10. 4	5. B 10. F	9–10. E, B	5. B 10. A

Chapter 16 (Shoplifter)

Ten Words in Context	*Matching Words/Defs*	*Sentence Check 1*	*Sentence Check 2*	*Final Check*
1. A 6. A	1. 3 6. 10	1. G 6. E	1–2. C, E	1. F 6. A
2. A 7. C	2. 6 7. 5	2. B 7. F	3–4. J, B	2. B 7. E
3. C 8. B	3. 7 8. 2	3. I 8. H	5–6. G, H	3. D 8. C
4. C 9. C	4. 9 9. 8	4. C 9. D	7–8. A, F	4. H 9. J
5. B 10. A	5. 1 10. 4	5. A 10. J	9–10. I, D	5. I 10. G

Chapter 17 (A Nutty Newspaper Office)

Ten Words in Context	*Matching Words/Defs*	*Sentence Check 1*	*Sentence Check 2*	*Final Check*
1. B 6. A	1. 6 6. 8	1. B 6. C	1–2. H, I	1. D 6. I
2. A 7. A	2. 1 7. 2	2. H 7. J	3–4. A, C	2. F 7. C
3. B 8. C	3. 5 8. 9	3. G 8. A	5–6. J, D	3. G 8. B
4. C 9. C	4. 10 9. 4	4. D 9. I	7–8. G, E	4. A 9. J
5. C 10. B	5. 3 10. 7	5. F 10. E	9–10. F, B	5. E 10. H

Chapter 18 (Roughing It)

Ten Words in Context	*Matching Words/Defs*	*Sentence Check 1*	*Sentence Check 2*	*Final Check*
1. C 6. C	1. 9 6. 2	1. J 6. B	1–2. I, C	1. J 6. G
2. B 7. A	2. 6 7. 5	2. E 7. H	3–4. D, F	2. H 7. B
3. C 8. B	3. 8 8. 10	3. I 8. F	5–6. G, J	3. C 8. D
4. A 9. A	4. 3 9. 4	4. A 9. G	7–8. B, A	4. A 9. E
5. C 10. C	5. 1 10. 7	5. D 10. C	9–10. E, H	5. F 10. I

Chapter 19 (Getting Scared)

Ten Words in Context	*Matching Words/Defs*	*Sentence Check 1*	*Sentence Check 2*	*Final Check*
1. B 6. B	1. 7 6. 2	1. I 6. J	1–2. C, J	1. A 6. G
2. C 7. A	2. 10 7. 6	2. D 7. C	3–4. A, B	2. I 7. C
3. B 8. C	3. 1 8. 3	3. B 8. A	5–6. G, I	3. J 8. D
4. A 9. C	4. 9 9. 8	4. G 9. E	7–8. H, E	4. F 9. B
5. C 10. B	5. 4 10. 5	5. H 10. F	9–10. F, D	5. H 10. E

Chapter 20 (My Sister's Date)

Ten Words in Context	*Matching Words/Defs*	*Sentence Check 1*	*Sentence Check 2*	*Final Check*
1. C 6. B	1. 4 6. 10	1. H 6. I	1–2. F, E	1. J 6. D
2. B 7. A	2. 7 7. 9	2. C 7. J	3–4. C, G	2. I 7. A
3. A 8. C	3. 8 8. 1	3. B 8. D	5–6. B, J	3. C 8. E
4. B 9. B	4. 5 9. 3	4. F 9. E	7–8. A, D	4. F 9. H
5. C 10. B	5. 2 10. 6	5. A 10. G	9–10. I, H	5. G 10. B

Answers to the Unit Reviews:
IMPROVING VOCABULARY SKILLS, SHORT VERSION

Unit One

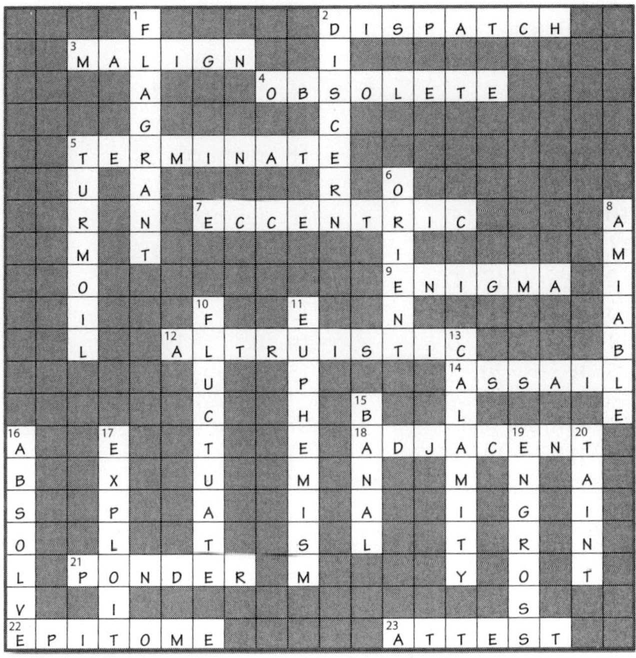

Unit Two

Unit Three

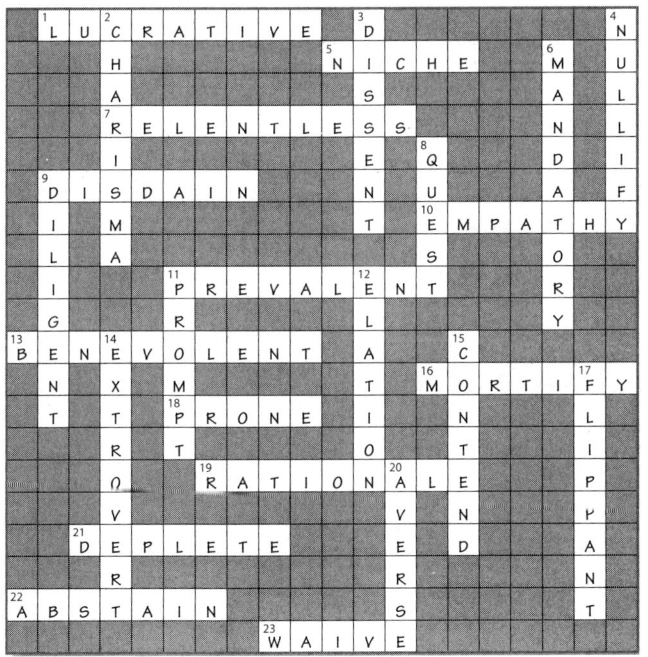

Unit Four

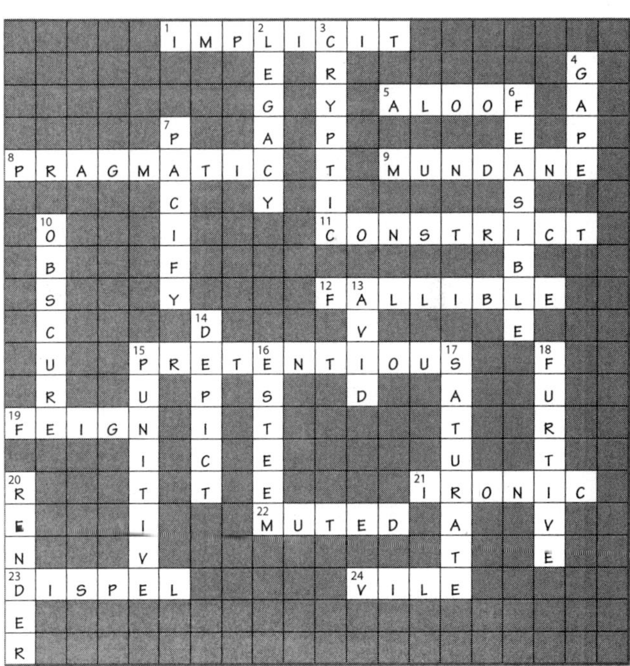

Answers to the Unit Tests: IMPROVING VOCABULARY SKILLS, SHORT VERSION

Unit One

Unit One, Test 1

1. escalates
2. euphemism
3. mercenary
4. obsolete
5. epitome
6. absolved
7. nocturnal
8. rehabilitate
9. dispatch
10. flagrant
11. D
12. C
13. A
14. C
15. B
16. B
17. C
18. D
19. B
20. A

Unit One, Test 2

1. K
2. D
3. J
4. M
5. F
6. H
7. E
8. G
9. A
10. B
11. L
12. C
13. I
14. I
15. C
16. I
17. I
18. C
19. I
20. I
21. C
22. C
23. I
24. I
25. C

Unit One, Test 3

1. D
2. C
3. A
4. C
5. B
6. B
7. A
8. B
9. D
10. C
11. B
12. A
13. B
14. D
15. D
16. B
17. A
18. C
19. B
20. A
21. A
22. C
23. C
24. D
25. A
26. D
27. B
28. C
29. D
30. B
31. C
32. A
33. C
34. B
35. A
36. C
37. D
38. D
39. B
40. D
41. A
42. C
43. A
44. B
45. B
46. B
47. B
48. D
49. A
50. B

Unit One, Test 4

1. A
2. D
3. B
4. C
5. C
6. D
7. B
8. A
9. D
10. A
11. D
12. A
13. C
14. A
15. B
16. D
17. A
18. B
19. B
20. A

Unit Two

Unit Two, Test 1

1. degenerate
2. implausible
3. concurrent
4. immaculate
5. curtailed
6. blight
7. default
8. covert
9. speculate
10. demise
11. C
12. D
13. D
14. A
15. C
16. D
17. B
18. C
19. C
20. A

Unit Two, Test 2

1. A
2. C
3. G
4. J
5. E
6. M
7. F
8. D
9. B
10. I
11. L
12. H
13. K
14. C
15. C
16. I
17. C
18. C
19. I
20. C
21. C
22. C
23. I
24. C
25. I

Unit Two, Test 3

1. B
2. D
3. C
4. B
5. A
6. B
7. D
8. A
9. D
10. C
11. B
12. B
13. D
14. B
15. A
16. C
17. D
18. A
19. D
20. C
21. D
22. C
23. A
24. B
25. C
26. C
27. B
28. A
29. D
30. A
31. D
32. D
33. B
34. A
35. C
36. C
37. A
38. D
39. B
40. C
41. D
42. A
43. A
44. D
45. B
46. A
47. C
48. A
49. B
50. D

Unit Two, Test 4

1. B
2. D
3. A
4. C
5. C
6. D
7. B
8. A
9. A
10. B
11. C
12. D
13. D
14. B
15. C
16. A
17. B
18. D
19. A
20. C

Unit Three

Unit Three, Test 1

1. niche
2. elation
3. Proponents
4. diligent
5. impasse
6. Prone
7. abstain
8. deficit
9. empathy
10. complacent
11. B
12. C
13. D
14. B
15. B
16. A
17. D
18. B
19. B
20. A

Unit Three, Test 2

1. H
2. K
3. A
4. E
5. L
6. G
7. J
8. M
9. C
10. D
11. B
12. I
13. F
14. I
15. I
16. C
17. I
18. C
19. I
20. C
21. I
22. C
23. I
24. C
25. I

Unit Three, Test 3

1. D
2. C
3. B
4. D
5. A
6. D
7. B
8. B
9. A
10. C
11. C
12. A
13. D
14. A
15. C
16. B
17. D
18. A
19. A
20. B
21. A
22. C
23. C
24. D
25. A
26. B
27. A
28. B
29. D
30. C
31. A
32. D
33. B
34. A
35. D
36. C
37. B
38. D
39. C
40. A
41. A
42. B
43. C
44. D
45. D
46. B
47. C
48. D
49. A
50. B

Unit Three, Test 4

1. C
2. A
3. B
4. B
5. C
6. D
7. A
8. B
9. B
10. D
11. B
12. B
13. D
14. A
15. B
16. D
17. B
18. A
19. D
20. C

Unit Four

Unit Four, Test 1

1. pretentious
2. explicit
3. depicted
4. implicit
5. esteem
6. formulated
7. exhaustive
8. ruptured
9. ironic
10. feigned
11. C
12. D
13. A
14. B
15. A
16. C
17. B
18. D
19. B
20. C

Unit Four, Test 2

1. K
2. E
3. J
4. M
5. A
6. B
7. D
8. F
9. C
10. I
11. G
12. H
13. L
14. I
15. C
16. C
17. I
18. C
19. C
20. C
21. I
22. C
23. I
24. C
25. I

Unit Four, Test 3

1. C
2. D
3. B
4. C
5. A
6. D
7. D
8. C
9. A
10. B
11. C
12. D
13. C
14. C
15. A
16. B
17. C
18. B
19. D
20. B
21. C
22. B
23. A
24. D
25. C
26. B
27. A
28. D
29. A
30. C
31. B
32. A
33. C
34. A
35. B
36. D
37. B
38. B
39. D
40. D
41. C
42. A
43. C
44. B
45. D
46. B
47. D
48. C
49. A
50. C

Unit Four, Test 4

1. A
2. C
3. D
4. C
5. B
6. C
7. B
8. A
9. D
10. A
11. A
12. B
13. C
14. D
15. C
16. B
17. B
18. A
19. C
20. D

Mastery Test: *Chapter 1 (Joseph Palmer)*

In the space provided, write the word from the box needed to complete each sentence. Then put the **letter** of that word in the column at the left. Use each word once.

A. **absolve**	B. **adamant**	C. **amiable**	D. **amoral**	E. **animosity**
F. **antagonist**	G. **eccentric**	H. **encounter**	I. **epitome**	J. **malign**

____ 1. Female students who took auto shop classes used to be considered ______________________. Now, however, it's not considered odd for women to learn to do car repairs.

____ 2. The husband and wife were such bitter ______________________s at their divorce hearing that it was hard to believe they had once loved each other.

____ 3. Frank hates the thought that his teacher believes he cheated. He'll go to any lengths to ______________________ himself.

____ 4. Elena intended to ask her father to lend her his car, but when she saw how grouchy he was, she decided to wait until he was in a more ______________________ mood.

____ 5. The great baseball player and civil rights leader Jackie Robinson was the ______________________ of both physical and moral strength.

____ 6. When Mrs. Haley visited the school she'd attended thirty years before, she unexpectedly had an ______________________ with one of her former teachers.

____ 7. Bill is ______________________ about going to the park for a picnic, even though the weather report is predicting severe thunderstorms.

____ 8. Although my emotionally disturbed neighbor makes rude comments to my visitors and scatters trash all over my steps, I don't feel any ______________________ toward her. I just feel sorry for her.

____ 9. A newborn baby is ______________________. It's only as a child grows older that he or she develops a sense of "right" and "wrong."

____ 10. People who say the female crocodile eats her young ______________________ her. She simply takes them into a protective pouch inside her mouth.

SCORE: (Number correct) ________ × 10 = __________ %

Mastery Test: *Chapter 2 (A Cruel Sport)*

In the space provided, write the word from the box needed to complete each sentence. Then put the **letter** of that word in the column at the left. Use each word once.

A. **acclaim**	B. **adjacent**	C. **elicit**	D. **engross**	E. **escalate**
F. **exploit**	G. **methodical**	H. **obsolete**	I. **tangible**	J. **terminate**

____ 1. The mystery story so ________________(e)d Donna that she jumped in fright when I entered the room.

____ 2. Dinah arranges the spices in her kitchen in a(n) ________________ way: in alphabetical order.

____ 3. The landlord would like to ________________ the lease of the family in 4-A. Their loud parties and shouting disturb everyone in the building.

____ 4. My woodworker friend lives ________________ to his work. His workshop is next door to his house.

____ 5. That supervisor knows how to ________________ workers. She makes them work overtime without extra pay.

____ 6. Electronic books are becoming more popular, but I don't think they'll ever make printed books ________________.

____ 7. Peter seems to think he deserves ________________ just for showing up for school. His teachers, however, think that's the least he can do.

____ 8. The protests of some small groups in Eastern Europe ________________(e)d into full-scale rebellions against their governments.

____ 9. Some people enjoy getting praised when they do a good job. I prefer a more ________________ reward, like a raise in pay.

____ 10. Flora is a bad-tempered child. Even the suggestion that she come to the dinner table is enough to ________________ a tantrum.

SCORE: (Number correct) ________ × 10 = ________ %

Mastery Test: *Chapter 3 (No Luck with Women)*

In the space provided, write the word from the box needed to complete each sentence. Then put the **letter** of that word in the column at the left. Use each word once.

A. **allusion**	B. **altruistic**	C. **appease**	D. **arbitrary**	E. **assail**
F. **banal**	G. **euphemism**	H. **mercenary**	I. **syndrome**	J. **taint**

____ 1. I expected the made-for-TV movie to be another ______________________ romance, but I was pleasantly surprised. It was both original and funny.

____ 2. The little boy's slow speech and clumsy movements are all part of a(n) ______________________ caused by his lack of oxygen at birth.

____ 3. A heckler in the audience ______________________(e)d the comedian with rude remarks until the bouncer forced the heckler to leave the club.

____ 4. I'm afraid my sister is encouraging her children to be ______________________. Every time they do a chore or an errand, she gives them a dollar. Soon they won't do anything unless they get paid.

____ 5. Being suspended for drug abuse ______________________s athletes' reputations.

____ 6. So many people are afraid of dying that we use ______________________s to describe it, such as "passing away."

____ 7. I admire Luis' ______________________ nature. He is truly more concerned for the welfare of those around him than he is for his own.

____ 8. Apologizing for tearing Danny's shirt isn't enough. Nothing will ______________________ him until you buy him a new one.

____ 9. Hoping to receive a cell phone for her birthday, Jeannie continually makes such ______________________s to it as "Mom, when I was at the mall today I saw a coat you would have loved! I wish I could have called you to tell you about it."

____ 10. That judge's sentencing seems completely ______________________. Yesterday she sent a shoplifter to jail for three months, but today she gave a car thief probation and a suspended sentence.

SCORE: (Number correct) ________ × 10 = __________ %

Mastery Test: *Chapter 4 (Accident and Recovery)*

In the space provided, write the word from the box needed to complete each sentence. Then put the **letter** of that word in the column at the left. Use each word once.

A. **calamity**	B. **comprehensive**	C. **conventional**	D. **flagrant**	E. **fluctuate**
F. **persevere**	G. **ponder**	H. **rehabilitate**	I. **turmoil**	J. **venture**

____ 1. The movie I saw last weekend really confused me. I have ____________(e)d its meaning all week.

____ 2. When a doctor sees a new patient, the doctor should ask for a ____________ health history, beginning with childhood illnesses and ending with the patient's present physical condition.

____ 3. After breaking his leg in a motorcycle accident, Lenny had to attend physical therapy classes to ____________ himself so he could walk normally again.

____ 4. The birthday party ended in complete ____________, as the children ran around the room screaming, breaking balloons, and grabbing presents.

____ 5. I'm not sure my answer is correct, but I'm feeling brave, so I'll ____________ a guess.

____ 6. While Fran enjoys unusual foods, such as curries and pasta, her husband Nick prefers more ____________ dinners, like steak and French fries.

____ 7. It takes a long time for Julio to know people well enough to trust them. You'll have to ____________ if you want to win his friendship.

____ 8. The recent earthquake was a terrible____________, killing thousands of people and leveling entire towns.

____ 9. I was shocked by the new student's ____________ refusal to observe the dress code at our school.

____ 10. My feelings about my job ____________ according to what kind of day I've had at work. Some days my job is good; some days it's terrible.

SCORE: (Number correct) ________ × 10 = __________ %

Mastery Test: *Chapter 5 (Animal Senses)*

In the space provided, write the word from the box needed to complete each sentence. Then put the **letter** of that word in the column at the left. Use each word once.

A. **attest**	B. **attribute**	C. **discern**	D. **dispatch**	E. **enhance**
F. **enigma**	G. **exemplify**	H. **mobile**	I. **nocturnal**	J. **orient**

____ 1. Every year our neighbors ______________________ the appearance of their home. Last year they redecorated the living room; this year, they planted a flowering tree in their front yard.

____ 2. One interesting ______________________ of my family is that everyone in it was born in July.

____ 3. Sailors used to ______________________ themselves by looking at the positions of the stars. Now they use modern instruments to figure out their location and direction at sea.

____ 4. For many people, Adolf Hitler and the Nazis ____________________ the human potential for evil.

____ 5. We keep our TV in the bedroom, but since it's on wheels, it's ______________________. We roll it into the living room or kitchen whenever we want to.

____ 6. The victim's neighbor ______________________(e)d to the fact that she had never returned from her shopping trip. Her newspapers and mail hadn't been picked up for a week.

____ 7. My brother's career plans are a(n) ______________________ to my parents. They can't understand why he wants to move to a small town in Maine and make furniture instead of getting an office job and making money.

____ 8. I can't ______________________ any difference between diet soft drinks and the nondiet ones. They taste exactly the same to me.

____ 9. Cats are ______________________ animals. They sleep most of the day and are active most of the night.

____ 10. As soon as the emergency call was received, police and paramedics were ____________________(e)d to the scene of the accident.

SCORE: (Number correct) ________ × 10 = __________ %

Mastery Test: *Chapter 6 (Money Problems)*

In the space provided, write the word from the box needed to complete each sentence. Then put the **letter** of that word in the column at the left. Use each word once.

A. **concurrent**	B. **confiscate**	C. **constitute**	D. **decipher**	E. **default**
F. **hypothetical**	G. **nominal**	H. **predominant**	I. **prerequisite**	J. **recession**

____ 1. Myra won her case in small-claims court when the man she was suing ____________________(e)d by not showing up.

____ 2. Although the delicious punch is made of a mixture of fruit juices, the ____________________ flavor is strawberry.

____ 3. After a water fight broke out in the fourth-grade classroom, the teacher ____________________(e)d all the squirt guns.

____ 4. During the ____________________, when business was bad, more than half the workers in the plastics factory were laid off.

____ 5. Since Velma couldn't ____________________ her teacher's handwriting, she had no idea how to go about revising her paper.

____ 6. I just realized that my school vacation and my sister's wedding are ____________________. I'll be able to help her get everything ready for the wedding.

____ 7. Two scoops of vanilla fudge ice cream, hot fudge sauce, marshmallow topping, and walnut pieces ____________________ my favorite dessert—a walnut-marshmallow-hot-fudge sundae.

____ 8. Let me ask you a ____________________ question. If you were teaching this course, what questions would you put on the final exam?

____ 9. Being at least 16 years old is the usual ____________________ for obtaining a driver's license.

____ 10. Although the dog fight looked serious, our German shepherd escaped with only ____________________ injuries.

SCORE: (Number correct) ________ × 10 = __________ %

Mastery Test: *Chapter 7 (The New French Employee)*

In the space provided, write the word from the box needed to complete each sentence. Then put the **letter** of that word in the column at the left. Use each word once.

A. **degenerate**	B. **implausible**	C. **incoherent**	D. **intercede**	E. **intricate**
F. **sanctuary**	G. **scrutiny**	H. **sinister**	I. **suffice**	J. **vulnerable**

____ 1. Because the novel's plot was so ____________________, Alfonso was beginning to get confused. Then he had the bright idea of writing down the names of the many characters and their relationships to one another.

____ 2. My close friendship with Ellen began to ____________________ after my school work began taking up most of my time. I then had no spare time in which to see her or have our usual long phone conversations.

____ 3. Since his divorce, my older brother has felt extremely ____________________. He's afraid to get involved with anyone and run the risk of getting hurt again.

____ 4. After the robbery, I gave the apartment a careful inspection to see what had been taken. My ____________________ extended even to the linen closet, where I counted the towels and sheets.

____ 5. "I'd love to go shopping with you," Cheryl said, "but my granddad says I have to finish my homework first. If you'd ____________________, maybe he'll change his mind and let me go."

____ 6. When Pat learned she had won the lottery, she became ____________________ with joy. She kept babbling: "You've got to be . . . Oh my . . . If this isn't . . ."

____ 7. The Women's ____________________ in town is a shelter for women who are being abused at home.

____ 8. "Who drew on the wall with crayon?" asked the angry mother. The little boy's ____________________ answer was, "A man came through the window and did it."

____ 9. The food in the refrigerator will have to ____________________ for the rest of the week. There's no grocery money until the next family paycheck.

____ 10. Everyone was shocked to learn that Mr. Johnson had once spent time in jail for a break-in and robbery. His cheerful, friendly manner gave no hint of his ____________________ past.

SCORE: (Number correct) ________ × 10 = __________ %

Mastery Test: *Chapter 8 (A Cruel Teacher)*

In the space provided, write the word from the box needed to complete each sentence. Then put the **letter** of that word in the column at the left. Use each word once.

A. **blatant**	B. **blight**	C. **contrive**	D. **garble**	E. **gaunt**
F. **gloat**	G. **immaculate**	H. **plagiarism**	I. **qualm**	J. **retaliate**

____ 1. When the boss announced that everyone would have to work an hour overtime, the staff ______________________(e)d by taking a two-hour lunch.

____ 2. Even though I knew I was doing the right thing, I felt a ______________________ of conscience as I told Mr. Lane that it was my friend who'd stolen his car.

____ 3. To the family's amazement, the teenager's room was ______________________. The bed was made, the records were put away, and there wasn't a single piece of clothing on the floor.

____ 4. It's hard not to ______________________ about Sharon being fired when she's been so unpleasant to all her coworkers.

____ 5. That dogwood tree must be suffering from a ______________________. It didn't flower this year, and half the branches have no leaves.

____ 6. Those ten-dollar bills are ______________________ forgeries. Even a ten-year-old could tell that they're fakes.

____ 7. My uncle's stroke has ______________________(e)d his speech. Now it's almost impossible to understand what he's saying.

____ 8. A writer accused a comedian of ______________________. He said that the comedian had taken the writer's script and turned it into a movie without paying the writer or giving him credit.

____ 9. After losing forty pounds, Alice thought her figure was perfect. Actually, though, she looked unpleasantly ______________________ —as if she'd not quite recovered from a long illness.

____ 10. Joanne has ______________________(e)d a clever way of making throw pillows. She sews two fancy washcloths together back to back and then stuffs them with foam rubber.

SCORE: (Number correct) ________ × 10 = ___________ %

Mastery Test: *Chapter 9 (Learning to Study)*

In the space provided, write the word from the box needed to complete each sentence. Then put the **letter** of that word in the column at the left. Use each word once.

A. **curtail**	B. **devastate**	C. **digress**	D. **incentive**	E. **incorporate**
F. **indispensable**	G. **intermittent**	H. **rigor**	I. **squander**	J. **succumb**

____ 1. My fantasy apartment ____________________s several very desirable features: a huge living room for parties, an all-electronic kitchen, a whirlpool, and a balcony overlooking the ocean.

____ 2. The ____________________s of camping are too much for Elaine. She likes to sleep on a sturdy mattress in a safe, warm room, not in a flimsy tent with biting insects.

____ 3. My grandmother refused to ____________________ even one bit of food. Today's leftovers always became tomorrow's soup or hash.

____ 4. Are you going to stick to your diet, or are you going to ____________________ to temptation and have a piece of chocolate fudge cake?

____ 5. I don't understand how people got along without VCR's. I find my VCR ____________________; without it, I'd never get to see my favorite shows at the few times I have to watch them.

____ 6. A bad case of flu forced Gerald to ____________________ his vacation. He came home after only three days and spent the rest of the week lying in bed.

____ 7. When employers offer their workers ____________________s, such as vacations or a share in the profits, the employees usually work harder.

____ 8. Rico was ____________________(e)d to learn that he hadn't gotten the promotion. He had already planned how he would spend the extra money.

____ 9. My e-mails to my friend Steve are ____________________. Sometimes I write once a month, other times once a year.

____ 10. The candidate for the state senate must not know much about taxes. Every time she's asked about this topic, she ____________________(e)s and talks about other matters, like the homeless or public transportation.

SCORE: (Number correct) ________ × 10 = __________ %

Mastery Test: *Chapter 10 (The Mad Monk)*

In the space provided, write the word from the box needed to complete each sentence. Then put the **letter** of that word in the column at the left. Use each word once.

A. **alleviate**	B. **benefactor**	C. **covert**	D. **cynic**	E. **demise**
F. **infamous**	G. **intrinsic**	H. **revulsion**	I. **speculate**	J. **virile**

____ 1. Everyone was shocked to learn of the sudden ____________________ of Michael Jackson, famous worldwide as the "King of Pop." He died at the age of only 50 while rehearsing for a series of concerts.

____ 2. My family photo album has little ____________________ value, but to me, it is worth more than any amount of money.

____ 3. Nicotine gum can ____________________ the withdrawal symptoms of quitting smoking.

____ 4. Someone once helped my uncle pay for college. Now that he can afford it, he's become a ____________________ to struggling students.

____ 5. Brenda took a(n) ____________________ look at her watch, hoping her hosts didn't notice her glance and think she was anxious to leave.

____ 6. Benjamin Franklin must have been a ____________________. He showed a lack of faith in human nature when he wrote, "Three may keep a secret if two of them are dead."

____ 7. In her lecture, the history teacher ____________________(e)d about why countries go to war. She came up with three reasons: to get territory, to gain natural resources such as oil, and to have power over others.

____ 8. In the past, men who cried or showed their emotions weren't considered ____________________. Today, though, it's acceptable for "real men" to be sensitive.

____ 9. My husband was filled with such ____________________ during the horror movie that he had to leave the theater. He couldn't bear to watch the scientist turn into a giant fly.

____ 10. Nearly every American has heard of John Wilkes Booth. He is ____________________ for murdering President Abraham Lincoln.

SCORE: (Number correct) ________ × 10 = ________ %

Mastery Test: *Chapter 11 (Conflict Over Holidays)*

In the space provided, write the word from the box needed to complete each sentence. Then put the **letter** of that word in the column at the left. Use each word once.

A. **abstain**	B. **affiliate**	C. **agnostic**	D. **aspire**	E. **benevolent**
F. **deficit**	G. **dissent**	H. **diversion**	I. **lucrative**	J. **mandatory**

____ 1. The famous American lawyer, Clarence Darrow, said it was impossible to know if God exists. "I do not consider it an insult, but a compliment, to be called an ______________________. I do not pretend to know where many ignorant men are sure."

____ 2. Laura loves salty foods, but she has to ______________________ from them. Her blood pressure is high, and salt makes it higher.

____ 3. Organizations such as the Boy Scouts and Girl Scouts reward their members for performing ______________________ actions like volunteering at a hospital or a shelter for the homeless.

____ 4. The Taylors were considering a divorce around Christmas time, so there was a noticeable ______________________ of good cheer in their house.

____ 5. To get a construction job, workers usually have to ______________________ with the union. Few bosses are willing to risk hiring non-union employees.

____ 6. The Johnsons were sorry to lose their favorite babysitter, but they understood that she needed a more ______________________ job in order to earn money for college.

____ 7. That teacher won't put up with any ______________________ in her classroom. The only opinions she likes to listen to are her own.

____ 8. Many Little League players ______________________ to become major league ballplayers. That's why they take the game so seriously.

____ 9. At this school, a course in writing is ______________________. Even art students must take it.

____ 10. JoJo the Clown visits Children's Hospital every Saturday to provide a(n) ______________________ for children who are bedridden or about to undergo operations.

SCORE: (Number correct) ________ × 10 = __________ %

Mastery Test: *Chapter 12 (Dr. Martin Luther King, Jr.)*

In the space provided, write the word from the box needed to complete each sentence. Then put the **letter** of that word in the column at the left. Use each word once.

A. **charisma**	B. **contemporary**	C. **contend**	D. **conversely**	E. **extrovert**
F. **poignant**	G. **prevalent**	H. **proponent**	I. **quest**	J. **traumatic**

____ 1. My little sister doesn't enjoy old classic movies like *The Wizard of Oz* or *Gone with the Wind.* She'd rather see something more ____________________, with actors who are still alive.

____ 2. My friend Bob is so outgoing that he can joke and make friends easily. I wish I were as much of a(n) ____________________ as he is.

____ 3. Holly's most ____________________ childhood experience was getting lost in a department store. She's never forgotten how frightened and upset she was before her parents found her.

____ 4. Many people in our community object to the plan to build a shopping mall in the center of town. They ____________________ that it will create too much traffic and noise, and they also insist it will be bad for the environment.

____ 5. Squirrels are ____________________ in our neighborhood. We see them everywhere.

____ 6. Gold was discovered in California in January, 1848. The following year, 80,000 people traveled there in a(n) ____________________ for the precious metal.

____ 7. My mother raised my brother and me after getting her college degree. ____________________, my aunt raised a family before getting her degree.

____ 8. Some sports stars have so much ____________________ that their fans will wait outside the stadium for hours just to get a look at them.

____ 9. Donna and Greg's wedding ceremony was full of touching details. An especially ____________________ moment came when the bride and groom gave a rose to each other's parents.

____ 10. Our doctor is a(n) ____________________ of home care. She sends patients home from the hospital as soon as possible, believing they'll recover more quickly in familiar surroundings.

SCORE: (Number correct) ________ × 10 = __________ %

Mastery Test: *Chapter 13 (Relating to Parents)*

In the space provided, write the word from the box needed to complete each sentence. Then put the **letter** of that word in the column at the left. Use each word once.

A. **congenial**	B. **flippant**	C. **impasse**	D. **perception**	E. **prompt**
F. **prone**	G. **rapport**	H. **rationale**	I. **relentless**	J. **reprisal**

____ 1. We were at a frustrating ______________________. Our old car needed major repairs in order to keep running, but it wasn't really worth saving. However, a new car would simply cost too much.

____ 2. The rain has been ______________________. It has poured down every day for the past week.

____ 3. Reba's ______________________ of big cities is that they're exciting, interesting places. Her husband, however, sees them only as noisy, dirty places to avoid.

____ 4. Why am I more ______________________ to upset stomachs on the days I have tests? I wish I didn't get so tense then.

____ 5. In the days when parents arranged their children's marriages, it could take a long time for the newlyweds to develop a ______________________.

____ 6. When the fourth-grade teacher asked her class, "Who discovered America?" my little brother gave the ______________________ answer, "Not me, Teacher!"

____ 7. The boss's ______________________ for not letting us leave the building during our lunch hour is "It gives you the chance to get to know each other better." We don't think that's a good enough reason for keeping us cooped up.

____ 8. The sing-along at Sally's party was so much fun that it ______________________(e)d my father to get out his dusty old guitar when we got home.

____ 9. Henry is such a ______________________ fellow that all the other waiters at the restaurant like him, even though he does get more tips than any of them.

____ 10. The Thompsons, our next-door neighbors, didn't invite us to their Fourth of July barbecue. In ______________________, we didn't invite them to our Labor Day picnic.

SCORE: (Number correct) ________ × 10 = __________ %

Mastery Test: *Chapter 14 (The Nightmare of Gym)*

In the space provided, write the word from the box needed to complete each sentence. Then put the **letter** of that word in the column at the left. Use each word once.

A. **averse**	B. **detract**	C. **disdain**	D. **divulge**	E. **elation**
F. **endow**	G. **expulsion**	H. **mortified**	I. **nullified**	J. **ominous**

____ 1. My parents couldn't give me much materially, but they did ______________________ me with a healthy self-confidence.

____ 2. Patti's ______________________ at being elected class president was lessened by the knowledge that her best friend had lost the election for class secretary.

____ 3. Some superstitious people are ______________________ to anything with the number thirteen on it.

____ 4. The still air and strangely green sky were signs of a(n) ______________________ change in the weather.

____ 5. Elise felt ______________________ when she jumped on the trampoline and her shorts fell off, but everyone else laughed.

____ 6. A year in college has made Gina feel superior. She now looks with ______________________ upon old friends who haven't gone beyond high school.

____ 7. Officials ______________________(e)d the results of the race when they learned that the winning horse had been given an illegal drug.

____ 8. Rudy's noisy and insulting behavior resulted in his ______________________ from the restaurant.

____ 9. The continual crying of a baby in the auditorium ______________________(e)d from our enjoyment of the movie.

____ 10. Because the Academy Awards program is so long, I fall asleep long before the names of the top winners are ______________________(e)d.

SCORE: (Number correct) ________ × 10 = __________ %

Mastery Test: *Chapter 15 (A Model Teacher)*

In the space provided, write the word from the box needed to complete each sentence. Then put the **letter** of that word in the column at the left. Use each word once.

A. **commemorate**	B. **complacent**	C. **consensus**	D. **deplete**	E. **diligent**
F. **empathy**	G. **menial**	H. **niche**	I. **transcend**	J. **waive**

____ 1. Although we have only one house guest, his huge appetite quickly ______________________s our supplies of certain foods. I've had to make three trips to the supermarket this week.

____ 2. To be a good therapist, one must have ______________________ for others.

____ 3. Tony never became ______________________ about his store's success. He continued to work as hard as he did the first day it was opened.

____ 4. To ______________________ my aunt and uncle's wedding anniversary, I made a donation to one of their favorite charities.

____ 5. Amy isn't skilled at dealing with people, but she has found a(n) ______________________ as a computer repair specialist, working mainly with machines, not humans.

____ 6. There was rarely a(n) ______________________ in our large family on where to eat. Three of us always wanted Mexican food, and the others usually preferred Italian or Chinese.

____ 7. With special training, Philip was able to ______________________ his learning disability and become a successful accountant.

____ 8. Ben cheerfully accepted a job as a dishwasher at a summer resort. He didn't mind the ______________________ work as long as he could enjoy the beautiful resort in his free time.

____ 9. Once the librarian gets to know you, she ______________________s the requirement that you show your student identification every time you wish to take out a book.

____ 10. Herb is not at the top of the honor roll month after month because he's so brilliant, but because he's very ______________________ about his school work.

SCORE: (Number correct) ________ × 10 = __________ %

Mastery Test: *Chapter 16 (Shoplifter)*

In the space provided, write the word from the box needed to complete each sentence. Then put the **letter** of that word in the column at the left. Use each word once.

A. **condone**	B. **contemplate**	C. **feasible**	D. **feign**	E. **fiscal**
F. **furtive**	G. **gape**	H. **pathetic**	I. **precedent**	J. **punitive**

____ 1. Although Dr. Simpson often seems rude, we ____________________ his bad manners because of the many kind things he's done for our family over the years.

____ 2. The ____________________ rules at some banks allowed them to lend huge amounts of money. When the economy turned bad and the loans weren't repaid, those banks failed.

____ 3. Many young people ____________________ joining the Army because of the free career training it could provide them.

____ 4. Should prisons only be ____________________? Or should they also teach prisoners useful skills?

____ 5. We ____________________(e)d in astonishment at the huge hole in the ground left by the earthquake.

____ 6. Alex's attempts to repair his car were so ____________________ that he made the situation even worse.

____ 7. Lawyers rely heavily on legal ____________________. When a question arises, they look for past cases in which similar questions were dealt with.

____ 8. Little Emily tried to act as if she wasn't thinking about her Christmas presents, but she kept taking ____________________ glances at the beautifully wrapped packages under the tree.

____ 9. I wonder if it will someday be ____________________ for an average person to take a vacation somewhere in space.

____ 10. When I open one of Grandma's birthday presents, I usually have to ____________________ delighted surprise. She often gives me something that's either ugly or useless.

SCORE: (Number correct) ________ × 10 = __________ %

Mastery Test: *Chapter 17 (A Nutty Newspaper Office)*

In the space provided, write the word from the box needed to complete each sentence. Then put the **letter** of that word in the column at the left. Use each word once.

A. **cryptic**	B. **deficient**	C. **depict**	D. **detrimental**	E. **implicit**
F. **inhibition**	G. **ironic**	H. **rupture**	I. **saturate**	J. **vindictive**

____ 1. The ______________________ note my girlfriend left on my door said only, "A bridge over troubled waters."

____ 2. Throughout the hilarious movie, my visiting cousin didn't laugh once or even crack a smile. He seemed completely ______________________ in a sense of humor.

____ 3. Most plants need as much sunshine as possible. But for shade-loving plants, direct sunlight is actually ______________________ to their well-being.

____ 4. The expensive two-week, eight-hour-a-day language course ______________________s students' minds with the new language.

____ 5. "Wouldn't you be more comfortable on the couch?" was a(n) ______________________ request for the 300-pound guest not to sit on Jane's fragile antique chair.

____ 6. Celia felt as if she'd kept all her anger at her roommate trapped in a box inside her. Suddenly, the box ______________________(e)d, and angry words came spilling out of her mouth.

____ 7. Although Denzel Washington was in the same elevator with me, my ______________________ against bothering celebrities kept me from asking for his autograph.

____ 8. "It's a(n) ______________________ fact of life," said Aunt Lucy, "that we are often attracted to our mates by the very qualities that later drive us crazy."

____ 9. Bertha had ______________________(e)d her father as such a monster that when I finally met him, I was surprised to find him soft-spoken and pleasant.

____ 10. Mona was angry because her brother had refused to lend her a favorite CD. Feeling ______________________, Mona went through her brother's room and removed everything she had ever given him.

SCORE: (Number correct) ________ × 10 = __________ %

Mastery Test: *Chapter 18 (Roughing It)*

In the space provided, write the word from the box needed to complete each sentence. Then put the **letter** of that word in the column at the left. Use each word once.

A. **constrict**	B. **exhaustive**	C. **fallible**	D. **formulate**	E. **genial**
F. **habitat**	G. **pragmatic**	H. **pretentious**	I. **reconcile**	J. **vile**

____ 1. The octopus is very good at squeezing into small spaces. It can ____________________ its flexible legs and body enough to slip into what seems an impossibly small area.

____ 2. My fifth-grade teacher's ____________________ manner disguised a truly unpleasant personality.

____ 3. Instead of denying it when she makes a mistake, our English teacher simply says, "Like everyone else, I'm ____________________."

____ 4. Jan doesn't often mention the fact that she has two doctoral degrees because she doesn't want to seem ____________________.

____ 5. I don't really like my biology lab partner, but he asked me out so suddenly that I didn't have time to ____________________ an excuse. Instead I just stammered, "Uh, well, I guess so."

____ 6. Although several specialists ran a(n) ____________________ series of tiring tests and exams, they could discover no cause for Eric's terrible headaches.

____ 7. My twelve-year-old sister enjoyed creating a natural ____________________ inside a large aquarium for her hermit crab.

____ 8. It's more ____________________ to buy clothing that can be mixed and matched into various outfits than to buy clothes that can be worn in only one outfit.

____ 9. When Sara decided to stay home with the baby, she and Andy ____________________(e)d themselves to living on considerably less money for a while.

____ 10. Why do millions of people enjoy seeing movies about such ____________________ subjects as chain-saw murders?

SCORE: (Number correct) ________ × 10 = __________ %

Mastery Test: *Chapter 19 (Getting Scared)*

In the space provided, write the word from the box needed to complete each sentence. Then put the **letter** of that word in the column at the left. Use each word once.

A. **avid**	B. **dwindle**	C. **esteem**	D. **evoke**	E. **legacy**
F. **mediate**	G. **muted**	H. **nurture**	I. **pacify**	J. **transient**

____ 1. If we aren't careful, our ______________________ to our children and grandchildren may be an environment damaged beyond saving.

____ 2. The children were annoyed to return from lunch and find that their formerly huge snowman had ______________________(e)d under the midday sun to only a stump.

____ 3. "I don't know what to say!" gasped the woman when she met her favorite actor. "I'm your most ______________________ fan. I've seen each of your movies at least three times."

____ 4. The smell of lilac cologne always ______________________s memories in me of my grandmother.

____ 5. Kay looks more attractive now that she's traded in her harsh, bright make-up for more ______________________ colors.

____ 6. It was hard for Toni to see the restaurant she had ______________________(e)d from a tiny take-out stand to a thriving pizzeria disappear in a blaze of fire.

____ 7. Al was about to offer to ______________________ the dispute between his two angry neighbors, but when he noticed one of them had a knife, he decided instead to call the police.

____ 8. My ______________________ for my rich uncle grew when I learned how much work he did for charities and how much money he gave them.

____ 9. When my brother is really angry, nothing I say can ______________________ him. I just listen until he's had his say, and then he quickly calms down again.

____ 10. My joy at seeing an A at the top of the returned math paper was ______________________, disappearing quickly when I realized the teacher had mistakenly given me someone else's paper.

SCORE: (Number correct) ________ × 10 = __________ %

Mastery Test: *Chapter 20 (My Sister's Date)*

In the space provided, write the word from the box needed to complete each sentence. Then put the **letter** of that word in the column at the left. Use each word once.

A. **aloof**	B. **ambivalent**	C. **augment**	D. **dispel**	E. **explicit**
F. **longevity**	G. **magnitude**	H. **mundane**	I. **obscure**	J. **render**

____ 1. I've tried to ____________________ superstitions from my mind, but I still find myself walking around ladders, not under them.

____ 2. I don't know how Tom could have made such a mess of painting the garage. He was given ____________________ instructions as to how it was to be done.

____ 3. Perry decided to ____________________ his muscles by lifting weights every other day.

____ 4. Cats are usually thought of as more ____________________ than dogs, keeping their distance from everyone but a chosen few.

____ 5. Doug is ____________________ about the job offer he's received. The job itself sounds great, but accepting it would mean moving far from his family and friends.

____ 6. Many scientists believe our sun will die someday, but since that event wouldn't happen for millions of years, it seems of little ____________________ today.

____ 7. People often marry expecting never-ending romance and excitement. However, marriages are full of ____________________ details like bill-paying and finding baby sitters.

____ 8. After staying awake all night, Duane wrote what he thought was a brilliant letter to his girlfriend. But this morning he found it so ____________________ that even he couldn't understand it all.

____ 9. A new coat of off-white paint ____________________(e)d the old kitchen much brighter and more attractive.

____ 10. Just when you are determined to stop all unhealthy habits, you read about some lively 100-year-old who says his or her ____________________ stems from daily doses of whiskey and cigars.

SCORE: (Number correct) ________ × 10 = __________ %

Answers to the Mastery Tests:
IMPROVING VOCABULARY SKILLS, SHORT VERSION

Chapter 1 (Joseph Palmer)

1. G
2. F
3. A
4. C
5. I
6. H
7. B
8. E
9. D
10. J

Chapter 2 (A Cruel Sport)

1. D
2. G
3. J
4. B
5. F
6. H
7. A
8. E
9. I
10. C

Chapter 3 (No Luck with Women)

1. F
2. I
3. E
4. H
5. J
6. G
7. B
8. C
9. A
10. D

Chapter 4 (Accident and Recovery)

1. G
2. B
3. H
4. I
5. J
6. C
7. F
8. A
9. D
10. E

Chapter 5 (Animal Senses)

1. E
2. B
3. J
4. G
5. H
6. A
7. F
8. C
9. I
10. D

Chapter 6 (Money Problems)

1. E
2. H
3. B
4. J
5. D
6. A
7. C
8. F
9. I
10. G

Chapter 7 (The New French Employee)

1. E
2. A
3. J
4. G
5. D
6. C
7. F
8. B
9. I
10. H

Chapter 8 (A Cruel Teacher)

1. J
2. I
3. G
4. F
5. B
6. A
7. D
8. H
9. E
10. C

Chapter 9 (Learning to Study)

1. E
2. H
3. I
4. J
5. F
6. A
7. D
8. B
9. G
10. C

Chapter 10 (The Mad Monk)

1. E
2. G
3. A
4. B
5. C
6. D
7. I
8. J
9. H
10. F

Chapter 11 (Conflict Over Holidays)

1. C
2. A
3. E
4. F
5. B
6. I
7. G
8. D
9. J
10. H

Chapter 12 (Dr. Martin Luther King, Jr.)

1. B
2. E
3. J
4. C
5. G
6. I
7. D
8. A
9. F
10. H

Chapter 13 (Relating to Parents)

1. C	6. B
2. I	7. H
3. D	8. E
4. F	9. A
5. G	10. J

Chapter 14 (The Nightmare of Gym)

1. F	6. C
2. E	7. I
3. A	8. G
4. J	9. B
5. H	10. D

Chapter 15 (A Model Teacher)

1. D	6. C
2. F	7. I
3. B	8. G
4. A	9. J
5. H	10. E

Chapter 16 (Shoplifter)

1. A	6. H
2. E	7. I
3. B	8. F
4. J	9. C
5. G	10. D

Chapter 17 (A Nutty Newspaper Office)

1. A	6. H
2. B	7. F
3. D	8. G
4. I	9. C
5. E	10. J

Chapter 18 (Roughing It)

1. A	6. B
2. E	7. F
3. C	8. G
4. H	9. I
5. D	10. J

Chapter 19 (Getting Scared)

1. E	6. H
2. B	7. F
3. A	8. C
4. D	9. I
5. G	10. J

Chapter 20 (My Sister's Date)

1. D	6. G
2. E	7. H
3. C	8. I
4. A	9. J
5. B	10. F

Mastery Test: *Unit One*

PART A

Complete each sentence in a way that clearly shows you understand the meaning of the **boldfaced** word. Take a minute to plan your answer before you write.

Example: Being **nocturnal** animals, raccoons ______raid our garbage cans only at night______.

1. The news program reported a **calamity** in which ______________________________

______________________________.

2. Typewriters are now almost **obsolete** because ______________________________

______________________________.

3. Three personal **attributes** that I possess are ______________________________

______________________________.

4. One **tangible** symbol of affection is ______________________________

______________________________.

5. When I'm alone, I often **ponder** ______________________________

______________________________.

6. The **eccentric** teacher has a habit of ______________________________

______________________________.

7. One advantage of a **mobile** library might be ______________________________

______________________________.

8. The most **altruistic** thing I ever saw anyone do was to ______________________________

______________________________.

9. The actor received this **acclaim** for his performance: "______________________________

______________________________."

10. I plan to **persevere** in ______________________________

______________________________.

(Continues on next page)

PART B

Use each of the following ten words in sentences of your own. Make it clear that you know the meaning of the word you use. Feel free to use the past tense or plural form of a word.

A. **absolve**	B. **animosity**	C. **antagonist**	D. **appease**	E. **banal**
F. **encounter**	G. **engross**	H. **euphemism**	I. **mercenary**	J. **turmoil**

11. ______________________________

____

12. ______________________________

____

13. ______________________________

____

14. ______________________________

____

15. ______________________________

____

16. ______________________________

____

17. ______________________________

____

18. ______________________________

____

19. ______________________________

____

20. ______________________________

____

SCORE: (Number correct) ________ × 5 = __________ %

Mastery Test: *Unit Two*

PART A

Complete each sentence in a way that clearly shows you understand the meaning of the **boldfaced** word. Take a minute to plan your answer before you write.

Example: As an **incentive** to work better, the company gives bonuses to workers who show special effort.

1. One of the most **infamous** people I've heard of is ______________________.

2. One sight that makes me feel **revulsion** is ______________________.

3. The reason the plan was **covert** was that ______________________.

4. When Carolyn saw her essay grade, she **gloated**, saying, "______________________."

5. During the math class, the teacher **digressed** by ______________________.

6. My apartment is so **immaculate** that ______________________.

7. A good friend of mine was once **devastated** by ______________________.

8. The novel's main character is a **sinister** doctor who ______________________.

9. When our neighbor cut lilacs off our bush for her home, we **retaliated** by ______________________.

10. One **prerequisite** for getting married ought to be ______________________.

(Continues on next page)

PART B

Use each of the following ten words in sentences of your own. Make it clear that you know the meaning of the word you use. Feel free to use the past tense or plural form of a word.

A. **blight**	B. **curtail**	C. **decipher**	D. **implausible**	E. **predominant**
F. **qualm**	G. **sanctuary**	H. **speculate**	I. **virile**	J. **vulnerable**

11. ______________________________

____

12. ______________________________

____

13. ______________________________

____

14. ______________________________

____

15. ______________________________

____

16. ______________________________

____

17. ______________________________

____

18. ______________________________

____

19. ______________________________

____

20. ______________________________

____

SCORE: (Number correct) ________ × 5 = __________ %

Mastery Test: *Unit Three*

PART A

Complete each sentence in a way that clearly shows you understand the meaning of the **boldfaced** word. Take a minute to plan your answer before you write.

Example: I **abstain** from ______staying up late and watching TV the night before a test______.

1. Luis showed his **elation** at the news by ______________________________

______________________________.

2. I **aspire** to ______________________________

______________________________.

3. Jon, who is a **proponent** of daily exercise, advised me, " ______________________________

______________________________."

4. At our school, it is **mandatory** to ______________________________

______________________________.

5. At parties, Shawna, who is an **extrovert** , likes to ______________________________

______________________________.

6. I find it **detracts** from a restaurant meal when ______________________________

______________________________.

7. Lamont is **averse** to city life because ______________________________

______________________________.

8. Our father told us how **traumatic** it was for him to ______________________________

______________________________.

9. My **rationale** for going to college is ______________________________

______________________________.

10. When asked by the restaurant owner to pay his bill, the young man's **flippant** reply was " ____________

______________________________."

(Continues on next page)

PART B

Use each of the following ten words in sentences of your own. Make it clear that you know the meaning of the word you use. Feel free to use the past tense or plural form of a word.

A. **consensus**	B. **deplete**	C. **dissent**	D. **empathy**	E. **niche**
F. **perception**	G. **prone**	H. **quest**	I. **rapport**	J. **waive**

11. ____________________

12. ____________________

13. ____________________

14. ____________________

15. ____________________

16. ____________________

17. ____________________

18. ____________________

19. ____________________

20. ____________________

SCORE: (Number correct) ________ × 5 = ____________ %

Mastery Test: *Unit Four*

PART A

Complete each sentence in a way that clearly shows you understand the meaning of the **boldfaced** word. Take a minute to plan your answer before you write.

Example: To increase your **longevity**, exercise frequently and avoid tobacco, alcohol, and high-fat foods.

1. **Pragmatic** Ramona spends her money on such things as ____________________ ____________________.

2. One thing the nursery-school teacher did to **nurture** each child each day was ____________________ ____________________.

3. The critic summed up how **pathetic** the actor's performance was with this comment: "____________________ ____________________."

4. The car accident **rendered** Philip ____________________ ____________________.

5. The **magnitude** of Carol's musical talent became clear to us when ____________________ ____________________.

6. A student **deficient** in study skills might ____________________ ____________________.

7. We learned how **fallible** the house builder was when ____________________ ____________________.

8. I have had to **reconcile** myself to the fact that ____________________ ____________________.

9. When he wasn't invited to the wedding, the bride's **vindictive** cousin ____________________ ____________________.

10. I'm such an **avid** fan of ____________________ that I'll ____________________ ____________________.

(Continues on next page)

PART B

Use each of the following ten words in sentences of your own. Make it clear that you know the meaning of the word you use. Feel free to use the past tense or plural form of a word.

A. **condone**	B. **contemplate**	C. **esteem**	D. **feign**	E. **furtive**
F. **gape**	G. **habitat**	H. **inhibition**	I. **pacify**	J. **vile**

11. ____

____

12. ____

____

13. ____

____

14. ____

____

15. ____

____

16. ____

____

17. ____

____

18. ____

____

19. ____

____

20. ____

____

SCORE: (Number correct) ________ × 5 = __________ %

ADVANCING VOCABULARY SKILLS

Pretest

NAME: ____________________

SECTION: __________ DATE: __________

SCORE: ____________________

This test contains 100 items. In the space provided, write the letter of the choice that is closest in meaning to the **boldfaced** word.

Important: Keep in mind that this test is for diagnostic purposes only. **If you do not know a word, leave the space blank rather than guess at it.**

____ 1. **scrupulous** **a)** sociable **b)** careless **c)** clean **d)** conscientious

____ 2. **vicarious** **a)** experienced indirectly **b)** lively **c)** inactive **d)** occasional

____ 3. **facetious** **a)** ill-mannered **b)** joking **c)** careless **d)** depressed

____ 4. **discretion** **a)** independence **b)** gladness **c)** slyness **d)** tact

____ 5. **gregarious** **a)** wordy **b)** depressed **c)** sociable **d)** religious

____ 6. **despondent** **a)** depressed **b)** tired **c)** encouraged **d)** well-behaved

____ 7. **rudimentary** **a)** rude **b)** planned **c)** partial **d)** elementary

____ 8. **retrospect** **a)** expecting **b)** repetition **c)** removal **d)** looking back

____ 9. **instigate** **a)** stir to action **b)** investigate **c)** prepare **d)** suppress

____ 10. **venerate** **a)** protect **b)** create **c)** make unfriendly **d)** respect

____ 11. **subsidize** **a)** support financially **b)** lift up **c)** fall over **d)** calculate

____ 12. **dissident** **a)** political supporter **b)** visitor **c)** candidate **d)** one who disagrees

____ 13. **juxtapose** **a)** replace **b)** place side by side **c)** remove **d)** imagine

____ 14. **embellish** **a)** remove **b)** keep **c)** decorate **d)** hide

____ 15. **inadvertent** **a)** unintentional **b)** not for sale **c)** distant **d)** near

____ 16. **relinquish** **a)** enjoy **b)** gather **c)** criticize **d)** give up

____ 17. **impetuous** **a)** lazy **b)** calm **c)** teasing **d)** impulsive

____ 18. **euphoric** **a)** undecided **b)** depressed **c)** lonely **d)** overjoyed

19. **infallible** **a)** incapable of error **b)** accident-prone **c)** human **d)** wild

____ 20. **regress** **a)** make progress **b)** restrict **c)** return to previous behavior **d)** adjust

____ 21. **fortuitous** **a)** lucky **b)** sad **c)** having never happened before **d)** brave

____ 22. **sham** **a)** type **b)** imitation **c)** disturbance **d)** belief

____ 23. **predisposed** **a)** against **b)** reluctant to speak **c)** undecided **d)** tending beforehand

____ 24. **propensity** **a)** relation **b)** job **c)** tendency **d)** hobby

____ 25. **reprehensible** **a)** blameworthy **b)** well-filled **c)** affordable **d)** admirable

(Continues on next page)

____ 26. **attrition** **a)** becoming fewer **b)** connection **c)** multiplying **d)** imitation

____ 27. **reticent** **a)** forgiving **b)** sad **c)** reluctant to speak **d)** contrary to reason

____ 28. **circumvent** **a)** avoid **b)** fail to notice **c)** distribute **d)** socialize

____ 29. **inundate** **a)** delay **b)** flood **c)** swallow **d)** approve

____ 30. **oblivious** **a)** courageous **b)** unaware **c)** quiet **d)** reliable

____ 31. **inquisitive** **a)** cheerful **b)** nervous **c)** curious **d)** in pain

____ 32. **relegate** **a)** bring back into use **b)** assign to a lesser place **c)** blend **d)** raise

____ 33. **bolster** **a)** support **b)** protect **c)** protest **d)** hide

____ 34. **terse** **a)** nervous **b)** sad **c)** brief **d)** cool

____ 35. **sedentary** **a)** sitting **b)** excessive **c)** harmless **d)** repeated

____ 36. **superfluous** **a)** extra **b)** unclear **c)** useful **d)** ahead

____ 37. **exonerate** **a)** encourage **b)** condemn **c)** hide **d)** free from blame

____ 38. **contingency** **a)** contest **b)** disapproval **c)** theory **d)** possibility

____ 39. **clandestine** **a)** well-lit **b)** secret **c)** noble **d)** harmless

____ 40. **liability** **a)** drawback **b)** hatred **c)** favor **d)** indirect remark

____ 41. **austere** **a)** wealthy **b)** plain **c)** complex **d)** far

____ 42. **perfunctory** **a)** unenthusiastic **b)** troubled **c)** on time **d)** well-prepared

____ 43. **provocative** **a)** careful **b)** able to improve **c)** inconsistent **d)** arousing interest

____ 44. **esoteric** **a)** public **b)** uniform **c)** well-written **d)** understood by few

____ 45. **metamorphosis** **a)** journey **b)** change **c)** secret plot **d)** fantasy

____ 46. **verbose** **a)** wordy **b)** active **c)** noisy **d)** forceful

____ 47. **connoisseur** **a)** one who likes to suffer **b)** egotist **c)** expert **d)** painter

____ 48. **contrite** **a)** indecent **b)** sorry **c)** lacking confidence **d)** careful

____ 49. **plight** **a)** difficult situation **b)** minor weakness **c)** environment **d)** travel

____ 50. **distraught** **a)** educated **b)** too noticeable **c)** troubled **d)** rehearsed

(Continues on next page)

____ 51. **encompass** **a)** include **b)** draw **c)** separate **d)** purchase

____ 52. **stringent** **a)** dry **b)** strict **c)** loose **d)** long

____ 53. **eradicate** **a)** wipe out **b)** scold **c)** restore **d)** hold onto

____ 54. **sordid** **a)** slow **b)** unprepared **c)** morally low **d)** injured

____ 55. **presumptuous** **a)** indecent **b)** lacking standards of selection **c)** nervous **d)** too bold

____ 56. **meticulous** **a)** broken-down **b)** curious **c)** careful and exact **d)** irregular

____ 57. **magnanimous** **a)** nameless **b)** proud **c)** generous in forgiving **d)** lacking standards

____ 58. **exhort** **a)** strongly urge **b)** travel **c)** escape **d)** hint

____ 59. **innocuous** **a)** delightful **b)** harmless **c)** dangerous **d)** disappointing

____ 60. **masochist** **a)** one who likes to suffer **b)** egotist **c)** fan
d) one who expects the worst

____ 61. **deplore** **a)** command **b)** disapprove of **c)** encourage **d)** prevent

____ 62. **atrophy** **a)** weaken **b)** reward **c)** expand **d)** strengthen

____ 63. **unprecedented** **a)** overly noticeable **b)** without authority **c)** unexpected
d) having never happened before

____ 64. **mitigate** **a)** make worse **b)** make less severe **c)** remove **d)** hide

____ 65. **exacerbate** **a)** make worse **b)** remove **c)** bring closer **d)** strengthen

____ 66. **exorbitant** **a)** absorbent **b)** excessive **c)** quarrelsome **d)** well-timed

____ 67. **facilitate** **a)** approve **b)** serve **c)** make easier **d)** clear from blame

____ 68. **synchronize** **a)** spread throughout **b)** separate **c)** reduce **d)** cause to occur together

____ 69. **extricate** **a)** run away **b)** confuse **c)** free from difficulty **d)** complicate

____ 70. **exhilaration** **a)** freedom **b)** thirst **c)** wisdom **d)** gladness

____ 71. **proficient** **a)** proud **b)** wise **c)** skilled **d)** well-known

____ 72. **annihilate** **a)** guide **b)** misunderstand **c)** carry out **d)** destroy

____ 73. **criterion** **a)** philosophy **b)** standard for judgment **c)** political theory
d) state of mind

____ 74. **vindicate** **a)** clear from blame **b)** ridicule **c)** escape **d)** formally question

____ 75. **subversive** **a)** being a servant **b)** acting to overthrow **c)** willing
d) planning to build

(Continues on next page)

____ 76. **forestall** a) prevent b) predict c) rent d) hurry

____ 77. **retribution** a) donation b) looking back c) evil d) punishment

____ 78. **insinuate** a) demand b) state c) deny d) hint

____ 79. **disparity** a) sadness b) inequality c) blemish d) similarity

____ 80. **opportune** a) generous b) more important c) well-timed d) belittling

____ 81. **fastidious** a) not planned b) attentive to details c) quick d) inferior

____ 82. **heinous** a) evil b) mischievous c) stubborn d) depressed

____ 83. **implement** a) encourage b) carry out c) insult d) prevent

____ 84. **complement** a) praise b) sin c) make fun of d) add what is needed

____ 85. **impromptu** a) forceful b) unplanned c) delayed d) on time

____ 86. **transgress** a) follow b) round out c) travel d) break a law

____ 87. **extenuating** a) excusing b) inferior c) forceful d) overly noticeable

____ 88. **vehement** a) forceful b) wicked c) rude d) calm

____ 89. **auspicious** a) threatening b) lazy c) favorable d) not trusting

____ 90. **rebuke** a) compromise b) fix c) scold d) admire

____ 91. **macabre** a) frightful b) depressed c) cheerful d) common

____ 92. **fabricate** a) misinterpret b) put away c) clothe d) invent

____ 93. **turbulent** a) ambitious b) wildly disturbed c) mixed d) fast

____ 94. **impending** a) about to happen b) illegal c) historical d) usual

____ 95. **paramount** a) dramatic b) disturbed c) unknown d) chief

____ 96. **emulate** a) be tardy b) misunderstand c) imitate d) prepare

____ 97. **antithesis** a) disorder b) theory c) effect d) opposite

____ 98. **incapacitate** a) disable b) allow c) increase d) fight

____ 99. **abrasive** a) rough b) friendly c) mild d) foolish

____ 100. **prognosis** a) hope b) memory c) opposite d) prediction

STOP. This is the end of the test. If there is time remaining, you may go back and recheck your answers. When the time is up, hand in both your answer sheet and this test booklet to your instructor.

ADVANCING VOCABULARY SKILLS

Posttest

NAME: ______________________

SECTION: __________ DATE: __________

SCORE: ______________________

This test contains 100 items. In the space provided, write the letter of the choice that is closest in meaning to the **boldfaced** word.

____ 1. **juxtapose** a) place side by side b) replace c) remove d) imagine

____ 2. **embellish** a) remove b) decorate c) keep d) hide

____ 3. **facetious** a) joking b) ill-mannered c) careless d) depressed

____ 4. **infallible** a) wild b) accident-prone c) incapable of error d) human

____ 5. **discretion** a) independence b) tact c) slyness d) gladness

____ 6. **inadvertent** a) near b) not for sale c) distant d) unintentional

____ 7. **gregarious** a) religious b) sociable c) depressed d) wordy

____ 8. **rudimentary** a) rude b) planned c) partial d) elementary

____ 9. **retrospect** a) repetition b) looking back c) removal d) expecting

____ 10. **regress** a) restrict b) make progress c) adjust d) return to previous behavior

____ 11. **instigate** a) stir to action b) suppress c) prepare d) investigate

____ 12. **venerate** a) protect b) respect c) make unfriendly d) create

____ 13. **propensity** a) hobby b) relation c) job d) tendency

____ 14. **subsidize** a) fall over b) lift up c) support financially d) calculate

____ 15. **dissident** a) political supporter b) candidate c) visitor d) one who disagrees

____ 16. **despondent** a) tired b) depressed c) encouraged d) well-behaved

____ 17. **relinquish** a) give up b) criticize c) gather d) enjoy

____ 18. **scrupulous** a) clean b) careless c) sociable d) conscientious

____ 19. **sham** a) type b) imitation c) disturbance d) belief

____ 20. **impetuous** a) impulsive b) lazy c) teasing d) calm

____ 21. **fortuitous** a) having never happened before b) brave c) lucky d) sad

____ 22. **predisposed** a) against b) reluctant to speak c) tending beforehand d) undecided

____ 23. **reprehensible** a) affordable b) well-filled c) blameworthy d) admirable

____ 24. **vicarious** a) occasional b) experienced indirectly c) lively d) inactive

____ 25. **euphoric** a) undecided b) depressed c) lonely d) overjoyed

(Continues on next page)

____ 26. **contrite** **a)** careful **b)** lacking confidence **c)** sorry **d)** indecent

____ 27. **attrition** **a)** becoming fewer **b)** imitation **c)** multiplying **d)** connection

____ 28. **terse** **a)** nervous **b)** sad **c)** brief **d)** cool

____ 29. **esoteric** **a)** public **b)** uniform **c)** well-written **d)** understood by few

____ 30. **clandestine** **a)** secret **b)** well-lit **c)** noble **d)** harmless

____ 31. **inquisitive** **a)** cheerful **b)** curious **c)** nervous **d)** in pain

____ 32. **contingency** **a)** contest **b)** disapproval **c)** theory **d)** possibility

____ 33. **relegate** **a)** blend **b)** assign to a lesser place **c)** bring back into use **d)** raise

____ 34. **verbose** **a)** noisy **b)** active **c)** wordy **d)** forceful

____ 35. **exonerate** **a)** encourage **b)** hide **c)** condemn **d)** free from blame

____ 36. **connoisseur** **a)** one who likes to suffer **b)** egotist **c)** expert **d)** painter

____ 37. **liability** **a)** hatred **b)** drawback **c)** indirect remark **d)** favor

____ 38. **circumvent** **a)** distribute **b)** socialize **c)** avoid **d)** fail to notice

____ 39. **bolster** **a)** hide **b)** protest **c)** protect **d)** support

____ 40. **austere** **a)** far **b)** wealthy **c)** plain **d)** complex

____ 41. **reticent** **a)** forgiving **b)** reluctant to speak **c)** sad **d)** contrary to reason

____ 42. **distraught** **a)** troubled **b)** too noticeable **c)** educated **d)** rehearsed

____ 43. **superfluous** **a)** useful **b)** unclear **c)** extra **d)** ahead

____ 44. **provocative** **a)** careful **b)** arousing interest **c)** inconsistent **d)** able to improve

____ 45. **metamorphosis** **a)** secret plot **b)** fantasy **c)** journey **d)** change

____ 46. **sedentary** **a)** excessive **b)** sitting **c)** repeated **d)** harmless

____ 47. **oblivious** **a)** courageous **b)** unaware **c)** quiet **d)** reliable

____ 48. **plight** **a)** minor weakness **b)** difficult situation **c)** travel **d)** environment

____ 49. **inundate** **a)** flood **b)** delay **c)** approve **d)** swallow

____ 50. **perfunctory** **a)** unenthusiastic **b)** on time **c)** troubled **d)** well-prepared

(Continues on next page)

____ 51. **encompass** **a)** separate **b)** draw **c)** include **d)** purchase

____ 52. **vindicate** **a)** ridicule **b)** escape **c)** clear from blame **d)** formally question

____ 53. **meticulous** **a)** irregular **b)** broken-down **c)** curious **d)** careful and exact

____ 54. **annihilate** **a)** destroy **b)** misunderstand **c)** carry out **d)** guide

____ 55. **exacerbate** **a)** bring closer **b)** strengthen **c)** make worse **d)** remove

____ 56. **magnanimous** **a)** nameless **b)** generous in forgiving **c)** proud **d)** lacking standards

____ 57. **exhort** **a)** hint **b)** strongly urge **c)** travel **d)** escape

____ 58. **stringent** **a)** long **b)** loose **c)** strict **d)** dry

____ 59. **innocuous** **a)** delightful **b)** harmless **c)** dangerous **d)** disappointing

____ 60. **facilitate** **a)** make easier **b)** serve **c)** approve **d)** clear from blame

____ 61. **presumptuous** **a)** indecent **b)** lacking standards of selection **c)** nervous **d)** too bold

____ 62. **unprecedented** **a)** overly noticeable **b)** without authority **c)** unexpected
d) having never happened before

____ 63. **mitigate** **a)** make less severe **b)** make worse **c)** hide **d)** remove

____ 64. **subversive** **a)** being a servant **b)** willing **c)** planning to build **d)** acting to overthrow

____ 65. **atrophy** **a)** strengthen **b)** reward **c)** expand **d)** weaken

____ 66. **sordid** **a)** slow **b)** morally low **c)** unprepared **d)** injured

____ 67. **extricate** **a)** run away **b)** free from difficulty **c)** confuse **d)** complicate

____ 68. **exhilaration** **a)** gladness **b)** freedom **c)** thirst **d)** wisdom

____ 69. **masochist** **a)** one who expects the worst **b)** egotist **c)** fan
d) one who likes to suffer

____ 70. **eradicate** **a)** wipe out **b)** scold **c)** restore **d)** hold onto

____ 71. **proficient** **a)** wise **b)** proud **c)** well-known **d)** skilled

____ 72. **exorbitant** **a)** excessive **b)** absorbent **c)** quarrelsome **d)** well-timed

____ 73. **synchronize** **a)** cause to occur together **b)** separate **c)** reduce **d)** spread throughout

____ 74. **deplore** **a)** command **b)** encourage **c)** disapprove of **d)** prevent

____ 75. **criterion** **a)** philosophy **b)** political theory **c)** standard for judgment
d) state of mind

(Continues on next page)

____ 76. **forestall** **a)** rent **b)** predict **c)** prevent **d)** hurry

____ 77. **complement** **a)** sin **b)** praise **c)** add what is needed **d)** make fun of

____ 78. **prognosis** **a)** memory **b)** hope **c)** prediction **d)** opposite

____ 79. **vehement** **a)** wicked **b)** forceful **c)** calm **d)** rude

____ 80. **auspicious** **a)** threatening **b)** lazy **c)** not trusting **d)** favorable

____ 81. **disparity** **a)** sadness **b)** similarity **c)** inequality **d)** blemish

____ 82. **heinous** **a)** depressed **b)** evil **c)** mischievous **d)** stubborn

____ 83. **impromptu** **a)** forceful **b)** on time **c)** delayed **d)** unplanned

____ 84. **antithesis** **a)** disorder **b)** theory **c)** opposite **d)** effect

____ 85. **incapacitate** **a)** allow **b)** disable **c)** increase **d)** fight

____ 86. **implement** **a)** carry out **b)** encourage **c)** insult **d)** prevent

____ 87. **insinuate** **a)** demand **b)** state **c)** deny **d)** hint

____ 88. **rebuke** **a)** compromise **b)** scold **c)** fix **d)** admire

____ 89. **impending** **a)** illegal **b)** about to happen **c)** historical **d)** usual

____ 90. **abrasive** **a)** foolish **b)** rough **c)** friendly **d)** mild

____ 91. **fastidious** **a)** not planned **b)** attentive to details **c)** quick **d)** inferior

____ 92. **macabre** **a)** depressed **b)** frightful **c)** common **d)** cheerful

____ 93. **opportune** **a)** well-timed **b)** more important **c)** generous **d)** belittling

____ 94. **turbulent** **a)** wildly disturbed **b)** ambitious **c)** mixed **d)** fast

____ 95. **transgress** **a)** round out **b)** follow **c)** break a law **d)** travel

____ 96. **extenuating** **a)** overly noticeable **b)** excusing **c)** inferior **d)** forceful

____ 97. **paramount** **a)** disturbed **b)** dramatic **c)** chief **d)** unknown

____ 98. **fabricate** **a)** put away **b)** misinterpret **c)** invent **d)** clothe

____ 99. **retribution** **a)** looking back **b)** donation **c)** punishment **d)** evil

____ 100. **emulate** **a)** be tardy **b)** imitate **c)** misunderstand **d)** prepare

STOP. This is the end of the test. If there is time remaining, you may go back and recheck your answers. When the time is up, hand in both your answer sheet and this test booklet to your instructor.

Name: ______________________

Unit One: *Pretest*

In the space provided, write the letter of the choice that is closest in meaning to the **boldfaced** word.

____ 1. **dexterous** a) young b) accidental c) skillful d) skinny

____ 2. **scrupulous** a) sociable b) careless c) clean d) conscientious

____ 3. **vicarious** a) experienced indirectly b) lively c) inactive d) occasional

____ 4. **sensory** a) in the mind b) sensible c) of the senses d) on the surface

____ 5. **facetious** a) ill-mannered b) joking c) careless d) depressed

____ 6. **discretion** a) independence b) gladness c) slyness d) tact

____ 7. **ostentatious** a) showy b) lazy c) courageous d) playfully witty

____ 8. **gregarious** a) wordy b) depressed c) sociable d) religious

____ 9. **despondent** a) depressed b) tired c) encouraged d) well-behaved

____ 10. **rudimentary** a) rude b) planned c) partial d) elementary

____ 11. **collaborate** a) respect b) work hard c) search d) work together

____ 12. **resilient** a) able to recover quickly b) strong c) heavy d) light

____ 13. **retrospect** a) expecting b) repetition c) removal d) looking back

____ 14. **instigate** a) stir to action b) investigate c) prepare d) suppress

____ 15. **scoff** a) impress b) inquire c) make fun of d) show off

____ 16. **venerate** a) protect b) create c) make unfriendly d) respect

____ 17. **ambiguous** a) under b) not clear c) widespread d) too large

____ 18. **subsidize** a) support financially b) lift up c) fall over d) calculate

____ 19. **inane** a) brilliant b) measurable c) causing pain d) silly

____ 20. **dissident** a) political supporter b) visitor c) candidate d) one who disagrees

____ 21. **juxtapose** a) replace b) place side by side c) remove d) imagine

____ 22. **fritter** a) waste b) prove c) wander d) collect

____ 23. **embellish** a) remove b) keep c) decorate d) hide

____ 24. **inadvertent** a) unintentional b) not for sale c) distant d) near

____ 25. **relinquish** a) enjoy b) gather c) criticize d) give up

(Continues on next page)

____ 26. **estrange** **a)** state again **b)** depart **c)** keep away **d)** enter

____ 27. **impetuous** **a)** lazy **b)** calm **c)** teasing **d)** impulsive

____ 28. **euphoric** **a)** undecided **b)** depressed **c)** lonely **d)** overjoyed

____ 29. **zenith** **a)** cure-all **b)** peak **c)** drawback **d)** authority

____ 30. **infallible** **a)** incapable of error **b)** accident-prone **c)** human **d)** wild

____ 31. **regress** **a)** make progress **b)** restrict **c)** return to previous behavior **d)** adjust

____ 32. **berate** **a)** urge **b)** criticize **c)** branch off **d)** lie

____ 33. **fortuitous** **a)** lucky **b)** sad **c)** having never happened before **d)** brave

____ 34. **impeccable** **a)** built-in **b)** unnecessary **c)** mischievous **d)** faultless

____ 35. **sham** **a)** type **b)** imitation **c)** disturbance **d)** belief

____ 36. **equivocate** **a)** be vague on purpose **b)** dedicate **c)** approve **d)** agree

____ 37. **predisposed** **a)** against **b)** reluctant to speak **c)** undecided **d)** tending beforehand

____ 38. **solicitous** **a)** trying to impress **b)** sitting **c)** showing concern **d)** negative

____ 39. **propensity** **a)** relation **b)** job **c)** tendency **d)** hobby

____ 40. **reprehensible** **a)** blameworthy **b)** well-filled **c)** affordable **d)** admirable

____ 41. **detriment** **a)** outward behavior **b)** something damaging **c)** failure **d)** silence

____ 42. **optimum** **a)** highest **b)** most favorable **c)** brightest **d)** heaviest

____ 43. **squelch** **a)** make fun of **b)** stretch **c)** suppress **d)** approve

____ 44. **zealot** **a)** dictator **b)** person devoted to a cause **c)** casual person **d)** leader

____ 45. **sporadic** **a)** tiny **b)** particular **c)** occasional **d)** wasteful

____ 46. **lethargy** **a)** strength **b)** highest point **c)** hunger **d)** lack of energy

____ 47. **maudlin** **a)** kind **b)** sentimental **c)** useful **d)** clever

____ 48. **ubiquitous** **a)** existing everywhere **b)** all-knowing **c)** all-powerful **d)** perfect

____ 49. **liaison** **a)** reference **b)** plan **c)** go-between **d)** accusation

____ 50. **solace** **a)** relaxation **b)** comfort **c)** sleep **d)** comedy

SCORE: (Number correct) ________ × 2 = ___________ %

Name: ______________________________

Unit One: *Posttest*

In the space provided, write the letter of the choice that is closest in meaning to the **boldfaced** word.

____ 1. **inane** a) silly b) brilliant c) measurable d) causing pain

____ 2. **juxtapose** a) place side by side b) replace c) remove d) imagine

____ 3. **dexterous** a) young b) skillful c) accidental d) skinny

____ 4. **ambiguous** a) under b) not clear c) widespread d) too large

____ 5. **embellish** a) remove b) decorate c) keep d) hide

____ 6. **facetious** a) joking b) ill-mannered c) careless d) depressed

____ 7. **infallible** a) wild b) accident-prone c) incapable of error d) human

____ 8. **zenith** a) cure-all b) drawback c) peak d) authority

____ 9. **resilient** a) able to recover quickly b) light c) heavy d) strong

____ 10. **discretion** a) independence b) tact c) slyness d) gladness

____ 11. **inadvertent** a) near b) not for sale c) distant d) unintentional

____ 12. **scoff** a) show off b) make fun of c) inquire d) impress

____ 13. **gregarious** a) religious b) sociable c) depressed d) wordy

____ 14. **solicitous** a) trying to impress b) showing concern c) sitting d) negative

____ 15. **rudimentary** a) rude b) planned c) partial d) elementary

____ 16. **collaborate** a) search b) work together c) respect d) work hard

____ 17. **retrospect** a) repetition b) looking back c) removal d) expecting

____ 18. **regress** a) restrict b) make progress c) adjust d) return to previous behavior

____ 19. **instigate** a) stir to action b) suppress c) prepare d) investigate

____ 20. **ostentatious** a) showy b) courageous c) playfully witty d) lazy

____ 21. **berate** a) lie b) urge c) branch off d) criticize

____ 22. **venerate** a) protect b) respect c) make unfriendly d) create

____ 23. **propensity** a) hobby b) relation c) job d) tendency

____ 24. **subsidize** a) fall over b) lift up c) support financially d) calculate

____ 25. **dissident** a) political supporter b) candidate c) visitor d) one who disagrees

(Continues on next page)

____ 26. **despondent** a) tired b) depressed c) encouraged d) well-behaved

____ 27. **relinquish** a) give up b) criticize c) gather d) enjoy

____ 28. **equivocate** a) approve b) dedicate c) be vague on purpose d) agree

____ 29. **estrange** a) enter b) depart c) keep away d) state again

____ 30. **scrupulous** a) clean b) careless c) sociable d) conscientious

____ 31. **sham** a) type b) imitation c) disturbance d) belief

____ 32. **impetuous** a) impulsive b) lazy c) teasing d) calm

____ 33. **fortuitous** a) having never happened before b) brave c) lucky d) sad

____ 34. **impeccable** a) mischievous b) unnecessary c) built-in d) faultless

____ 35. **sensory** a) in the mind b) sensible c) of the senses d) on the surface

____ 36. **predisposed** a) against b) reluctant to speak c) tending beforehand d) undecided

____ 37. **fritter** a) collect b) wander c) prove d) waste

____ 38. **reprehensible** a) affordable b) well-filled c) blameworthy d) admirable

____ 39. **vicarious** a) occasional b) experienced indirectly c) lively d) inactive

____ 40. **euphoric** a) undecided b) depressed c) lonely d) overjoyed

____ 41. **sporadic** a) tiny b) particular c) occasional d) wasteful

____ 42. **liaison** a) accusation b) plan c) go-between d) reference

____ 43. **maudlin** a) clever b) sentimental c) useful d) kind

____ 44. **squelch** a) make fun of b) stretch c) suppress d) approve

____ 45. **lethargy** a) highest point b) strength c) hunger d) lack of energy

____ 46. **ubiquitous** a) existing everywhere b) all-knowing c) all-powerful d) perfect

____ 47. **solace** a) sleep b) comfort c) relaxation d) comedy

____ 48. **zealot** a) dictator b) person devoted to a cause c) casual person d) leader

____ 49. **detriment** a) silence b) something damaging c) failure d) outward behavior

____ 50. **optimum** a) heaviest b) brightest c) highest d) most favorable

SCORE: (Number correct) ________ × 2 = ____________ %

 Name: ____________________

Unit Two: *Pretest*

In the space provided, write the letter of the choice that is closest in meaning to the **boldfaced** word.

____ 1. **grievous** **a)** funny **b)** boring **c)** impressive **d)** causing pain

____ 2. **attrition** **a)** becoming fewer **b)** connection **c)** multiplying **d)** imitation

____ 3. **reticent** **a)** forgiving **b)** sad **c)** reluctant to speak **d)** contrary to reason

____ 4. **robust** **a)** extremely careful **b)** vigorous **c)** tall **d)** loyal

____ 5. **circumvent** **a)** avoid **b)** fail to notice **c)** distribute **d)** socialize

____ 6. **sanction** **a)** present **b)** prepare **c)** authorize **d)** free from a difficulty

____ 7. **inundate** **a)** delay **b)** flood **c)** swallow **d)** approve

____ 8. **oblivious** **a)** courageous **b)** unaware **c)** quiet **d)** reliable

____ 9. **inquisitive** **a)** cheerful **b)** nervous **c)** curious **d)** in pain

____ 10. **depreciate** **a)** set free **b)** come forth **c)** support **d)** fall in value

____ 11. **relegate** **a)** bring back into use **b)** assign to a lesser place **c)** blend **d)** raise

____ 12. **bolster** **a)** support **b)** protect **c)** protest **d)** hide

____ 13. **terse** **a)** nervous **b)** sad **c)** brief **d)** cool

____ 14. **sedentary** **a)** sitting **b)** excessive **c)** harmless **d)** repeated

____ 15. **indiscriminate** **a)** self-centered **b)** especially generous **c)** painful **d)** not choosing carefully

____ 16. **nebulous** **a)** contrary to reason **b)** unclear **c)** complete **d)** calm

____ 17. **prolific** **a)** wise **b)** overly cautious **c)** fertile **d)** holding firmly

____ 18. **superfluous** **a)** extra **b)** unclear **c)** useful **d)** ahead

____ 19. **exonerate** **a)** encourage **b)** condemn **c)** hide **d)** free from blame

____ 20. **contingency** **a)** contest **b)** disapproval **c)** theory **d)** possibility

____ 21. **reinstate** **a)** make more severe **b)** suggest **c)** restore **d)** visit

____ 22. **egocentric** **a)** unbalanced **b)** circular **c)** square **d)** self-centered

____ 23. **clandestine** **a)** well-lit **b)** secret **c)** noble **d)** harmless

____ 24. **liability** **a)** drawback **b)** hatred **c)** favor **d)** indirect remark

____ 25. **austere** **a)** wealthy **b)** plain **c)** complex **d)** far

(Continues on next page)

____ 26. **notorious** **a)** too bold **b)** written **c)** known widely but unfavorably **d)** lacking skill

____ 27. **facsimile** **a)** authority **b)** copy **c)** comparison **d)** accusation

____ 28. **perfunctory** **a)** unenthusiastic **b)** troubled **c)** on time **d)** well-prepared

____ 29. **mesmerize** **a)** wipe out **b)** control **c)** hypnotize **d)** slow down

____ 30. **provocative** **a)** careful **b)** able to improve **c)** inconsistent **d)** arousing interest

____ 31. **esoteric** **a)** public **b)** uniform **c)** well-written **d)** understood by few

____ 32. **metamorphosis** **a)** journey **b)** change **c)** secret plot **d)** fantasy

____ 33. **verbose** **a)** wordy **b)** active **c)** noisy **d)** forceful

____ 34. **connoisseur** **a)** one who likes to suffer **b)** egotist **c)** expert **d)** painter

____ 35. **contrite** **a)** indecent **b)** sorry **c)** lacking confidence **d)** careful

____ 36. **lucid** **a)** clear **b)** generous in forgiving **c)** careful **d)** bold

____ 37. **conspiracy** **a)** robbery **b)** revenge **c)** project **d)** secret plot

____ 38. **superficially** **a)** strictly **b)** carefully **c)** totally **d)** hastily

____ 39. **plight** **a)** difficult situation **b)** minor weakness **c)** environment **d)** travel

____ 40. **distraught** **a)** educated **b)** too noticeable **c)** troubled **d)** rehearsed

____ 41. **cohesive** **a)** slippery **b)** risky **c)** separating **d)** sticking together

____ 42. **vociferous** **a)** vicious **b)** talented **c)** noisy **d)** busy

____ 43. **tenet** **a)** principle **b)** apartment dweller **c)** disadvantage **d)** peculiarity

____ 44. **replete** **a)** unclear **b)** well-filled **c)** finished **d)** empty

____ 45. **indigenous** **a)** underground **b)** native **c)** following established rules **d)** distant

____ 46. **incongruous** **a)** not noticeable **b)** inborn **c)** inconsistent **d)** gathered together

____ 47. **travesty** **a)** mockery **b)** copy **c)** campaign **d)** ill will

____ 48. **grotesque** **a)** harmless **b)** unclear **c)** dirty **d)** distorted

____ 49. **germane** **a)** evil **b)** chief **c)** relevant **d)** growing

____ 50. **symmetrical** **a)** extra **b)** balanced **c)** threatening **d)** colorful

SCORE: (Number correct) ________ × 2 = ___________ %

Name: ______________________________

Unit Two: *Posttest*

In the space provided, write the letter of the choice that is closest in meaning to the **boldfaced** word.

____ 1. **nebulous** a) contrary to reason b) unclear c) complete d) calm

____ 2. **egocentric** a) self-centered b) square c) circular d) unbalanced

____ 3. **prolific** a) holding firmly b) fertile c) overly cautious d) wise

____ 4. **grievous** a) boring b) impressive c) funny d) causing pain

____ 5. **contrite** a) careful b) lacking confidence c) sorry d) indecent

____ 6. **facsimile** a) comparison b) accusation c) authority d) copy

____ 7. **attrition** a) becoming fewer b) imitation c) multiplying d) connection

____ 8. **terse** a) nervous b) sad c) brief d) cool

____ 9. **esoteric** a) public b) uniform c) well-written d) understood by few

____ 10. **clandestine** a) secret b) well-lit c) noble d) harmless

____ 11. **inquisitive** a) cheerful b) curious c) nervous d) in pain

____ 12. **depreciate** a) set free b) come forth c) fall in value d) support

____ 13. **contingency** a) contest b) disapproval c) theory d) possibility

____ 14. **relegate** a) blend b) assign to a lesser place c) bring back into use d) raise

____ 15. **verbose** a) noisy b) active c) wordy d) forceful

____ 16. **indiscriminate** a) painful b) especially generous c) self-centered d) not choosing carefully

____ 17. **exonerate** a) encourage b) hide c) condemn d) free from blame

____ 18. **connoisseur** a) one who likes to suffer b) egotist c) expert d) painter

____ 19. **reinstate** a) restore b) suggest c) make more severe d) visit

____ 20. **superficially** a) strictly b) carefully c) totally d) hastily

____ 21. **liability** a) hatred b) drawback c) indirect remark d) favor

____ 22. **circumvent** a) distribute b) socialize c) avoid d) fail to notice

____ 23. **bolster** a) hide b) protest c) protect d) support

____ 24. **austere** a) far b) wealthy c) plain d) complex

____ 25. **conspiracy** a) secret plot b) revenge c) project d) robbery

(Continues on next page)

____ 26. **reticent** **a)** forgiving **b)** reluctant to speak **c)** sad **d)** contrary to reason

____ 27. **distraught** **a)** troubled **b)** too noticeable **c)** educated **d)** rehearsed

____ 28. **robust** **a)** extremely careful **b)** vigorous **c)** tall **d)** loyal

____ 29. **notorious** **a)** too bold **b)** written **c)** known widely but unfavorably **d)** lacking skill

____ 30. **mesmerize** **a)** control **b)** hypnotize **c)** wipe out **d)** slow down

____ 31. **superfluous** **a)** useful **b)** unclear **c)** extra **d)** ahead

____ 32. **provocative** **a)** careful **b)** arousing interest **c)** inconsistent **d)** able to improve

____ 33. **metamorphosis** **a)** secret plot **b)** fantasy **c)** journey **d)** change

____ 34. **sanction** **a)** authorize **b)** prepare **c)** present **d)** free from a difficulty

____ 35. **sedentary** **a)** excessive **b)** sitting **c)** repeated **d)** harmless

____ 36. **oblivious** **a)** courageous **b)** unaware **c)** quiet **d)** reliable

____ 37. **lucid** **a)** clear **b)** generous in forgiving **c)** careful **d)** bold

____ 38. **plight** **a)** minor weakness **b)** difficult situation **c)** travel **d)** environment

____ 39. **inundate** **a)** flood **b)** delay **c)** approve **d)** swallow

____ 40. **perfunctory** **a)** unenthusiastic **b)** on time **c)** troubled **d)** well-prepared

____ 41. **grotesque** **a)** harmless **b)** unclear **c)** dirty **d)** distorted

____ 42. **travesty** **a)** campaign **b)** ill will **c)** mockery **d)** copy

____ 43. **tenet** **a)** peculiarity **b)** principle **c)** disadvantage **d)** apartment dweller

____ 44. **symmetrical** **a)** threatening **b)** balanced **c)** extra **d)** colorful

____ 45. **indigenous** **a)** native **b)** underground **c)** following established rules **d)** distant

____ 46. **germane** **a)** evil **b)** chief **c)** relevant **d)** growing

____ 47. **cohesive** **a)** sticking together **b)** risky **c)** separating **d)** slippery

____ 48. **incongruous** **a)** not noticeable **b)** gathered together **c)** inconsistent **d)** inborn

____ 49. **replete** **a)** empty **b)** unclear **c)** well-filled **d)** finished

____ 50. **vociferous** **a)** busy **b)** talented **c)** noisy **d)** vicious

SCORE: (Number correct) ________ × 2 = ___________ %

Name: ____

Unit Three: *Pretest*

In the space provided, write the letter of the choice that is closest in meaning to the **boldfaced** word.

____ 1. **encompass** a) include b) draw c) separate d) purchase

____ 2. **stringent** a) dry b) strict c) loose d) long

____ 3. **adept** a) forceful b) exact c) balanced d) skilled

____ 4. **eradicate** a) wipe out b) scold c) restore d) hold onto

____ 5. **sordid** a) slow b) unprepared c) morally low d) injured

____ 6. **entrepreneur** a) lawyer b) business investor c) college educator d) police officer

____ 7. **stint** a) period of work b) sequence of events c) exercise d) stunt

____ 8. **presumptuous** a) indecent b) lacking standards of selection c) nervous d) too bold

____ 9. **meticulous** a) broken-down b) curious c) careful and exact d) irregular

____ 10. **repugnant** a) scornful b) offensive c) harmful d) impressive

____ 11. **foible** a) character flaw b) ambition c) noble quality d) accident

____ 12. **magnanimous** a) nameless b) proud c) generous in forgiving d) lacking standards

____ 13. **exhort** a) strongly urge b) travel c) escape d) hint

____ 14. **rancor** a) pride b) fear c) strong desire d) ill will

____ 15. **innocuous** a) delightful b) harmless c) dangerous d) disappointing

____ 16. **masochist** a) one who likes to suffer b) egotist c) fan
d) one who expects the worst

____ 17. **deplore** a) command b) disapprove of c) encourage d) prevent

____ 18. **atrophy** a) weaken b) reward c) expand d) strengthen

____ 19. **unprecedented** a) overly noticeable b) without authority c) unexpected
d) having never happened before

____ 20. **mitigate** a) make worse b) make less severe c) remove d) hide

____ 21. **deprivation** a) lack of a basic necessity b) depth c) disapproval d) privacy

____ 22. **imperative** a) thoughtful b) more harmful than at first evident c) likely d) necessary

____ 23. **objective** a) useful b) poorly supported c) based on facts d) emotional

____ 24. **exacerbate** a) make worse b) remove c) bring closer d) strengthen

____ 25. **rejuvenate** a) set free b) grow c) refresh d) make easier

(Continues on next page)

____ 26. **exorbitant** **a)** absorbent **b)** excessive **c)** quarrelsome **d)** well-timed

____ 27. **decorum** **a)** correctness in manners **b)** talent **c)** repayment **d)** indirect remark

____ 28. **facilitate** **a)** approve **b)** serve **c)** make easier **d)** clear from blame

____ 29. **synchronize** **a)** spread throughout **b)** separate **c)** reduce **d)** cause to occur together

____ 30. **espouse** **a)** prolong **b)** support **c)** delay **d)** marry

____ 31. **extricate** **a)** run away **b)** confuse **c)** free from difficulty **d)** complicate

____ 32. **exhilaration** **a)** freedom **b)** thirst **c)** wisdom **d)** gladness

____ 33. **proficient** **a)** proud **b)** wise **c)** skilled **d)** well-known

____ 34. **annihilate** **a)** guide **b)** misunderstand **c)** carry out **d)** destroy

____ 35. **criterion** **a)** philosophy **b)** standard for judgment **c)** political theory **d)** state of mind

____ 36. **vindicate** **a)** clear from blame **b)** ridicule **c)** escape **d)** formally question

____ 37. **emanate** **a)** go above **b)** run through **c)** go down **d)** come forth

____ 38. **holistic** **a)** democratic **b)** secretive **c)** emphasizing the whole **d)** little-known

____ 39. **subversive** **a)** being a servant **b)** acting to overthrow **c)** willing **d)** planning to build

____ 40. **analogy** **a)** original **b)** sample **c)** summary **d)** comparison

____ 41. **standardize** **a)** allow **b)** simplify **c)** limit **d)** make uniform

____ 42. **homogeneous** **a)** pure **b)** smooth **c)** uniform **d)** separate

____ 43. **recrimination** **a)** environment **b)** ambition **c)** robbery **d)** countercharge

____ 44. **flamboyant** **a)** talkative **b)** courageous **c)** showy **d)** exact

____ 45. **panacea** **a)** cure-all **b)** state of uncertainty **c)** reward **d)** false medicine

____ 46. **utilitarian** **a)** useless **b)** built-in **c)** practical **d)** beautiful

____ 47. **orthodox** **a)** firm **b)** favorable **c)** traditional **d)** new

____ 48. **tenuous** **a)** weak **b)** boring **c)** showy **d)** well-supported

____ 49. **staunch** **a)** loyal **b)** in doubt **c)** proud **d)** easy to handle

____ 50. **placebo** **a)** standard **b)** harmless substance used as medicine **c)** wish **d)** the whole

SCORE: (Number correct) ________ × 2 = __________ %

Name: ______________________________

Unit Three: *Posttest*

In the space provided, write the letter of the choice that is closest in meaning to the **boldfaced** word.

____ 1. **decorum** a) indirect remark b) correctness in manners c) repayment d) talent

____ 2. **encompass** a) separate b) draw c) include d) purchase

____ 3. **vindicate** a) ridicule b) escape c) clear from blame d) formally question

____ 4. **analogy** a) sample b) original c) comparison d) summary

____ 5. **objective** a) poorly supported b) useful c) emotional d) based on facts

____ 6. **meticulous** a) irregular b) broken-down c) curious d) careful and exact

____ 7. **annihilate** a) destroy b) misunderstand c) carry out d) guide

____ 8. **repugnant** a) impressive b) harmful c) offensive d) scornful

____ 9. **exacerbate** a) bring closer b) strengthen c) make worse d) remove

____ 10. **emanate** a) go above b) come forth c) go down d) run through

____ 11. **foible** a) noble quality b) ambition c) character flaw d) accident

____ 12. **magnanimous** a) nameless b) generous in forgiving c) proud d) lacking standards

____ 13. **exhort** a) hint b) strongly urge c) travel d) escape

____ 14. **stringent** a) long b) loose c) strict d) dry

____ 15. **holistic** a) emphasizing the whole b) secretive c) democratic d) little-known

____ 16. **rancor** a) ill will b) fear c) strong desire d) pride

____ 17. **innocuous** a) delightful b) harmless c) dangerous d) disappointing

____ 18. **facilitate** a) make easier b) serve c) approve d) clear from blame

____ 19. **presumptuous** a) indecent b) lacking standards of selection c) nervous d) too bold

____ 20. **unprecedented** a) overly noticeable b) without authority c) unexpected d) having never happened before

____ 21. **mitigate** a) make less severe b) make worse c) hide d) remove

____ 22. **subversive** a) being a servant b) willing c) planning to build d) acting to overthrow

____ 23. **adept** a) forceful b) exact c) skilled d) balanced

____ 24. **atrophy** a) strengthen b) reward c) expand d) weaken

____ 25. **sordid** a) slow b) morally low c) unprepared d) injured

(Continues on next page)

____ 26. **deprivation** **a)** disapproval **b)** depth **c)** lack of a basic necessity **d)** privacy

____ 27. **imperative** **a)** thoughtful **b)** more harmful than at first evident **c)** likely **d)** necessary

____ 28. **extricate** **a)** run away **b)** free from difficulty **c)** confuse **d)** complicate

____ 29. **exhilaration** **a)** gladness **b)** freedom **c)** thirst **d)** wisdom

____ 30. **masochist** **a)** one who expects the worst **b)** egotist **c)** fan **d)** one who likes to suffer

____ 31. **rejuvenate** **a)** set free **b)** refresh **c)** grow **d)** make easier

____ 32. **eradicate** **a)** wipe out **b)** scold **c)** restore **d)** hold onto

____ 33. **exorbitant** **a)** excessive **b)** absorbent **c)** quarrelsome **d)** well-timed

____ 34. **synchronize** **a)** cause to occur together **b)** separate **c)** reduce **d)** spread throughout

____ 35. **deplore** **a)** command **b)** encourage **c)** disapprove of **d)** prevent

____ 36. **stint** **a)** stunt **b)** sequence of events **c)** exercise **d)** period of work

____ 37. **espouse** **a)** prolong **b)** support **c)** delay **d)** marry

____ 38. **proficient** **a)** wise **b)** proud **c)** well-known **d)** skilled

____ 39. **entrepreneur** **a)** business investor **b)** lawyer **c)** college educator **d)** police officer

____ 40. **criterion** **a)** philosophy **b)** political theory **c)** standard for judgment **d)** state of mind

____ 41. **staunch** **a)** easy to handle **b)** loyal **c)** proud **d)** in doubt

____ 42. **flamboyant** **a)** showy **b)** exact **c)** talkative **d)** courageous

____ 43. **orthodox** **a)** new **b)** favorable **c)** traditional **d)** firm

____ 44. **placebo** **a)** wish **b)** harmless substance used as medicine **c)** the whole **d)** standard

____ 45. **panacea** **a)** reward **b)** state of uncertainty **c)** cure-all **d)** false medicine

____ 46. **utilitarian** **a)** built-in **b)** practical **c)** useless **d)** beautiful

____ 47. **tenuous** **a)** showy **b)** boring **c)** weak **d)** well-supported

____ 48. **homogeneous** **a)** separate **b)** uniform **c)** smooth **d)** pure

____ 49. **recrimination** **a)** environment **b)** robbery **c)** countercharge **d)** ambition

____ 50. **standardize** **a)** make uniform **b)** allow **c)** simplify **d)** limit

SCORE: (Number correct) ________ × 2 = ___________ %

Name: ______________________________

Unit Four: *Pretest*

In the space provided, write the letter of the choice that is closest in meaning to the **boldfaced** word.

____ 1. **forestall** a) prevent b) predict c) rent d) hurry

____ 2. **retribution** a) donation b) looking back c) evil d) punishment

____ 3. **interrogate** a) put into practice b) invent c) formally question d) blame sharply

____ 4. **obsequious** a) too anxious to serve b) harmful c) overly ambitious d) tactful

____ 5. **insinuate** a) demand b) state c) deny d) hint

____ 6. **disparity** a) sadness b) inequality c) blemish d) similarity

____ 7. **omnipotent** a) all-powerful b) forgiving c) altogether d) cure-all

____ 8. **opportune** a) generous b) more important c) well-timed d) belittling

____ 9. **fastidious** a) not planned b) attentive to details c) quick d) inferior

____ 10. **heinous** a) evil b) mischievous c) stubborn d) depressed

____ 11. **intuition** a) inequality b) instinct c) punishment d) wish

____ 12. **implement** a) encourage b) carry out c) insult d) prevent

____ 13. **discreet** a) tactful b) intense c) knowledgeable d) open

____ 14. **inference** a) rumor b) meeting c) assumption d) speech

____ 15. **complement** a) praise b) sin c) make fun of d) add what is needed

____ 16. **impromptu** a) forceful b) unplanned c) delayed d) on time

____ 17. **transgress** a) follow b) round out c) travel d) break a law

____ 18. **extenuating** a) excusing b) inferior c) forceful d) overly noticeable

____ 19. **fraudulent** a) intense b) dishonest c) creative d) dangerous

____ 20. **redeem** a) show to be true b) restore to favor c) select d) ignore

____ 21. **vehement** a) forceful b) wicked c) rude d) calm

____ 22. **auspicious** a) threatening b) lazy c) favorable d) not trusting

____ 23. **subordinate** a) irritating b) inferior c) quiet d) chief

____ 24. **rebuke** a) compromise b) fix c) scold d) admire

____ 25. **validate** a) dislike b) prove c) discover d) notice

(Continues on next page)

____ 26. **macabre** **a)** frightful **b)** depressed **c)** cheerful **d)** common

____ 27. **quandary** **a)** wild disorder **b)** peak **c)** state of uncertainty **d)** opposite

____ 28. **fabricate** **a)** misinterpret **b)** put away **c)** clothe **d)** invent

____ 29. **derogatory** **a)** healthful **b)** unable to be repaired **c)** belittling **d)** proud

____ 30. **turbulent** **a)** ambitious **b)** wildly disturbed **c)** mixed **d)** fast

____ 31. **impending** **a)** about to happen **b)** illegal **c)** historical **d)** usual

____ 32. **paramount** **a)** dramatic **b)** disturbed **c)** unknown **d)** chief

____ 33. **emulate** **a)** be tardy **b)** misunderstand **c)** imitate **d)** prepare

____ 34. **abrasive** **a)** rough **b)** friendly **c)** mild **d)** foolish

____ 35. **docile** **a)** violent **b)** early **c)** easy to discipline **d)** irritating

____ 36. **antithesis** **a)** disorder **b)** theory **c)** effect **d)** opposite

____ 37. **incapacitate** **a)** disable **b)** allow **c)** increase **d)** fight

____ 38. **admonish** **a)** imitate **b)** scold **c)** publicize **d)** frighten

____ 39. **prognosis** **a)** hope **b)** memory **c)** opposite **d)** prediction

____ 40. **tumult** **a)** series **b)** uncertainty **c)** uproar **d)** scolding

____ 41. **permeate** **a)** imitate **b)** spread throughout **c)** pollute **d)** deny the authority of

____ 42. **insidious** **a)** more harmful than at first evident **b)** sly
c) more noticeable than desired **d)** slow

____ 43. **flout** **a)** beat **b)** surprise **c)** suggest **d)** disobey

____ 44. **obtrusive** **a)** about to happen **b)** too near **c)** undesirably noticeable **d)** shocking

____ 45. **expedite** **a)** speed up **b)** explore **c)** sadden **d)** elect

____ 46. **innuendo** **a)** threat **b)** challenge **c)** impression **d)** indirect remark

____ 47. **deride** **a)** repair **b)** take **c)** ridicule **d)** ease

____ 48. **misconstrue** **a)** misunderstand **b)** dislike **c)** reject **d)** admire

____ 49. **culmination** **a)** country **b)** highest point **c)** edge **d)** bottom

____ 50. **hierarchy** **a)** theory **b)** employment **c)** ranking **d)** highest point

SCORE: (Number correct) ________ × 2 = __________ %

Name: ______________________________

Unit Four: *Posttest*

In the space provided, write the letter of the choice that is closest in meaning to the **boldfaced** word.

____ 1. **redeem** a) show to be true b) restore to favor c) select d) ignore

____ 2. **forestall** a) rent b) predict c) prevent d) hurry

____ 3. **intuition** a) inequality b) punishment c) instinct d) wish

____ 4. **complement** a) sin b) praise c) add what is needed d) make fun of

____ 5. **interrogate** a) put into practice b) formally question c) invent d) blame sharply

____ 6. **prognosis** a) memory b) hope c) prediction d) opposite

____ 7. **vehement** a) wicked b) forceful c) calm d) rude

____ 8. **auspicious** a) threatening b) lazy c) not trusting d) favorable

____ 9. **disparity** a) sadness b) similarity c) inequality d) blemish

____ 10. **heinous** a) depressed b) evil c) mischievous d) stubborn

____ 11. **docile** a) easy to discipline b) early c) violent d) irritating

____ 12. **impromptu** a) forceful b) on time c) delayed d) unplanned

____ 13. **tumult** a) scolding b) uproar c) uncertainty d) series

____ 14. **fraudulent** a) intense b) creative c) dishonest d) dangerous

____ 15. **subordinate** a) inferior b) irritating c) chief d) quiet

____ 16. **abrasive** a) foolish b) rough c) friendly d) mild

____ 17. **obsequious** a) overly ambitious b) harmful c) too anxious to serve d) tactful

____ 18. **antithesis** a) disorder b) theory c) opposite d) effect

____ 19. **incapacitate** a) allow b) disable c) increase d) fight

____ 20. **implement** a) carry out b) encourage c) insult d) prevent

____ 21. **insinuate** a) demand b) state c) deny d) hint

____ 22. **inference** a) rumor b) assumption c) meeting d) speech

____ 23. **rebuke** a) compromise b) scold c) fix d) admire

____ 24. **impending** a) illegal b) about to happen c) historical d) usual

____ 25. **validate** a) dislike b) prove c) discover d) notice

(Continues on next page)

_____ 26. **omnipotent** **a)** cure-all **b)** forgiving **c)** all-powerful **d)** altogether

_____ 27. **admonish** **a)** publicize **b)** frighten **c)** imitate **d)** scold

_____ 28. **fastidious** **a)** not planned **b)** attentive to details **c)** quick **d)** inferior

_____ 29. **macabre** **a)** depressed **b)** frightful **c)** common **d)** cheerful

_____ 30. **discreet** **a)** open **b)** knowledgeable **c)** intense **d)** tactful

_____ 31. **quandary** **a)** state of uncertainty **b)** peak **c)** wild disorder **d)** opposite

_____ 32. **opportune** **a)** well-timed **b)** more important **c)** generous **d)** belittling

_____ 33. **derogatory** **a)** healthful **b)** unable to be repaired **c)** belittling **d)** proud

_____ 34. **turbulent** **a)** wildly disturbed **b)** ambitious **c)** mixed **d)** fast

_____ 35. **transgress** **a)** round out **b)** follow **c)** break a law **d)** travel

_____ 36. **extenuating** **a)** overly noticeable **b)** excusing **c)** inferior **d)** forceful

_____ 37. **paramount** **a)** disturbed **b)** dramatic **c)** chief **d)** unknown

_____ 38. **fabricate** **a)** put away **b)** misinterpret **c)** invent **d)** clothe

_____ 39. **retribution** **a)** looking back **b)** donation **c)** punishment **d)** evil

_____ 40. **emulate** **a)** be tardy **b)** imitate **c)** misunderstand **d)** prepare

_____ 41. **hierarchy** **a)** theory **b)** employment **c)** ranking **d)** highest point

_____ 42. **culmination** **a)** country **b)** highest point **c)** edge **d)** bottom

_____ 43. **deride** **a)** repair **b)** take **c)** ease **d)** ridicule

_____ 44. **insidious** **a)** sly **b)** more harmful than at first evident **c)** more noticeable than desired **d)** slow

_____ 45. **innuendo** **a)** impression **b)** challenge **c)** threat **d)** indirect remark

_____ 46. **obtrusive** **a)** shocking **b)** too near **c)** undesirably noticeable **d)** about to happen

_____ 47. **permeate** **a)** imitate **b)** spread throughout **c)** deny the authority of **d)** pollute

_____ 48. **misconstrue** **a)** dislike **b)** misunderstand **c)** reject **d)** admire

_____ 49. **expedite** **a)** elect **b)** speed up **c)** explore **d)** sadden

_____ 50. **flout** **a)** beat **b)** surprise **c)** disobey **d)** suggest

SCORE: (Number correct) ________ × 2 = __________ %

ADVANCING VOCABULARY SKILLS

Pretest / Posttest

NAME: ____________________

SECTION: __________ DATE: __________

SCORE: ____________________

ANSWER SHEET

1. ____	26. ____	51. ____	76. ____
2. ____	27. ____	52. ____	77. ____
3. ____	28. ____	53. ____	78. ____
4. ____	29. ____	54. ____	79. ____
5. ____	30. ____	55. ____	80. ____
6. ____	31. ____	56. ____	81. ____
7. ____	32. ____	57. ____	82. ____
8. ____	33. ____	58. ____	83. ____
9. ____	34. ____	59. ____	84. ____
10. ____	35. ____	60. ____	85. ____
11. ____	36. ____	61. ____	86. ____
12. ____	37. ____	62. ____	87. ____
13. ____	38. ____	63. ____	88. ____
14. ____	39. ____	64. ____	89. ____
15. ____	40. ____	65. ____	90. ____
16. ____	41. ____	66. ____	91. ____
17. ____	42. ____	67. ____	92. ____
18. ____	43. ____	68. ____	93. ____
19. ____	44. ____	69. ____	94. ____
20. ____	45. ____	70. ____	95. ____
21. ____	46. ____	71. ____	96. ____
22. ____	47. ____	72. ____	97. ____
23. ____	48. ____	73. ____	98. ____
24. ____	49. ____	74. ____	99. ____
25. ____	50. ____	75. ____	100. ____

Pretest

ANSWER KEY

1. d	26. a	51. a	76. a
2. a	27. c	52. b	77. d
3. b	28. a	53. a	78. d
4. d	29. b	54. c	79. b
5. c	30. b	55. d	80. c
6. a	31. c	56. c	81. b
7. d	32. b	57. c	82. a
8. d	33. a	58. a	83. b
9. a	34. c	59. b	84. d
10. d	35. a	60. a	85. b
11. a	36. a	61. b	86. d
12. d	37. d	62. a	87. a
13. b	38. d	63. d	88. a
14. c	39. b	64. b	89. c
15. a	40. a	65. a	90. c
16. d	41. b	66. b	91. a
17. d	42. a	67. c	92. d
18. d	43. d	68. d	93. b
19. a	44. d	69. c	94. a
20. c	45. b	70. d	95. d
21. a	46. a	71. c	96. c
22. b	47. c	72. d	97. d
23. d	48. b	73. b	98. a
24. c	49. a	74. a	99. a
25. a	50. c	75. b	100. d

ADVANCING VOCABULARY SKILLS

Posttest

ANSWER KEY

1. a
2. b
3. a
4. c
5. b
6. d
7. b
8. d
9. b
10. d
11. a
12. b
13. d
14. c
15. d
16. b
17. a
18. d
19. b
20. a
21. c
22. c
23. c
24. b
25. d
26. c
27. a
28. c
29. d
30. a
31. b
32. d
33. b
34. c
35. d
36. c
37. b
38. c
39. d
40. c
41. b
42. a
43. c
44. b
45. d
46. b
47. b
48. b
49. a
50. a
51. c
52. c
53. d
54. a
55. c
56. b
57. b
58. c
59. b
60. a
61. d
62. d
63. a
64. d
65. d
66. b
67. b
68. a
69. d
70. a
71. d
72. a
73. a
74. c
75. c
76. c
77. c
78. c
79. b
80. d
81. c
82. b
83. d
84. c
85. b
86. a
87. d
88. b
89. b
90. b
91. b
92. b
93. a
94. a
95. c
96. b
97. c
98. c
99. c
100. b

Answers to the Pretests and Posttests: ADVANCING VOCABULARY SKILLS, SHORT VERSION

Unit One		Unit Two		Unit Three		Unit Four	
Pretest	*Posttest*	*Pretest*	*Posttest*	*Pretest*	*Posttest*	*Pretest*	*Posttest*
1. c	1. a	1. d	1. b	1. a	1. b	1. a	1. b
2. d	2. a	2. a	2. a	2. b	2. c	2. d	2. c
3. a	3. b	3. c	3. b	3. d	3. c	3. c	3. c
4. c	4. b	4. b	4. d	4. a	4. c	4. a	4. c
5. b	5. b	5. a	5. c	5. c	5. d	5. d	5. b
6. d	6. a	6. c	6. d	6. b	6. d	6. b	6. c
7. a	7. c	7. b	7. a	7. a	7. a	7. a	7. b
8. c	8. c	8. b	8. c	8. d	8. c	8. c	8. d
9. a	9. a	9. c	9. d	9. c	9. c	9. b	9. c
10. d	10. b	10. d	10. a	10. b	10. b	10. a	10. b
11. d	11. d	11. b	11. b	11. a	11. c	11. b	11. a
12. a	12. b	12. a	12. c	12. c	12. b	12. b	12. d
13. d	13. b	13. c	13. d	13. a	13. b	13. a	13. b
14. a	14. b	14. a	14. b	14. d	14. c	14. c	14. c
15. c	15. d	15. d	15. c	15. b	15. a	15. d	15. a
16. d	16. b	16. b	16. d	16. a	16. a	16. b	16. b
17. b	17. b	17. c	17. d	17. b	17. b	17. d	17. c
18. a	18. d	18. a	18. c	18. a	18. a	18. a	18. c
19. d	19. a	19. d	19. a	19. d	19. d	19. b	19. b
20. d	20. a	20. d	20. d	20. b	20. d	20. b	20. a
21. b	21. d	21. c	21. b	21. a	21. a	21. a	21. d
22. a	22. b	22. d	22. c	22. d	22. d	22. c	22. b
23. c	23. d	23. b	23. d	23. c	23. c	23. b	23. b
24. a	24. c	24. a	24. c	24. a	24. d	24. c	24. b
25. d	25. d	25. b	25. a	25. c	25. b	25. b	25. b
26. c	26. b	26. c	26. b	26. b	26. c	26. a	26. c
27. d	27. a	27. b	27. a	27. a	27. d	27. c	27. d
28. d	28. c	28. a	28. b	28. c	28. b	28. d	28. b
29. b	29. c	29. c	29. c	29. d	29. a	29. c	29. b
30. a	30. d	30. d	30. b	30. b	30. d	30. b	30. d
31. c	31. b	31. d	31. c	31. c	31. b	31. a	31. a
32. b	32. a	32. b	32. b	32. d	32. a	32. d	32. a
33. a	33. c	33. a	33. d	33. c	33. a	33. c	33. c
34. d	34. d	34. c	34. a	34. d	34. a	34. a	34. a
35. b	35. c	35. b	35. b	35. b	35. c	35. c	35. c
36. a	36. c	36. a	36. b	36. a	36. d	36. d	36. b
37. d	37. d	37. d	37. a	37. d	37. b	37. a	37. c
38. c	38. c	38. d	38. b	38. c	38. d	38. b	38. c
39. c	39. b	39. a	39. a	39. b	39. a	39. d	39. c
40. a	40. d	40. c	40. a	40. d	40. c	40. c	40. b
41. b	41. c	41. d	41. d	41. d	41. b	41. b	41. c
42. b	42. c	42. c	42. c	42. c	42. a	42. a	42. b
43. c	43. b	43. a	43. b	43. d	43. c	43. d	43. d
44. b	44. c	44. b	44. b	44. c	44. b	44. c	44. b
45. c	45. d	45. b	45. a	45. a	45. c	45. a	45. d
46. d	46. a	46. c	46. c	46. c	46. b	46. d	46. c
47. b	47. b	47. a	47. a	47. c	47. c	47. c	47. b
48. a	48. b	48. d	48. c	48. a	48. b	48. a	48. b
49. c	49. b	49. c	49. c	49. a	49. c	49. b	49. b
50. b	50. d	50. b	50. c	50. b	50. a	50. c	50. c

Answers to the Chapter Activities:
ADVANCING VOCABULARY SKILLS, SHORT VERSION

Chapter 1 (Apartment Problems)

Ten Words in Context	*Matching Words/Defs*	*Sentence Check 1*	*Sentence Check 2*	*Final Check*
1. C 6. A	1. 4 6. 2	1. C 6. G	1–2. C, H	1. E 6. I
2. A 7. B	2. 7 7. 8	2. A 7. J	3–4. D, B	2. C 7. J
3. B 8. A	3. 6 8. 5	3. B 8. F	5–6. F, A	3. A 8. D
4. C 9. A	4. 1 9. 3	4. E 9. I	7–8. E, G	4. B 9. H
5. B 10. B	5. 10 10. 9	5. H 10. D	9–10. I, J	5. G 10. F

Chapter 2 (Hardly a Loser)

Ten Words in Context	*Matching Words/Defs*	*Sentence Check 1*	*Sentence Check 2*	*Final Check*
1. C 6. A	1. 3 6. 8	1. F 6. G	1–2. F, A	1. C 6. D
2. B 7. A	2. 6 7. 9	2. B 7. A	3–4. G, D	2. F 7. A
3. C 8. B	3. 4 8. 2	3. C 8. H	5–6. I, B	3. G 8. J
4. C 9. B	4. 1 9. 5	4. J 9. E	7–8. C, E	4. H 9. I
5. A 10. A	5. 10 10. 7	5. I 10. D	9–10. H, J	5. B 10. E

Chapter 3 (Grandfather at the Art Museum)

Ten Words in Context	*Matching Words/Defs*	*Sentence Check 1*	*Sentence Check 2*	*Final Check*
1. A 6. A	1. 7 6. 3	1. H 6. C	1–2. H, I	1. E 6. H
2. A 7. B	2. 8 7. 10	2. I 7. G	3–4. G, B	2. B 7. J
3. B 8. A	3. 1 8. 4	3. J 8. B	5–6. J, C	3. G 8. D
4. C 9. B	4. 6 9. 5	4. E 9. A	7–8. D, F	4. C 9. F
5. C 10. A	5. 2 10. 9	5. D 10. F	9–10. A, E	5. A 10. I

Chapter 4 (My Brother's Mental Illness)

Ten Words in Context	*Matching Words/Defs*	*Sentence Check 1*	*Sentence Check 2*	*Final Check*
1. C 6. C	1. 8 6. 10	1. G 6. E	1–2. E, H	1. C 6. F
2. B 7. A	2. 4 7. 2	2. J 7. A	3–4. D, A	2. J 7. I
3. A 8. B	3. 6 8. 5	3. C 8. I	5–6. I, F	3. E 8. B
4. A 9. C	4. 1 9. 3	4. H 9. F	7–8. B, G	4. D 9. A
5. A 10. C	5. 9 10. 7	5. B 10. D	9–10. J, C	5. H 10. G

Chapter 5 (A Phony Friend)

Ten Words in Context	*Matching Words/Defs*	*Sentence Check 1*	*Sentence Check 2*	*Final Check*
1. B 6. B	1. 6 6. 1	1. I 6. H	1–2. F, A	1. D 6. J
2. A 7. A	2. 7 7. 3	2. C 7. F	3–4. I, D	2. F 7. C
3. A 8. A	3. 2 8. 10	3. E 8. B	5–6. E, J	3. E 8. B
4. C 9. C	4. 9 9. 5	4. J 9. D	7–8. B, G	4. I 9. H
5. B 10. B	5. 4 10. 8	5. G 10. A	9–10. C, H	5. A 10. G

Chapter 6 (Coco the Gorilla)

Ten Words in Context	*Matching Words/Defs*	*Sentence Check 1*	*Sentence Check 2*	*Final Check*
1. B 6. B	1. 9 6. 3	1. F 6. C	1–2. E, F	1. A 6. J
2. A 7. B	2. 5 7. 10	2. J 7. D	3–4. I, A	2. C 7. H
3. A 8. C	3. 2 8. 1	3. I 8. E	5–6. D, G	3. F 8. B
4. C 9. A	4. 7 9. 4	4. H 9. A	7–8. H, B	4. I 9. E
5. A 10. C	5. 8 10. 6	5. B 10. G	9–10. J, C	5. G 10. D

Chapter 7 (Our Annual Garage Sale)

Ten Words in Context	*Matching Words/Defs*	*Sentence Check 1*	*Sentence Check 2*	*Final Check*
1. C 6. A	1. 2 6. 1	1. J 6. G	1–2. B, E	1. F 6. G
2. B 7. B	2. 3 7. 4	2. C 7. F	3–4. F, H	2. A 7. J
3. C 8. C	3. 8 8. 7	3. A 8. E	5–6. D, A	3. H 8. C
4. C 9. A	4. 9 9. 5	4. B 9. H	7–8. G, I	4. I 9. D
5. A 10. C	5. 10 10. 6	5. I 10. D	9–10. J, C	5. E 10. B

Chapter 8 (My Large Family)

Ten Words in Context	*Matching Words/Defs*	*Sentence Check 1*	*Sentence Check 2*	*Final Check*
1. C 6. B	1. 7 6. 10	1. E 6. D	1–2. E, F	1. F 6. C
2. A 7. B	2. 1 7. 8	2. I 7. H	3–4. D, I	2. H 7. G
3. A 8. A	3. 5 8. 4	3. G 8. A	5–6. H, J	3. J 8. A
4. C 9. C	4. 2 9. 3	4. F 9. J	7–8. C, G	4. I 9. E
5. A 10. A	5. 6 10. 9	5. B 10. C	9–10. A, B	5. D 10. B

Chapter 9 (A Costume Party)

Ten Words in Context	*Matching Words/Defs*	*Sentence Check 1*	*Sentence Check 2*	*Final Check*
1. B 6. A	1. 5 6. 9	1. J 6. B	1–2. D, J	1. H 6. E
2. A 7. A	2. 6 7. 3	2. G 7. E	3–4. G, A	2. A 7. B
3. C 8. A	3. 10 8. 2	3. I 8. H	5–6. I, E	3. I 8. F
4. A 9. C	4. 8 9. 1	4. D 9. A	7–8. H, F	4. C 9. J
5. B 10. A	5. 7 10. 4	5. C 10. F	9–10. C, B	5. G 10. D

Chapter 10 (The Missing Painting)

Ten Words in Context	*Matching Words/Defs*	*Sentence Check 1*	*Sentence Check 2*	*Final Check*
1. B 6. A	1. 4 6. 3	1. C 6. B	1–2. D, B	1. D 6. I
2. A 7. C	2. 10 7. 9	2. G 7. E	3–4. A, H	2. A 7. H
3. C 8. B	3. 8 8. 1	3. I 8. D	5–6. C, G	3. F 8. B
4. A 9. C	4. 5 9. 7	4. A 9. F	7–8. E, I	4. G 9. E
5. B 10. B	5. 6 10. 2	5. J 10. H	9–10. J, F	5. J 10. C

Chapter 11 (An Ohio Girl in New York)

Ten Words in Context	*Matching Words/Defs*	*Sentence Check 1*	*Sentence Check 2*	*Final Check*
1. A 6. A	1. 3 6. 10	1. F 6. E	1–2. C, A	1. I 6. C
2. C 7. B	2. 1 7. 8	2. A 7. B	3–4. I, J	2. G 7. F
3. A 8. B	3. 9 8. 2	3. G 8. J	5–6. D, G	3. E 8. H
4. C 9. A	4. 6 9. 5	4. I 9. C	7–8. F, B	4. J 9. B
5. B 10. C	5. 4 10. 7	5. D 10. H	9–10. H, E	5. A 10. D

Chapter 12 (How Neat Is Neat Enough)

Ten Words in Context	*Matching Words/Defs*	*Sentence Check 1*	*Sentence Check 2*	*Final Check*
1. C 6. B	1. 8 6. 3	1. J 6. D	1–2. A, G	1. G 6. A
2. A 7. A	2. 4 7. 9	2. E 7. H	3–4. H, E	2. E 7. J
3. B 8. B	3. 10 8. 1	3. F 8. I	5–6. F, J	3. C 8. F
4. A 9. C	4. 6 9. 5	4. C 9. G	7–8. C, D	4. B 9. I
5. A 10. A	5. 2 10. 7	5. A 10. B	9–10. I, B	5. D 10. H

Chapter 13 (Thomas Dooley)

Ten Words in Context	*Matching Words/Defs*	*Sentence Check 1*	*Sentence Check 2*	*Final Check*
1. B 6. A	1. 4 6. 3	1. C 6. J	1–2. F, C	1. A 6. G
2. A 7. B	2. 6 7. 5	2. F 7. G	3–4. B, I	2. D 7. H
3. A 8. C	3. 9 8. 7	3. D 8. H	5–6. D, A	3. B 8. F
4. C 9. A	4. 8 9. 10	4. I 9. E	7–8. G, E	4. C 9. J
5. C 10. B	5. 1 10. 2	5. B 10. A	9–10. J, H	5. E 10. I

Chapter 14 (Twelve Grown Men in a Bug)

Ten Words in Context	*Matching Words/Defs*	*Sentence Check 1*	*Sentence Check 2*	*Final Check*
1. C 6. C	1. 3 6. 2	1. A 6. F	1–2. C, I	1. G 6. A
2. A 7. B	2. 5 7. 9	2. J 7. E	3–4. G, J	2. B 7. F
3. B 8. C	3. 10 8. 6	3. H 8. B	5–6. D, H	3. H 8. I
4. C 9. A	4. 1 9. 7	4. D 9. I	7–8. A, E	4. D 9. E
5. A 10. A	5. 8 10. 4	5. C 10. G	9–10. B, F	5. J 10. C

Chapter 15 (A Different Kind of Doctor)

Ten Words in Context	*Matching Words/Defs*	*Sentence Check 1*	*Sentence Check 2*	*Final Check*
1. B 6. A	1. 10 6. 3	1. I 6. E	1–2. D, B	1. E 6. B
2. C 7. A	2. 6 7. 9	2. B 7. D	3–4. C, G	2. A 7. J
3. A 8. C	3. 4 8. 8	3. H 8. A	5–6. J, I	3. D 8. G
4. B 9. B	4. 1 9. 5	4. C 9. J	7–8. E, A	4. I 9. H
5. B 10. A	5. 2 10. 7	5. G 10. F	9–10. H, F	5. F 10. C

Chapter 16 (My Devilish Older Sister)

Ten Words in Context	*Matching Words/Defs*	*Sentence Check 1*	*Sentence Check 2*	*Final Check*
1. B 6. B	1. 6 6. 9	1. I 6. A	1–2. A, D	1. A 6. D
2. A 7. C	2. 4 7. 8	2. B 7. C	3–4. C, I	2. G 7. I
3. B 8. A	3. 10 8. 2	3. H 8. G	5–6. J, H	3. F 8. E
4. A 9. B	4. 1 9. 7	4. E 9. D	7–8. G, B	4. B 9. C
5. A 10. C	5. 3 10. 5	5. J 10. F	9–10. E, F	5. H 10. J

Chapter 17 (Harriet Tubman)

Ten Words in Context	*Matching Words/Defs*	*Sentence Check 1*	*Sentence Check 2*	*Final Check*
1. A 6. B	1. 4 6. 7	1. I 6. F	1–2. I, C	1. E 6. F
2. B 7. A	2. 9 7. 5	2. D 7. C	3–4. A, G	2. J 7. G
3. C 8. B	3. 6 8. 8	3. E 8. A	5–6. B, H	3. A 8. B
4. A 9. C	4. 10 9. 1	4. G 9. H	7–8. F, E	4. I 9. H
5. A 10. A	5. 2 10. 3	5. B 10. J	9–10. D, J	5. C 10. D

Chapter 18 (Tony's Rehabilitation)

Ten Words in Context	*Matching Words/Defs*	*Sentence Check 1*	*Sentence Check 2*	*Final Check*
1. C 6. A	1. 5 6. 1	1. H 6. A	1–2. I, G	1. I 6. F
2. A 7. B	2. 2 7. 3	2. I 7. J	3–4. F, D	2. C 7. B
3. A 8. A	3. 6 8. 9	3. D 8. F	5–6. A, C	3. D 8. J
4. B 9. C	4. 10 9. 8	4. B 9. E	7–8. J, H	4. A 9. E
5. C 10. A	5. 4 10. 7	5. G 10. C	9–10. E, B	5. H 10. G

Chapter 19 (Rumors)

Ten Words in Context	*Matching Words/Defs*	*Sentence Check 1*	*Sentence Check 2*	*Final Check*
1. B 6. A	1. 9 6. 6	1. E 6. C	1–2. I, G	1. C 6. E
2. A 7. A	2. 5 7. 1	2. G 7. J	3–4. H, E	2. F 7. H
3. C 8. A	3. 8 8. 3	3. D 8. H	5–6. J, C	3. B 8. I
4. A 9. A	4. 2 9. 4	4. F 9. I	7–8. D, B	4. A 9. G
5. C 10. B	5. 10 10. 7	5. B 10. A	9–10. F, A	5. D 10. J

Chapter 20 (Firing Our Boss)

Ten Words in Context	*Matching Words/Defs*	*Sentence Check 1*	*Sentence Check 2*	*Final Check*
1. B 6. B	1. 10 6. 2	1. J 6. B	1–2. C, E	1. B 6. E
2. B 7. A	2. 8 7. 3	2. A 7. I	3–4. I, H	2. A 7. D
3. A 8. C	3. 5 8. 4	3. H 8. E	5–6. G, D	3. C 8. G
4. C 9. A	4. 1 9. 6	4. C 9. D	7–8. F, A	4. F 9. J
5. A 10. B	5. 9 10. 7	5. G 10. F	9–10. J, B	5. H 10. I

Answers to the Unit Reviews:
ADVANCING VOCABULARY SKILLS, SHORT VERSION

Unit One

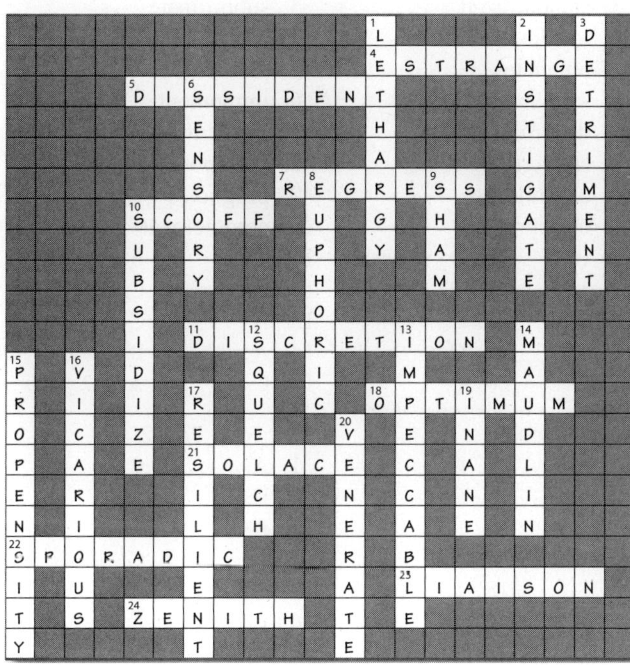

Unit Two

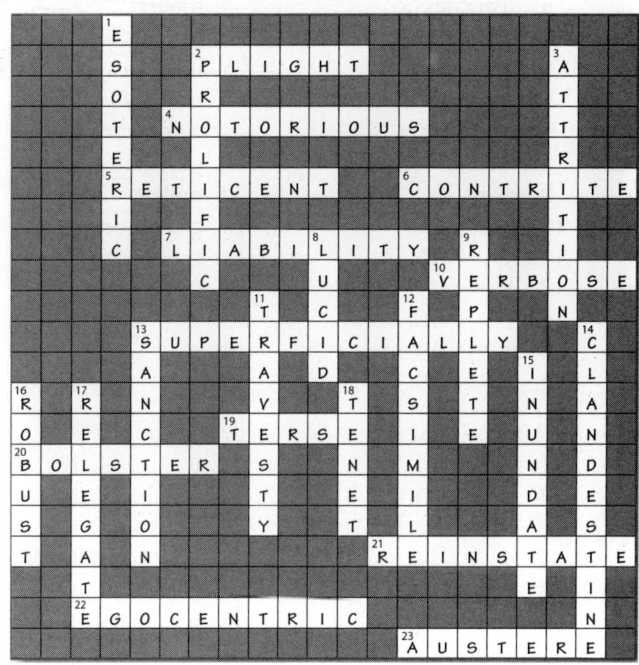

Unit Three

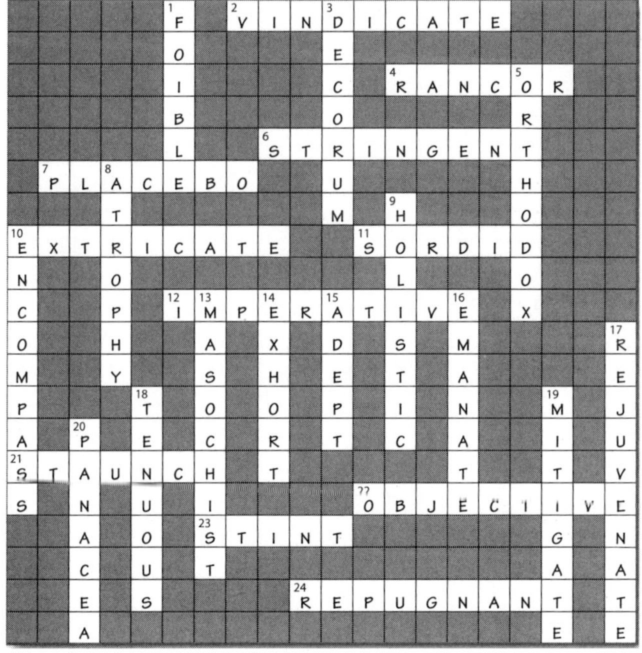

Unit Four

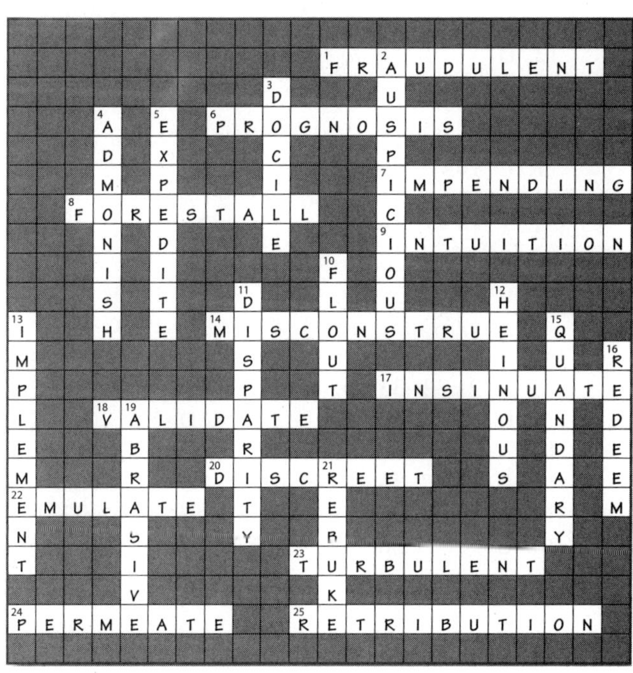

Answers to the Unit Tests: ADVANCING VOCABULARY SKILLS, SHORT VERSION

Unit One

Unit One, Test 1

1. propensity
2. venerate
3. instigates
4. equivocated
5. sensory
6. facetious
7. detriment
8. squelch
9. sham
10. scrupulous

11. A 16. A
12. A 17. D
13. C 18. D
14. B 19. A
15. B 20. C

Unit One, Test 2

1. M 14. I
2. D 15. C
3. E 16. C
4. H 17. C
5. K 18. I
6. J 19. C
7. B 20. C
8. C 21. I
9. F 22. I
10. I 23. C
11. A 24. C
12. G 25. I
13. L

Unit One, Test 3

1. C 14. D 26. B 39. C
2. D 15. B 27. D 40. A
3. A 16. A 28. C 41. D
4. A 17. C 29. A 42. B
5. D 18. D 30. D 43. A
6. A 19. D 31. A 44. B
7. B 20. A 32. B 45. D
8. D 21. B 33. D 46. B
9. C 22. C 34. B 47. C
10. A 23. A 35. C 48. B
11. D 24. C 36. A 49. D
12. B 25. B 37. C 50. B
13. C 38. D

Unit One, Test 4

1. D 11. B
2. A 12. A
3. B 13. D
4. A 14. C
5. C 15. A
6. D 16. D
7. B 17. C
8. B 18. B
9. A 19. A
10. D 20. B

Unit Two

Unit Two, Test 1

1. cohesive
2. liability
3. robust
4. connoisseur
5. notorious
6. travesty
7. clandestine
8. sanction
9. replete
10. grotesque

11. D 16. D
12. C 17. C
13. A 18. A
14. A 19. C
15. A 20. D

Unit Two, Test 2

1. F 14. I
2. H 15. I
3. B 16. C
4. E 17. I
5. C 18. I
6. A 19. I
7. L 20. C
8. D 21. C
9. J 22. I
10. G 23. C
11. M 24. C
12. I 25. C
13. K

Unit Two, Test 3

1. D 14. A 26. B 39. C
2. A 15. C 27. D 40. B
3. B 16. D 28. D 41. C
4. A 17. A 29. C 42. D
5. C 18. B 30. B 43. C
6. B 19. C 31. A 44. B
7. C 20. B 32. A 45. B
8. B 21. B 33. B 46. B
9. D 22. A 34. C 47. B
10. C 23. B 35. D 48. C
11. D 24. C 36. D 49. A
12. A 25. D 37. C 50. C
13. B 38. A

Unit Two, Test 4

1. D 11. C
2. C 12. B
3. D 13. B
4. B 14. D
5. C 15. B
6. D 16. A
7. C 17. C
8. A 18. B
9. D 19. C
10. A 20. D

Unit Three

Unit Three, Test 1

1. stint
2. sordid
3. standardized
4. exhilaration
5. emanates
6. synchronize
7. decorum
8. subversive
9. annihilate
10. entrepreneur

11. B 16. D
12. D 17. D
13. A 18. C
14. A 19. C
15. D 20. C

Unit Three, Test 2

1. M 14. C
2. H 15. C
3. E 16. I
4. F 17. I
5. I 18. I
6. B 19. C
7. D 20. I
8. G 21. C
9. L 22. I
10. C 23. C
11. A 24. I
12. K 25. C
13. J

Unit Three, Test 3

1. A 14. A 26. D 39. A
2. B 15. D 27. B 40. B
3. C 16. A 28. A 41. C
4. B 17. C 29. B 42. D
5. C 18. D 30. C 43. A
6. A 19. B 31. C 44. B
7. C 20. B 32. B 45. C
8. B 21. C 33. D 46. A
9. D 22. A 34. A 47. C
10. A 23. D 35. C 48. A
11. C 24. C 36. A 49. C
12. A 25. C 37. D 50. B
13. B 38. C

Unit Three, Test 4

1. C 11. C
2. D 12. B
3. B 13. D
4. C 14. C
5. A 15. A
6. B 16. C
7. D 17. B
8. C 18. C
9. D 19. D
10. C 20. B

Unit Four

Unit Four, Test 1

1. incapacitates
2. heinous
3. subordinate
4. rebuked
5. permeated
6. implement
7. expedite
8. omnipotent
9. prognosis
10. complement

11. A 16. B
12. D 17. C
13. A 18. C
14. A 19. B
15. C 20. A

Unit Four, Test 2

1. A 14. C
2. H 15. I
3. B 16. I
4. J 17. C
5. C 18. I
6. I 19. I
7. E 20. C
8. L 21. C
9. D 22. I
10. F 23. C
11. K 24. I
12. G 25. C
13. M

Unit Four, Test 3

1. D 14. B 26. D 39. B
2. A 15. A 27. B 40. D
3. D 16. A 28. A 41. C
4. B 17. C 29. B 42. B
5. B 18. B 30. D 43. C
6. A 19. C 31. C 44. A
7. D 20. D 32. A 45. D
8. C 21. B 33. D 46. B
9. D 22. A 34. B 47. A
10. D 23. D 35. C 48. C
11. B 24. A 36. D 49. A
12. C 25. A 37. D 50. D
13. D 38. A

Unit Four, Test 4

1. C 11. B
2. B 12. D
3. A 13. C
4. C 14. C
5. D 15. D
6. A 16. B
7. C 17. C
8. B 18. C
9. C 19. D
10. A 20. B

Mastery Test: *Chapter 1 (Apartment Problems)*

In the space provided, write the word from the box needed to complete each sentence. Then put the **letter** of that word in the column at the left. Use each word once.

A. **detriment**	B. **dexterous**	C. **discretion**	D. **facetious**	E. **gregarious**
F. **optimum**	G. **ostentatious**	H. **scrupulous**	I. **sensory**	J. **vicarious**

____ 1. Babies benefit from a great deal of ________________________ stimulation: different textures to feel, shapes and colors to look at, and various sounds to hear.

____ 2. The boys' club has made Hank more comfortable with others. In the past, he usually stayed by himself, but now he's much more ________________________.

____ 3. Anita is ________________________ about not wasting her employer's time. Although she uses a computer all day, she never sends personal e-mail or plays computer games until she gets home.

____ 4. When Brian said he spent all the money I had lent him on a new sports car, I wasn't sure if he was being serious or ________________________.

____ 5. It will be many years before I can afford to travel much, but in the meantime, I get ________________________ pleasure from hearing about my friends' exciting vacations.

____ 6. Not being able to read well is a(n) ________________________ to most careers.

____ 7. To be great performers, piano players must be ________________________ with their hands.

____ 8. Experts say that the ________________________ age for receiving the measles vaccine is 15 months. Children younger than that aren't well protected by the injection.

____ 9. It's________________________ of the Millers to build a huge fancy vacation home that they'll use only once or twice a year. Why must they make such a show of having money?

____ 10. It's difficult to make a child understand the need for ________________________. What parent hasn't had the experience of hearing his child yell out some true, but embarrassing fact, such as "Look! That man doesn't have any hair on his head!"

SCORE: (Number correct) ________ × 10 = __________ %

Mastery Test: *Chapter 2 (Hardly a Loser)*

In the space provided, write the word from the box needed to complete each sentence. Then put the **letter** of that word in the column at the left. Use each word once.

A. **collaborate**	B. **despondent**	C. **instigate**	D. **resilient**	E. **retrospect**
F. **rudimentary**	G. **scoff**	H. **squelch**	I. **venerate**	J. **zealot**

____ 1. In ______________________, Tim believes his marriage to Lily could have been saved. But at the time, he was convinced that they should split up.

____ 2. The world ______________________s Isaac Newton for discovering the laws of gravity.

____ 3. After breaking her hip, Mrs. Murphy was ______________________, but she became more hopeful and cheerful when she was discharged from the hospital.

____ 4. Our neighbor is a ______________________ about keeping his yard neat. When a single leaf falls off a tree, he rushes out of his house to rake it up.

____ 5. Winnie was a happy, fun-loving girl when she got married. But five years of living with her sour, serious husband has ______________________(e)d her bubbly personality.

____ 6. Joan didn't take part in the snowball fight, but she ______________________(e)d it by giving the boys huge piles of snowballs.

____ 7. John Lennon and Paul McCartney ______________________(e)d in writing many of the Beatles' hit songs, including "Yesterday" and "Yellow Submarine."

____ 8. People with AIDS are much less ______________________ than others. A flu attack that most of us can easily shake off is life-threatening to them.

____ 9. Anyone with even a(n) ______________________ understanding of electricity knows it's not a good idea to use a metal fork to take a piece of toast from the toaster.

____ 10. My little sister's friends ______________________(e)d at her when she claimed she could do magic tricks. Their laughter stopped, however, when she made a pair of pigeons appear from nowhere.

SCORE: (Number correct) ________ × 10 = __________ %

Mastery Test: *Chapter 3 (Grandfather at the Art Museum)*

In the space provided, write the word from the box needed to complete each sentence. Then put the **letter** of that word in the column at the left. Use each word once.

A. **ambiguous**	B. **dissident**	C. **embellish**	D. **fritter**	E. **inadvertent**
F. **inane**	G. **juxtapose**	H. **lethargy**	I. **sporadic**	J. **subsidize**

____ 1. Nita allows her son to ______________________ away his weekly allowance on junk. She says he'll soon learn that it's better to save his money for something he really wants.

____ 2. We watched in wonder as the baker ______________________(e)d the wedding cake with colorful flowers, hearts, and birds.

____ 3. Dr. Green was disturbed to see such ______________________ in young Lisa. Usually, children her age have a great amount of energy.

____ 4. Here's one of the ______________________ excuses people have given on insurance forms for accidents: "Coming home, I drove into the wrong driveway and hit a tree I don't have."

____ 5. Every member of the school board but one voted to hire the new teacher. The ______________________ kept saying, "There's something about him that I just don't like."

____ 6. The laundry soap ad ______________________(e)d an ugly, stained shirt with a beautiful, bright shirt that had supposedly been washed in the soap.

____ 7. The town business association has established a scholarship to ______________________ a needy business student each year at the local college.

____ 8. Instead of having a steady job, Lila stays home with her children and makes a little extra money now and then by doing ______________________ sewing jobs for friends.

____ 9. Cora's failure to send Rachel a wedding invitation was entirely______________________. As soon as Cora realized her mistake, she telephoned Rachel to invite her.

____ 10. One famous psychological test involves showing people inkblots in shapes purposely made ______________________ enough so that a variety of different things can be "seen" in each design.

SCORE: (Number correct) ________ × 10 = __________ %

Mastery Test: *Chapter 4 (My Brother's Mental Illness)*

In the space provided, write the word from the box needed to complete each sentence. Then put the **letter** of that word in the column at the left. Use each word once.

A. **berate**	B. **estrange**	C. **euphoric**	D. **impetuous**	E. **infallible**
F. **maudlin**	G. **regress**	H. **relinquish**	I. **ubiquitous**	J. **zenith**

____ 1. McDonald's is certainly a(n) ________________________ restaurant chain. It's almost impossible to find a city that doesn't contain a set of the "golden arches."

____ 2. "Don't ________________________ the child so," Mrs. Lopez told her husband. "He'll learn more if you just explain what he's done wrong instead of scolding him so harshly."

____ 3. My older brother seems to believe he's really ________________________. Whenever someone disagrees with him, he won't even consider the possibility that he's mistaken.

____ 4. Since so many people who diet eventually ________________________ to their old weights, wouldn't it make more sense simply to eat sensibly than to diet constantly?

____ 5. The young woman ________________________(e)d custody of her baby to adoptive parents because she wanted the child to have a good home, and she knew she wasn't able to provide one.

____ 6. Timmy was ________________________ when his parents, at last, agreed to let him have the puppy he'd been begging for. He walked around singing and smiling all day.

____ 7. Some child stars reached the ________________________ of their careers at a very young age and later felt like failures because they couldn't stay at the top.

____ 8. Last Friday night, my sister and I popped popcorn, put on our pajamas, and cried together over a silly, sentimental movie. Then we laughed at ourselves for being so ________________________.

____ 9. Harry's relationship with his two sisters had always been poor, but he completely ________________________(e)d them when, without their knowledge, he took several of their mother's belongings from her home on the day their mother died.

____ 10. Phyllis stole a tube of mascara just because she felt like it. She later discovered that her ________________________ act wasn't worth the humiliation and grief that resulted when she was caught.

SCORE: (Number correct) ________ × 10 = ___________ %

Mastery Test: *Chapter 5 (A Phony Friend)*

In the space provided, write the word from the box needed to complete each sentence. Then put the **letter** of that word in the column at the left. Use each word once.

A. **equivocate**	B. **fortuitous**	C. **impeccable**	D. **liaison**	E. **predisposed**
F. **propensity**	G. **reprehensible**	H. **sham**	I. **solace**	J. **solicitous**

____ 1. Alice knows she has a(n) ______________________ to overspend on clothes, so she has put herself on a clothing budget.

____ 2. Because my grandmother is ______________________ to pneumonia, I make sure she stays warm and healthy during the flu season.

____ 3. Teenagers often ______________________ about their plans. When asked where they're going, they say "Out," and when asked what they'll be doing, they say "Nothing much."

____ 4. Because Julie speaks both Vietnamese and English well, she acts as a(n) ______________________ between various Vietnamese immigrants and the telephone company, banks, and so on.

____ 5. Children traveling alone on airplanes generally get very ______________________ attention from the flight attendants, who keep them well supplied with coloring books, snacks, and pillows.

____ 6. Stealing money is bad enough, but stealing from a charity is really ______________________.

____ 7. Bob and Tina's meeting was unusually ______________________: intending to visit someone else, Bob knocked on Tina's apartment door by mistake.

____ 8. I used to envy my neighbor's ______________________ housekeeping until I realized how much time she spends cleaning. I live a messier but more balanced life.

____ 9. Mrs. Walker has been lonely since all her children moved to other areas. Her children hope that their frequent e-mails and photographs provide her with some ______________________.

____ 10. After Billy spent ten of his hard-earned dollars on an autographed picture of his baseball hero, he was heartbroken to learn that the player's signature was a(n) ______________________.

SCORE: (Number correct) ________ × 10 = __________ %

Mastery Test: *Chapter 6 (Coco the Gorilla)*

In the space provided, write the word from the box needed to complete each sentence. Then put the **letter** of that word in the column at the left. Use each word once.

A. **attrition**	B. **circumvent**	C. **cohesive**	D. **grievous**	E. **inundate**
F. **oblivious**	G. **reticent**	H. **robust**	I. **sanction**	J. **vociferous**

____ 1. Our house was so ______________________(e)d by carpenter ants that we finally were forced to call an exterminator.

____ 2. The baseball player's protest was ______________________—he stamped his feet and screamed at the umpire.

____ 3. There are many possible explanations as to why some families fall apart and have little contact while others are so much more ______________________.

____ 4. The rate of ______________________ in William's high school class was terrible. Of the 104 students who entered ninth grade with him, only 47 graduated.

____ 5. After the car accident, Rodrigo wandered around in a daze, ______________________ to the blood that was running down his face and soaking his shirt.

____ 6. The pilot ______________________(e)d the storm by flying above it.

____ 7. Many actors are quite happy to talk about their film careers, but ______________________about their private lives.

____ 8. The earthquake was especially ______________________ for those victims who lost friends and family as well as possessions.

____ 9. The principal wouldn't ______________________ the use of the gym for an after-school dance club, even though one of the teachers agreed to be in charge of it.

____ 10. It's hard to believe that Ana and Tomas's baby, who was so tiny and weak when she was born prematurely, has grown into such a ______________________ one-year-old.

SCORE: (Number correct) ________ × 10 = __________ %

Mastery Test: *Chapter 7 (Our Annual Garage Sale)*

In the space provided, write the word from the box needed to complete each sentence. Then put the **letter** of that word in the column at the left. Use each word once.

A. **bolster**	B. **depreciate**	C. **indiscriminate**	D. **inquisitive**	E. **nebulous**
F. **relegate**	G. **replete**	H. **sedentary**	I. **tenet**	J. **terse**

____ 1. A flaw in a diamond will cause the gem's market value to ______________________.

____ 2. Being accepted to two good schools ______________________(e)d Amy's confidence in her ability to do well in college.

____ 3. If the tax laws sometimes seem ______________________ to IRS agents, how is the average person supposed to make sense of them?

____ 4. My sister's______________________ shopping has resulted in a closet full of clothes that don't go together and that she doesn't even especially like.

____ 5. Scott was such a(n) ______________________ child that his father teased him by saying, "You ask so many questions that you'll probably be a game show host when you grow up."

____ 6. One ______________________ of the Ben & Jerry's ice cream company is that a percentage of their profits will be donated to peace efforts.

____ 7. Our car was too old and broken-down to trade in. It could only be ______________________(e)d to the junk pile.

____ 8. Since Carla is a receptionist, her work is very ______________________. As a result, she makes a special effort to exercise every day.

____ 9. One expensive kennel guarantees that your dog will be well cared for during your vacation. It offers cages ______________________ with such luxuries as air conditioning and pillows.

____ 10. Writer Dorothy Parker was well-known for her brief, witty statements. She once suggested this ______________________ sentence for her own gravestone: "Excuse my dust."

SCORE: (Number correct) ________ × 10 = __________ %

Mastery Test: *Chapter 8 (My Large Family)*

In the space provided, write the word from the box needed to complete each sentence. Then put the **letter** of that word in the column at the left. Use each word once.

A. **clandestine**	B. **contingency**	C. **egocentric**	D. **exonerate**	E. **incongruous**
F. **indigenous**	G. **liability**	H. **prolific**	I. **reinstate**	J. **superfluous**

____ 1. Mint is ______________________ to the town of North Judson, Indiana. Each summer, the town hosts a "Mint Festival" to celebrate its favorite native crop.

____ 2. ______________________ people do not necessarily feel good about themselves. Sometimes people focus on themselves too much because of self-doubt and insecurity.

____ 3. To prepare everyone for the ______________________ of a car accident, many states require drivers to buy accident insurance.

____ 4. After spending 45 minutes cramming our belongings into the back of our station wagon, Dad said, "The next time we go camping, we take only the necessities. All this ______________________ junk stays home!"

____ 5. Johann Sebastian Bach was ______________________ as both a composer and a parent. In addition to writing numerous pieces of music, he fathered twenty children.

____ 6. People who oppose the death penalty point out that occasionally, a person who has been put to death has later been ______________________(e)d of the crime.

____ 7. My little brother loves belonging to a "secret society." Only its members know where and when the society's ______________________ meetings are held.

____ 8. My brother's shyness is a great ______________________. Whenever he meets someone who interests him, he's usually too embarrassed to speak.

____ 9. Madeline's boss ______________________(e)d her in her old job as shop manager when she returned to work after maternity leave.

____ 10. Hal and Lisa spent so much on their new house that they had almost no money left to furnish it. It seems ______________________ to have this lovely, expensive home filled with cast-off sofas and chairs from thrift shops and garage sales.

SCORE: (Number correct) ________ × 10 = __________ %

Mastery Test: *Chapter 9 (A Costume Party)*

In the space provided, write the word from the box needed to complete each sentence. Then put the **letter** of that word in the column at the left. Use each word once.

A. **austere**	B. **esoteric**	C. **facsimile**	D. **grotesque**	E. **mesmerize**
F. **metamorphosis**	G. **notorious**	H. **perfunctory**	I. **provocative**	J. **travesty**

____ 1. Hitler is so ________________________ that his name has come to represent evil to most people.

____ 2. A native of Kansas, Randy was ________________________(e)d by the towering skyline of New York City.

____ 3. My brother's major—nuclear physics—is so ________________________ that he finds it difficult to discuss it at length with most people.

____ 4. Quaker meeting houses tend to be very ________________________ because the worshippers don't want to be distracted by a lot of decoration.

____ 5. I spend a little more money by buying my clothes at Bloom's, but it's worth it. The salespeople there give me sincere personal attention, instead of the ______________________ treatment I've experienced at other stores.

____ 6. Common ways to make ads ________________________ are the use of humor and famous singers.

____ 7. Numerous bee stings caused Levi's face to swell in such a ____________________ manner that he was barely recognizable.

____ 8. In the front window of a local French restaurant is a ____________________ of the Eiffel Tower—in miniature, of course.

____ 9. With its violence and phony drama, most so-called "professional" wrestling is really a ________________________ of the sport.

____ 10. Panicked by his wife's leaving him, Travis immediately promised to undergo a complete ________________________: from a cold workaholic to a warm person who makes time for his family. To do so, he's even willing to go into therapy.

SCORE: (Number correct) ________ × 10 = __________ %

Mastery Test: *Chapter 10 (The Missing Painting)*

In the space provided, write the word from the box needed to complete each sentence. Then put the **letter** of that word in the column at the left. Use each word once.

A. **connoisseur**	B. **conspiracy**	C. **contrite**	D. **distraught**	E. **germane**
F. **lucid**	G. **plight**	H. **superficially**	I. **symmetrical**	J. **verbose**

____ 1. Someone who admires all things French—food, art, wine, and literature—is called a Francophile, while a __________________________ of everything English is called an Anglophile.

____ 2. To argue fairly, stick to the topic. Don't bring up old sore points that aren't ____________________ to the issue at hand.

____ 3. In Shakespeare's well-known tragedy *Julius Caesar*, a group of Roman senators join in a ____________________ to assassinate Caesar.

____ 4. When the young mother first missed her little boy in the park, she wasn't too disturbed, but after ten minutes of searching without success, she became ________________________.

____ 5. The day-care teacher was disturbed to see Emily's father's reaction to the birthday card Emily had so carefully made for him. He glanced at it only ________________________ and said, "That's nice. Now get in the car."

____ 6. Wendy's financial ________________________ is severe. She's out of work and has barely enough money for the bus fare to interview for a new job.

____ 7. Because humans are basically __________________________—their left and right sides are mirror images of each other—they have a well-balanced appearance.

____ 8. When my dog is scolded for some misdeed, her drooping tail and saddened eyes make it seem that she's ________________________.

____ 9. If your essay is ________________________, it doesn't necessarily mean you're naturally wordier than other students. You just haven't taken the time to edit out repetitions and unnecessary words.

____ 10. Cheryl was so helpless with laughter that she couldn't provide a ____________________ explanation of what had happened. She could only gasp out fragments of sentences, such as "And then the chair. . . . But Thomas was trying. . . . And the *noise!*"

SCORE: (Number correct) ________ × 10 = ___________ %

Mastery Test: *Chapter 11 (An Ohio Girl in New York)*

In the space provided, write the word from the box needed to complete each sentence. Then put the **letter** of that word in the column at the left. Use each word once.

A. **adept**	B. **encompass**	C. **entrepreneur**	D. **eradicate**	E. **homogeneous**
F. **presumptuous**	G. **sordid**	H. **standardize**	I. **stint**	J. **stringent**

____ 1. The principal called a special meeting to address the ____________________ problem of drug use in the school system.

____ 2. Nancy has tried to ____________________ the ants in her kitchen, but no matter how often she sprays, they soon reappear.

____ 3. The two-week survival course ____________________(e)d all we would need to know, from starting a campfire to building a shelter to finding food in the wilderness.

____ 4. Some people would like all countries to adopt the metric system in order to ____________________ the system of weights and measures worldwide.

____ 5. When Helen needed a kidney transplant, several of her friends insisted she take one of theirs. They didn't realize there are ____________________ guidelines determining who can be a successful donor.

____ 6. When we were young, our grandfather would tell us colorful stories about his ____________________ as a circus clown.

____ 7. I was annoyed with Eileen yesterday. I felt it was ____________________ of her to try to sell me magazine subscriptions since I had invited her over for a social visit.

____ 8. An excellent public speaker with a likable personality, Jim is ____________________ at getting others to see things from his point of view.

____ 9. On hot summer days in our small town, you can see many young ____________________s operating their own lemonade or iced-tea stands.

____ 10. When we decided to get rid of our chickens, I offered our three white hens to a neighboring egg farmer, but he refused them. He wanted to keep his all-brown flock ____________________.

SCORE: (Number correct) ________ × 10 = __________ %

Mastery Test: *Chapter 12 (How Neat Is Neat Enough?)*

In the space provided, write the word from the box needed to complete each sentence. Then put the **letter** of that word in the column at the left. Use each word once.

A. **exhort**	B. **flamboyant**	C. **foible**	D. **innocuous**	E. **magnanimous**
F. **masochist**	G. **meticulous**	H. **rancor**	I. **recrimination**	J. **repugnant**

____ 1. Determined that the casting director would notice her, the would-be actress wore a ______________________ costume—featuring feathers, pearls, and spangles—to the audition.

____ 2. Elizabeth is so kind and good-natured that her friends cheerfully overlook her ______________________ of talking too much.

____ 3. The scratch on our car's fender seemed ______________________ at first, but it soon began to rust. We ended up paying $275 to have it fixed.

____ 4. Because he'd had so much difficulty with his studies, Oscar's parents ______________________(e)d him to go to summer school.

____ 5. It's amazing how ______________________ a formerly appetizing dish can become after it's spent a few weeks forgotten in the back of the refrigerator.

____ 6. It certainly was ______________________ of Charlie to forgive Eric for losing Charlie's winning lottery ticket worth $500.

____ 7. Karen's friends called her a ______________________ when they learned that she planned to run in two marathons in one weekend.

____ 8. The home-team fans felt such ______________________ for the visiting team that they began booing and shouting insults before the game even began.

____ 9. Henry is ______________________ about his car's upkeep. He washes the car by hand every Saturday, changes the oil four times a year, and won't allow anyone to eat in it.

____ 10. The warring couple spent their first session with the marriage counselor trading ______________________s such as "You're never home at night!" and "Well, if you weren't so grouchy, I might stay home more!"

SCORE: (Number correct) ________ × 10 = __________ %

Mastery Test: *Chapter 13 (Thomas Dooley)*

In the space provided, write the word from the box needed to complete each sentence. Then put the **letter** of that word in the column at the left. Use each word once.

A. **atrophy**	B. **deplore**	C. **deprivation**	D. **exacerbate**	E. **imperative**
F. **mitigate**	G. **objective**	H. **panacea**	I. **unprecedented**	J. **utilitarian**

____ 1. You can ________________________ the stress of preparing for finals by studying carefully throughout the semester.

____ 2. David's mother left an urgent message on his answering machine: "It's ________________________ that you call me before Thursday!"

____ 3. The doctors explained that Uncle Tim's muscles will gradually ________________________, making it increasingly more difficult for him to walk.

____ 4. My brother's dorm room is strictly ________________________. The room is empty except for the necessities: a desk, chair, bed, dresser, and bookcase.

____ 5. Marie wished her husband would be more ________________________ and consider the facts instead of always judging things by his own narrow point of view, without even thinking.

____ 6. Karen believes that moving away from home would be a(n) ________________________ for her problems, but I think it will take more than that to cure all her difficulties.

____ 7. People who suffer a(n) ________________________ of foods containing vitamin C develop a disease called scurvy.

____ 8. Luis doesn't simply ________________________ the evils in the world; he tries to work to make the world better.

____ 9. The high-school band has won the state competition for a(n) ________________________ six straight years. The previous record was five years in a row.

____ 10. Bonnie thought ice water would cool the burning in her mouth from the Chinese mustard, but a drink did just the opposite—the water ________________________(e)d her discomfort.

SCORE: (Number correct) ________ × 10 = __________ %

Mastery Test: *Chapter 14 (Twelve Grown Men in a Bug)*

In the space provided, write the word from the box needed to complete each sentence. Then put the **letter** of that word in the column at the left. Use each word once.

A. **decorum**	B. **espouse**	C. **exhilaration**	D. **exorbitant**	E. **extricate**
F. **facilitate**	G. **orthodox**	H. **rejuvenate**	I. **synchronize**	J. **tenuous**

____ 1. A man on the street corner handed out pamphlets that ______________________(e)d the cause of the homeless.

____ 2. The injured deer carefully ______________________(e)d itself from the thorny brush by the side of the road.

____ 3. The ski trip was worthwhile just to see the ______________________ on Joanne's face the first time she made it down the hill without falling.

____ 4. People hired for the staff of the elegant new hotel must have a strong sense of ______________________. Guests there will expect to be treated with formal politeness.

____ 5. Dawn's boyfriend sometimes shows poor judgment. Although he makes a very low salary, he spends a(n) ______________________ amount of money on fancy sneakers and leather jackets.

____ 6. Uncle Richard loves his power tools because they ______________________ tasks he finds difficult because of his arthritis.

____ 7. "A cup of warm cocoa will ______________________ you," said Mom. And sure enough, I soon felt as good as new.

____ 8. My friendship with Debby is ______________________. If it were subjected to the least bit of conflict, I don't think it would survive.

____ 9. The differing times on the clocks in the living room, kitchen, and bedroom drive me crazy. Before going to bed tonight, I'm going to ______________________ them.

____ 10. ______________________ standards of dress vary from culture to culture. While men in the United States are expected to wear pants, men in other countries often wear long robes.

SCORE: (Number correct) ________ × 10 = ___________ %

Mastery Test: *Chapter 15 (A Different Kind of Doctor)*

In the space provided, write the word from the box needed to complete each sentence. Then put the **letter** of that word in the column at the left. Use each word once.

A. **analogy**	B. **annihilate**	C. **criterion**	D. **emanate**	E. **holistic**
F. **placebo**	G. **proficient**	H. **staunch**	I. **subversive**	J. **vindicate**

____ 1. To ______________________ himself, Joe produced evidence that he had been out of town the day that green paint was sprayed all over school.

____ 2. One widely used ______________________ is the comparison of the pastor of a congregation to the shepherd of a flock of sheep.

____ 3. A delicious aroma of baking bread ______________________(e)d from the kitchen.

____ 4. It made me angry when my parents judged my boyfriends only by the ______________________ of the length of their hair.

____ 5. I feel sorry for ants when they work so hard to construct an anthill, only to have a child come along and ______________________ it with one blow of his foot.

____ 6. Dr. Wyatt is a ______________________ practitioner. She considers the health of the entire body when attempting to heal one of its parts.

____ 7. The sports fans in our town are ______________________ supporters of the home team. They're loyal even during a losing season.

____ 8. Zamil used to be a ______________________ secretary, but since she hadn't worked in a while, she decided to brush up on her office skills before going back to work.

____ 9. The old movie was about a ______________________ plot that failed to overthrow a powerful, cruel dictator.

____ 10. Carl was furious when he realized his doctor had been treating his headaches with ______________________s. He felt this treatment meant the doctor believed Carl was only imagining his headaches.

SCORE: (Number correct) ________ × 10 = ___________ %

Mastery Test: *Chapter 16 (My Devilish Older Sister)*

In the space provided, write the word from the box needed to complete each sentence. Then put the **letter** of that word in the column at the left. Use each word once.

A. **disparity**	B. **forestall**	C. **insidious**	D. **insinuate**	E. **interrogate**
F. **obsequious**	G. **omnipotent**	H. **opportune**	I. **permeate**	J. **retribution**

____ 1. To ______________________ any chance of the chicken salad spoiling, do not let it sit outside all afternoon at the picnic.

____ 2. As ______________________ for starting a rebellion against the government, the leaders of the uprising were jailed.

____ 3. Don't tell Jasmin that her new striped dress makes her look slender. She'll think you mean to ______________________ that she's overweight.

____ 4. Lead poisoning may not be immediately apparent. It can be ______________________, eventually leading to effects as harmful as brain damage.

____ 5. My grandfather believes his 22-year-old fiancée loves him, but the ______________________ in their ages makes it seem more likely that she loves his money.

____ 6. In describing a(n) ______________________ coworker, Elizabeth explained, "If a superior says 'Jump like a frog!' her only response is 'How high?' "

____ 7. Quicksand is formed when water ______________________s loose sand and makes its surface so soft that it cannot support weight.

____ 8. In a democracy, no single person is ______________________. Even the President has to get approval from Congress in order to carry out his policies.

____ 9. Since my parents were so pleased with my grades, I thought it was a(n) ______________________ time to ask if I could borrow the car.

____ 10. When rumors began about steroids in the weight room, the principal kept all members of the weightlifting club after school to ______________________ them about drugs.

SCORE: (Number correct) ________ × 10 = __________ %

Mastery Test: *Chapter 17 (Harriet Tubman)*

In the space provided, write the word from the box needed to complete each sentence. Then put the **letter** of that word in the column at the left. Use each word once.

A. **complement**	B. **discreet**	C. **fastidious**	D. **flout**	E. **heinous**
F. **implement**	G. **impromptu**	H. **inference**	I. **intuition**	J. **obtrusive**

____ 1. Cynthia's all-white living room is a little dull. If it were my house, I'd ____________________ it with some colorful pillows and pictures.

____ 2. Bookkeepers and accountants must be ____________________. Overlooking even one little detail can cause problems in their work.

____ 3. The new people next door seem to actually want to create bad feelings with their neighbors. They ____________________ neighborhood standards by never cutting the grass, leaving an abandoned car in the yard, and dumping trash everywhere.

____ 4. When our school ____________________s the reduced budget, there will no longer be money to support extracurricular activities.

____ 5. Politicians must be ____________________ about their personal lives because revealing sensitive information can give other candidates something to use against them in an election campaign.

____ 6. Leila's bright red dress was certainly ____________________ at the funeral.

____ 7. My parents haven't said what they think of my new boyfriend, but since they are silent, my ____________________ is that they dislike him.

____ 8. Obviously, some people enjoy reading about ____________________ crimes. Books about murders are often best-sellers, and the more gruesome the crime, the better the book sells.

____ 9. One group that had no time to rehearse a skit gave a(n) ____________________ performance so funny and lively that it may even have benefited from the lack of practice.

____ 10. I just knew Emil's business partner would let him down, but he wouldn't believe me until it happened. Now Emil says he should have trusted my "feminine ____________________."

SCORE: (Number correct) ________ × 10 = __________ %

Mastery Test: *Chapter 18 (Tony's Rehabilitation)*

In the space provided, write the word from the box needed to complete each sentence. Then put the **letter** of that word in the column at the left. Use each word once.

A. **auspicious**	B. **expedite**	C. **extenuating**	D. **fraudulent**	E. **innuendo**
F. **rebuke**	G. **redeem**	H. **subordinate**	I. **transgress**	J. **vehement**

____ 1. People who believe in astrology often plan important events for days that the stars "say" are ______________________.

____ 2. Any ad for a product that promises to help you lose weight without dieting or exercising must be ______________________.

____ 3. Needing his order soon, a customer spoke to the manager, who promised to ______________________ a rapid delivery.

____ 4. I'll never forgive myself for gossiping so cruelly about our new neighbor. Now that I know and like her, I've ______________________(e)d myself for my behavior a hundred times.

____ 5. "It's true I lied to you about being out of town last weekend," Jan admitted to Brian, "but there were ______________________ circumstances. I had promised your mother that I wouldn't see you over the weekend so that you could concentrate on studying for Monday's exam."

____ 6. Turning away from a life of crime, the robber ______________________(e)d himself by teaching citizens how to protect themselves against theft.

____ 7. Malik reports to his boss—the vice president of the company. She, in turn, is ______________________ to the executive vice president.

____ 8. Joey's parents had laid down so many rules for him that it was impossible for the little boy not to ______________________ once in a while.

____ 9. My uncle is so ______________________ in his opinions on politics that it's impossible to have a casual conversation with him on the topic. He gets too carried away by his passion.

____ 10. Richard listened politely to the information about where to buy a hairpiece, but he resented the ______________________ that his baldness made him unattractive.

SCORE: (Number correct) ________ × 10 = __________ %

Mastery Test: *Chapter 19 (Rumors)*

In the space provided, write the word from the box needed to complete each sentence. Then put the **letter** of that word in the column at the left. Use each word once.

A. **deride**	B. **derogatory**	C. **fabricate**	D. **impending**	E. **macabre**
F. **misconstrue**	G. **paramount**	H. **quandary**	I. **turbulent**	J. **validate**

____ 1. Children like to frighten each other at slumber parties by telling __________________ stories about demons, ghosts, and vampires.

____ 2. Being with Fred can be depressing because of all his __________________ remarks. Just once, I'd like to hear him say something good about someone else.

____ 3. When the staff heard that a huge snowstorm was on its way, everyone in the office left for home early, hoping to miss the __________________ bad weather.

____ 4. You may get some laughs when you __________________ someone's appearance, but some of us find your scornful remarks more in bad taste than amusing.

____ 5. Gina was so anxious to impress her college friends that she pretended to have a boyfriend at Harvard. The guy she __________________(e)d was rich, intelligent, and spoke five foreign languages.

____ 6. My low opinion of Brian was __________________(e)d when I learned he had faked an auto accident in order to file a dishonest insurance claim.

____ 7. I enjoy sailing when the water is calm, but if the lake becomes __________________, I promptly become "seasick."

____ 8. Vicky always __________________s my compliments, somehow finding an insult in every comment I intend to be encouraging.

____ 9. When your boss says a job is of __________________ importance, you should consider it more important than any other project you're working on.

____ 10. Linda's adoptive parents were in a __________________ about what to tell her regarding her birth. Should she be told the truth, or would it be too painful to know that she'd been left at the entrance of a hospital emergency room the day she was born?

SCORE: (Number correct) ________ × 10 = __________ %

Mastery Test: *Chapter 30 (Firing Our Boss)*

In the space provided, write the word from the box needed to complete each sentence. Then put the **letter** of that word in the column at the left. Use each word once.

A. **abrasive**	B. **admonish**	C. **antithesis**	D. **culmination**	E. **docile**
F. **emulate**	G. **hierarchy**	H. **incapacitate**	I. **prognosis**	J. **tumult**

____ 1. Dee's parrot is so ______________________ that you can hand-feed it without fear of getting bitten.

____ 2. Sandpaper comes in different degrees of roughness. The most ______________________ type has large pieces of sand.

____ 3. When it comes to work, Marco is the ______________________ of Lee. Marco is ambitious and finds work challenging, while Lee tries to wriggle out of work whenever possible.

____ 4. It's appropriate to ______________________ a worker who forgets to punch the timecard only once or twice, but a stronger reaction is needed for someone who forgets almost every day.

____ 5. The Fourth of July show begins with a band concert. Next, there's a sing-along. The ______________________ of the evening is a fifteen-minute display of spectacular fireworks.

____ 6. There's no way I'll be able to give a speech tomorrow. I've just begun to lose my voice, and the doctor's ______________________ is that it'll get even weaker for at least two more days.

____ 7. What is the point of having a band play at that restaurant? The ______________________ from the diners is so great that you can't possibly appreciate the music.

____ 8. My broken arm was beneficial in that it ______________________(e)d me for most household chores.

____ 9. My brother quit smoking the day he saw his six-year-old pick up one of his cigarettes and put it in her own mouth. "I want my daughter to ______________________ my good behaviors, not my bad ones," he said.

____ 10. If I ever entered the military service, I'd have to learn the ______________________ of ranks. I have no idea if a major is higher than a lieutenant or vice versa.

SCORE: (Number correct) ________ × 10 = __________ %

Answers to the Mastery Tests:
ADVANCING VOCABULARY SKILLS, SHORT VERSION

Chapter 1 (Apartment Problems)

1. I
2. E
3. H
4. D
5. J
6. A
7. B
8. F
9. G
10. C

Chapter 2 (Hardly a Loser)

1. E
2. I
3. B
4. J
5. H
6. C
7. A
8. D
9. F
10. G

Chapter 3 (Grandfather at the Art Museum)

1. D
2. C
3. H
4. F
5. B
6. G
7. J
8. I
9. E
10. A

Chapter 4 (My Brother's Mental Illness)

1. I
2. A
3. E
4. G
5. H
6. C
7. J
8. F
9. B
10. D

Chapter 5 (A Phony Friend)

1. F
2. E
3. A
4. D
5. J
6. G
7. B
8. C
9. I
10. H

Chapter 6 (Coco the Gorilla)

1. E
2. J
3. C
4. A
5. F
6. B
7. G
8. D
9. I
10. H

Chapter 7 (Our Annual Garage Sale)

1. B
2. A
3. E
4. C
5. D
6. I
7. F
8. H
9. G
10. J

Chapter 8 (My Large Family)

1. F
2. C
3. B
4. J
5. H
6. D
7. A
8. G
9. I
10. E

Chapter 9 (A Costume Party)

1. G
2. E
3. B
4. A
5. H
6. I
7. D
8. C
9. J
10. F

Chapter 10 (The Missing Painting)

1. A
2. E
3. B
4. D
5. H
6. G
7. I
8. C
9. J
10. F

Chapter 11 (An Ohio Girl in New York)

1. G
2. D
3. B
4. H
5. J
6. I
7. F
8. A
9. C
10. E

Chapter 12 (How Neat Is Neat Enough?)

1. B
2. C
3. D
4. A
5. J
6. E
7. F
8. H
9. G
10. I

Chapter 13 (Thomas Dooley)

1. F
2. E
3. A
4. J
5. G
6. H
7. C
8. B
9. I
10. D

Chapter 14 (Twelve Grown Men in a Bug)

1. B
2. E
3. C
4. A
5. D
6. F
7. H
8. J
9. I
10. G

Chapter 15 (A Different Kind of Doctor)

1. J
2. A
3. D
4. C
5. B
6. E
7. H
8. G
9. I
10. F

Chapter 16 (My Devilish Older Sister)

1. B
2. J
3. D
4. C
5. A
6. F
7. I
8. G
9. H
10. E

Chapter 17 (Harriet Tubman)

1. A
2. C
3. D
4. F
5. B
6. J
7. H
8. E
9. G
10. I

Chapter 18 (Tony's Rehabilitation)

1. A
2. D
3. B
4. F
5. C
6. G
7. H
8. I
9. J
10. E

Chapter 19 (Rumors)

1. E
2. B
3. D
4. A
5. C
6. J
7. I
8. F
9. G
10. H

Chapter 20 (Firing Our Boss)

1. E
2. A
3. C
4. B
5. D
6. I
7. J
8. H
9. F
10. G

Mastery Test: *Unit One*

PART A

Complete each sentence in a way that clearly shows you understand the meaning of the **boldfaced** word. Take a minute to plan your answer before you write.

Example: I was being **facetious** when I said that ___my parrot can tell the future. In fact, he's always wrong___.

1. I would be **euphoric** if ______________________________

______________________________.

2. I have a **propensity** to ______________________________. For example, ______________________________

______________________________.

3. Rhetta **frittered** away her money on ______________________________

______________________________.

4. A **zealot** in the environmental movement would never ______________________________

______________________________.

5. Being **gregarious**, Marisol wants to celebrate her birthday by ______________________________

______________________________.

6. I was **despondent** because ______________________________

______________________________.

7. An **inane** way to study for final exams is to ______________________________

______________________________.

8. At the mall, my **impetuous** friend ______________________________

______________________________.

9. The mayor **estranged** many voters when he ______________________________

______________________________.

10. In **retrospect**, I realized that ______________________________

______________________________.

(Continues on next page)

PART B

Use each of the following ten words in sentences of your own. Make it clear that you know the meaning of the word you use. Feel free to use the past tense or plural form of a word.

A. **ambiguous**	B. **embellish**	C. **infallible**	D. **ostentatious**	E. **scoff**
F. **scrupulous**	G. **sensory**	H. **sham**	I. **vicarious**	J. **zenith**

11. ______________________________

____

12. ______________________________

____

13. ______________________________

____

14. ______________________________

____

15. ______________________________

____

16. ______________________________

____

17. ______________________________

____

18. ______________________________

____

19. ______________________________

____

20. ______________________________

____

SCORE: (Number correct) ________ × 5 = __________ %

Mastery Test: *Unit Two*

PART A

Complete each sentence in a way that clearly shows you understand the meaning of the **boldfaced** word. Take a minute to plan your answer before you write.

Example: On our picnic, we carried a basket **replete** with ___a complete meal and plenty of snacks___.

1. A very **terse** answer to the question "Did you have fun at the dentist's office?" is "______________________________."
2. A loud voice would probably be a **liability** in ______________________________.
3. One good way to **bolster** a friend's spirits is to ______________________________.
4. One **verbose** way of saying no is "______________________________."
5. Reverend Patterson's appearance is **incongruous** with my image of a minister. He wears ______________________________.
6. As a child, I was **contrite** after ______________________________.
7. Vanessa is so **egocentric** that ______________________________.
8. I was **distraught** when ______________________________.
9. One way to **circumvent** rush-hour traffic is to ______________________________.
10. One of the most **notorious** people I've ever heard of is ____________, who became notorious because ______________________________.

(Continues on next page)

PART B

Use each of the following ten words in sentences of your own. Make it clear that you know the meaning of the word you use. Feel free to use the past tense or plural form of a word.

A. **clandestine**	B. **depreciate**	C. **exonerate**	D. **inquisitive**	E. **mesmerize**
F. **metamorphosis**	G. **plight**	H. **relegate**	I. **sedentary**	J. **superficially**

11. ______________________________

____

12. ______________________________

____

13. ______________________________

____

14. ______________________________

____

15. ______________________________

____

16. ______________________________

____

17. ______________________________

____

18. ______________________________

____

19. ______________________________

____

20. ______________________________

____

SCORE: (Number correct) ________ × 5 = __________ %

Mastery Test: *Unit Three*

PART A

Complete each sentence in a way that clearly shows you understand the meaning of the **boldfaced** word. Take a minute to plan your answer before you write.

Example: Kim must be an **adept** manager because ______ she was just promoted again ______.

1. My parents often **exhort** me to ______________________________

______________________________.

2. A good way to **exacerbate** a sore throat is to ______________________________

______________________________.

3. My best friend has an odd **foible**: ______________________________

______________________________.

4. The **magnanimous** boss ______________________________

______________________________.

5. Usual classroom **decorum** forbids ______________________________

______________________________.

6. The singer's **flamboyant** outfit consisted of ______________________________

______________________________.

7. I **deplore** ______________ because ______________________________

______________________________.

8. I can count on ______________________________ to **rejuvenate** me because

______________________________.

9. **Emanating** from the kitchen was ______________________________

______________________________.

10. I am quite **proficient** at ______________________. For example, ______________

______________________________.

(Continues on next page)

PART B

Use each of the following ten words in sentences of your own. Make it clear that you know the meaning of the word you use. Feel free to use the past tense or plural form of a word.

A. **analogy**	B. **criterion**	C. **eradicate**	D. **exorbitant**	E. **imperative**
F. **meticulous**	G. **objective**	H. **repugnant**	I. **stint**	J. **synchronize**

11. ____

____

12. ____

____

13. ____

____

14. ____

____

15. ____

____

16. ____

____

17. ____

____

18. ____

____

19. ____

____

20. ____

____

SCORE: (Number correct) ________ × 5 = __________ %

Mastery Test: *Unit Four*

PART A

Complete each sentence in a way that clearly shows you understand the meaning of the **boldfaced** word. Take a minute to plan your answer before you write.

Example: Jeff should be **discreet** about the party because ______it's meant to be a surprise______.

1. The **docile** dog ____

____.

2. Ted **flouted** the traffic laws by ____

____.

3. There was a huge **tumult** when ____

____.

4. An **obsequious** secretary, Agnes often ____

____.

5. Charles **misconstrued** my dinner invitation. He ____

____.

6. Maureen obviously had **fabricated** her excuse. She told the teacher, "______________________________

____."

7. To **implement** her vacation plans, Ruth started to ____

____.

8. After getting a D in chemistry, I tried to **redeem** myself by ____

____.

9. You can tell that my sister is **fastidious** by looking at her bedroom, where ______________________________

____.

10. When Len said that his brother wouldn't even give him the time of day, he meant to **insinuate** that ______

____

____.

(Continues on next page)

PART B

Use each of the following ten words in sentences of your own. Make it clear that you know the meaning of the word you use. Feel free to use the past tense or plural form of a word.

A. **antithesis**	B. **complement**	C. **derogatory**	D. **emulate**	E. **inference**
F. **intuition**	G. **paramount**	H. **prognosis**	I. **quandary**	J. **rebuke**

11. ____________________

____

12. ____________________

____

13. ____________________

____

14. ____________________

____

15. ____________________

____

16. ____________________

____

17. ____________________

____

18. ____________________

____

19. ____________________

____

20. ____________________

____

SCORE: (Number correct) ________ × 5 = ________ %

TP THE TOWNSEND PRESS

Vocabulary Placement Test

NAME: ____________________

SECTION: __________ DATE: __________

SCORE: ____________________

This test contains 100 items. You have 30 minutes to take the test. In the space provided, write the letter of the choice that is closest in meaning to the **boldfaced** word.

Important: Keep in mind that this test is for placement purposes only. **If you do not know a word, leave the space blank rather than guess at it.**

____ 1. to **deceive** **a)** prove **b)** mislead **c)** reach **d)** get back

____ 2. **earnest** **a)** serious and sincere **b)** illegal **c)** wealthy **d)** hidden

____ 3. **inferior** **a)** not proper **b)** clear **c)** poor in quality **d)** inside

____ 4. to **comprehend** **a)** describe **b)** understand **c)** make use of **d)** prepare

____ 5. **unanimous** **a)** alone **b)** animal-like **c)** unfriendly **d)** in full agreement

____ 6. the **vicinity** **a)** area nearby **b)** city **c)** enemy **d)** information

____ 7. **current** **a)** healthy **b)** modern **c)** well-known **d)** necessary

____ 8. **internal** **a)** forever **b)** inside **c)** outside **d)** brief

____ 9. **maximum** **a)** least **b)** expensive **c)** cheap **d)** greatest

____ 10. an **objective** **a)** goal **b)** puzzle **c)** cause **d)** supply

____ 11. a **potential** **a)** favorite **b)** possibility **c)** refusal **d)** desire

____ 12. to **detect** **a)** discover **b)** make **c)** follow **d)** commit a crime

____ 13. to **establish** **a)** receive **b)** delay **c)** set up **d)** attract

____ 14. to **pursue** **a)** follow **b)** run from **c)** suggest **d)** create

____ 15. **vague** **a)** missing **b)** unclear **c)** kind **d)** necessary

____ 16. **suitable** **a)** simple **b)** needed **c)** profitable **d)** proper

____ 17. a **category** **a)** kindness **b)** horror **c)** type **d)** question

____ 18. **reluctant** **a)** unwilling **b)** lost **c)** unhappy **d)** well-known

____ 19. to **coincide** **a)** pay **b)** decide **c)** get in the way **d)** happen together

____ 20. to **inhabit** **a)** enter **b)** live in **c)** get used to **d)** understand

____ 21. **apparent** **a)** together **b)** obvious **c)** motherly **d)** welcome

____ 22. **accustomed** **a)** in the habit **b)** specially made **c)** necessary **d)** extra

____ 23. to **revise** **a)** give advice **b)** go back **c)** change **d)** awaken

____ 24. a **contrast** **a)** purpose **b)** choice **c)** agreement **d)** difference

____ 25. **awkward** **a)** forward **b)** boring **c)** clumsy **d)** clever

(Continues on next page)

____ 26. **urban** **a)** of a city **b)** circular **c)** not allowed **d)** large

____ 27. **lenient** **a)** light **b)** not strict **c)** delayed **d)** not biased

____ 28. to **endorse** **a)** suggest **b)** stop **c)** support **d)** start

____ 29. a **novice** **a)** book **b)** false impression **c)** beginner **d)** servant

____ 30. to **deter** **a)** prevent **b)** make last longer **c)** refuse **d)** damage

____ 31. to **verify** **a)** imagine **b)** prove **c)** keep going **d)** cancel

____ 32. **moderate** **a)** generous **b)** not final **c)** medium **d)** bright

____ 33. a **diversity** **a)**separation **b)** conclusion **c)** enthusiasm **d)** variety

____ 34. **accessible** **a)** easily reached **b)** itchy **c)** difficult **d)** folded

____ 35. **lethal** **a)** sweet-smelling **b)** ancient **c)** deadly **d)** healthy

____ 36. **vivid** **a)** brightly colored **b)** local **c)** large **d)** very talkative

____ 37. to **convey** **a)** allow **b)** communicate **c)** invent **d)** approve

____ 38. **inevitable** **a)** unavoidable **b)** dangerous **c)** spiteful **d)** doubtful

____ 39. a **ritual** **a)** business deal **b)** war **c)** ceremony **d)** show

____ 40. **elaborate** **a)** large **b)** complex **c)** expensive **d)** boring

____ 41. the **essence** **a)** fundamental characteristic **b)** tiny part **c)** much later **d)** rule

____ 42. to **coerce** **a)** attract **b)** refuse **c)** remove **d)** force

____ 43. **skeptical** **a)** stubborn **b)** forceful **c)** generous **d)** doubting

____ 44. **vital** **a)** weak **b)** stiff **c)** necessary **d)** unimportant

____ 45. **innate** **a)** learned **b)** underneath **c)** inborn **d)** clever

____ 46. a **vocation** **a)** hobby **b)** trip **c)** report **d)** profession

____ 47. to **defy** **a)** send for **b)** resist **c)** improve **d)** approve

____ 48. **adverse** **a)** strict **b)** profitable **c)** rhyming **d)** harmful

____ 49. **consecutive** **a)** late **b)** following one after another **c)** able **d)** at the same time

____ 50. **audible** **a)** able to be heard **b)** believable **c)** willing **d)** nearby

(Continues on next page)

____ 51. to **encounter** **a)** come upon **b)** count up **c)** depart from **d)** attack

____ 52. **obsolete** **a)** modern **b)** difficult to believe **c)** out-of-date **d)** not sold

____ 53. to **terminate** **a)** stop **b)** continue **c)** begin **d)** approach

____ 54. **altruistic** **a)** honest **b)** lying **c)** proud **d)** unselfish

____ 55. to **enhance** **a)** reject **b)** get **c)** improve **d)** free

____ 56. **nocturnal** **a)** supposed **b)** not logical **c)** complex **d)** active at night

____ 57. to **suffice** **a)** think up **b)** be good enough **c)** allow **d)** reject

____ 58. to **retaliate** **a)** repair **b)** repeat **c)** renew **d)** pay back

____ 59. to **incorporate** **a)** combine **b)** anger **c)** separate **d)** calm

____ 60. an **incentive** **a)** fear **b)** pride **c)** concern **d)** encouragement

____ 61. **covert** **a)** distant **b)** hidden **c)** changed **d)** adjusted

____ 62. to **alleviate** **a)** make anxious **b)** depart **c)** infect **d)** relieve

____ 63. to **aspire** **a)** dislike **b)** strongly desire **c)** impress **d)** respect

____ 64. an **extrovert** **a)** shy person **b)** magnet **c)** main point **d)** outgoing person

____ 65. **prone** **a)** disliked **b)** tending **c)** active **d)** rested

____ 66. **ominous** **a)** happy **b)** threatening **c)** depressed **d)** friendly

____ 67. **complacent** **a)** workable **b)** lazy **c)** self-satisfied **d)** healthy

____ 68. a **consensus** **a)** majority opinion **b)** total **c)** study **d)** approval

____ 69. to **condone** **a)** forgive **b)** represent **c)** arrest **d)** appoint

____ 70. **deficient** **a)** forgotten **b)** lacking **c)** complete **d)** well-known

____ 71. **fallible** **a)** capable of error **b)** complete **c)** incomplete **d)** simple

____ 72. **pragmatic** **a)** ordinary **b)** slow **c)** wise **d)** practical

____ 73. **avid** **a)** bored **b)** disliked **c)** enthusiastic **d)** plentiful

____ 74. **explicit** **a)** everyday **b)** distant **c)** permanent **d)** stated exactly

____ 75. **ambivalent** **a)** unknown **b)** having mixed feelings **c)** temporary **d)** able to be done

(Continues on next page)

____ 76. **vicarious** **a)** experienced indirectly **b)** lively **c)** inactive **d)** occasional

____ 77. **rudimentary** **a)** rude **b)** planned **c)** partial **d)** elementary

____ 78. to **collaborate** **a)** respect **b)** work hard **c)** work together **d)** search

____ 79. to **venerate** **a)** protect **b)** create **c)** make unfriendly **d)** respect

____ 80. **inadvertent** **a)** unintentional **b)** not for sale **c)** distant **d)** near

____ 81. **predisposed** **a)** against **b)** unwilling to speak **c)** undecided **d)** tending beforehand

____ 82. **robust** **a)** extremely careful **b)** healthy and strong **c)** tall **d)** loyal

____ 83. **sedentary** **a)** sitting **b)** excessive **c)** harmless **d)** repeated

____ 84. **clandestine** **a)** well-lit **b)** secret **c)** noble **d)** harmless

____ 85. **austere** **a)** wealthy **b)** complex **c)** plain **d)** far

____ 86. **notorious** **a)** too bold **b)** written **c)** known widely but unfavorably **d)** lacking skill

____ 87. **lucid** **a)** clear **b)** generous in forgiving **c)** careful **d)** bold

____ 88. to **encompass** **a)** include **b)** draw **c)** separate **d)** purchase

____ 89. **meticulous** **a)** broken-down **b)** curious **c)** careful and exact **d)** irregular

____ 90. **innocuous** **a)** delightful **b)** harmless **c)** dangerous **d)** disappointing

____ 91. to **rejuvenate** **a)** set free **b)** grow **c)** refresh **d)** make easier

____ 92. to **facilitate** **a)** approve **b)** make easier **c)** serve **d)** clear from blame

____ 93. **proficient** **a)** proud **b)** wise **c)** skilled **d)** well-known

____ 94. to **emanate** **a)** go above **b)** run through **c)** go down **d)** come forth

____ 95. to **implement** **a)** encourage **b)** carry out **c)** insult **d)** prevent

____ 96. to **fabricate** **a)** misinterpret **b)** put away **c)** clothe **d)** invent

____ 97. to **emulate** **a)** be tardy **b)** misunderstand **c)** imitate **d)** prepare

____ 98. a **prognosis** **a)** hope **b)** prediction **c)** opposite **d)** memory

____ 99. a **tumult** **a)** uproar **b)** uncertainty **c)** series **d)** scolding

____ 100. to **insinuate** **a)** demand **b)** state **c)** deny **d)** hint

STOP. This is the end of the test. If there is time remaining, you may go back and recheck your answers. When the time is up, hand in both your answer sheet and this test booklet to your instructor.

To the Instructor: Use these guidelines to match your students with the appropriate TP vocabulary book.

Score	0–9	10–24	25–49	50–74	75–90	91–100
Recommended Book	*VB*	*GBV*	*BVS*	*IVS*	*AVS*	*AWP*

NAME: ____________________

SECTION: __________ DATE: __________

SCORE: ____________________

ANSWER SHEET

1. _____	26. _____	51. _____	76. _____
2. _____	27. _____	52. _____	77. _____
3. _____	28. _____	53. _____	78. _____
4. _____	29. _____	54. _____	79. _____
5. _____	30. _____	55. _____	80. _____
6. _____	31. _____	56. _____	81. _____
7. _____	32. _____	57. _____	82. _____
8. _____	33. _____	58. _____	83. _____
9. _____	34. _____	59. _____	84. _____
10. _____	35. _____	60. _____	85. _____
11. _____	36. _____	61. _____	86. _____
12. _____	37. _____	62. _____	87. _____
13. _____	38. _____	63. _____	88. _____
14. _____	39. _____	64. _____	89. _____
15. _____	40. _____	65. _____	90. _____
16. _____	41. _____	66. _____	91. _____
17. _____	42. _____	67. _____	92. _____
18. _____	43. _____	68. _____	93. _____
19. _____	44. _____	69. _____	94. _____
20. _____	45. _____	70. _____	95. _____
21. _____	46. _____	71. _____	96. _____
22. _____	47. _____	72. _____	97. _____
23. _____	48. _____	73. _____	98. _____
24. _____	49. _____	74. _____	99. _____
25. _____	50. _____	75. _____	100. _____

ANSWER KEY

1. b	26. a	51. a	76. a
2. a	27. b	52. c	77. d
3. c	28. c	53. a	78. c
4. b	29. c	54. d	79. d
5. d	30. a	55. c	80. a
6. a	31. b	56. d	81. d
7. b	32. c	57. b	82. b
8. b	33. d	58. d	83. a
9. d	34. a	59. a	84. b
10. a	35. c	60. d	85. c
11. b	36. a	61. b	86. c
12. a	37. b	62. d	87. a
13. c	38. a	63. b	88. a
14. a	39. c	64. d	89. c
15. b	40. b	65. b	90. b
16. d	41. a	66. b	91. c
17. c	42. a	67. c	92. b
18. a	43. d	68. a	93. c
19. d	44. c	69. a	94. d
20. b	45. c	70. b	95. b
21. b	46. d	71. a	96. d
22. a	47. b	72. d	97. c
23. c	48. d	73. c	98. b
24. d	49. b	74. d	99. a
25. c	50. a	75. b	100. d

To the Instructor: Use these guidelines to match your students with the appropriate TP vocabulary book.

Score	0–9	10–24	25–49	50–74	75–90	91–100
Recommended Book	*VB*	*GBV*	*BVS*	*IVS*	*AVS*	*AWP*

List of the 200 Words in
BUILDING VOCABULARY SKILLS, SHORT VERSION

accelerate
accessible
acknowledge
acute
adapt
adverse
advocate
affirm
alleged
allude
alternative
anecdote
anonymous
apprehensive
appropriate
arrogant
audible
avert
awe
bestow
candid
cite
coerce
coherent
comparable
compatible
compel
compensate
competent
comply
concede
conceive
concise
confirm
consecutive
consequence
conservative
conspicuous
contrary
convey
data
deceptive
defer
defy
delete
delusion
denounce
derive
destiny
detain
deter
deteriorate
devise
dialog
diminish
disclose
discriminate
dismal
dismay
dispense
diversity
donor
drastic
elaborate
elapse
elite
emerge
endeavor
endorse
equate
erode
erratic
essence
evasive
exempt
exile
exotic
extensive
fluent
forfeit
fortify
frugal
futile
gesture
gruesome
harass
hypocrite
idealistic
illuminate
illusion
immunity
impact
impair
impartial
imply
impose
impulsive
indifferent
indignant
indulgent
inept
inevitable
infer
inhibit
innate
integrity
intervene
isolate
lament
legitimate
lenient
lethal
liberal
malicious
mediocre
menace
moderate
morale
morbid
naive
notable
novice
obsession
obstacle
obstinate
option
ordeal
overt
parallel
passive
patron
perceptive
persistent
phobia
plausible
prevail
procrastinate
profound
prominent
propel
provoke
prudent
query
rational
recede
recipient
reciprocate
recur
refuge
refute
reminisce
reprimand
restrain
retain
retort
retrieve
revert
revoke
ridicule
ritual
sadistic
savor
scapegoat
seclusion
sedate
severity
shrewd
simultaneous
site
skeptical
stereotype
stimulate
strategy
submit
subside
subtle
summon
superficial
supplement
surpass
susceptible
sustain
tactic
tedious
tentative
theoretical
transaction
transition
transmit
undermine
unique
universal
urban
valid
verify
versatile
vigorous
vital
vivid
vocation

List of the 200 Words in
IMPROVING VOCABULARY SKILLS, SHORT VERSION

absolve
abstain
acclaim
adamant
adjacent
affiliate
agnostic
alleviate
allusion
aloof
altruistic
ambivalent
amiable
amoral
animosity
antagonist
appease
arbitrary
aspire
assail
attest
attribute
augment
averse
avid
banal
benefactor
benevolent
blatant
blight
calamity
charisma
commemorate
complacent
comprehensive
concurrent
condone
confiscate
congenial
consensus
constitute
constrict
contemplate
contemporary
contend
contrive
conventional
conversely
covert
cryptic
curtail
cynic
decipher
default
deficient
deficit
degenerate
demise
depict
deplete
detract
detrimental
devastate
digress
diligent
discern
disdain
dispatch
dispel
dissent
diversion
divulge
dwindle
eccentric
elation
elicit
empathy
encounter
endow
engross
enhance
enigma
epitome
escalate
esteem
euphemism
evoke
exemplify
exhaustive
explicit
exploit
expulsion
extrovert
fallible
feasible
feign
fiscal
flagrant
flippant
fluctuate
formulate
furtive
gape
garble
gaunt
genial
gloat
habitat
hypothetical
immaculate
impasse
implausible
implicit
incentive
incoherent
incorporate
indispensable
infamous
inhibition
intercede
intermittent
intricate
intrinsic
ironic
legacy
longevity
lucrative
magnitude
malign
mandatory
mediate
menial
mercenary
methodical
mobile
mortify
mundane
muted
niche
nocturnal
nominal
nullify
nurture
obscure
obsolete
ominous
orient
pacify
pathetic
perception
persevere
plagiarism
poignant
ponder
pragmatic
precedent
predominant
prerequisite
pretentious
prevalent
prompt
prone
proponent
punitive
qualm
quest
rapport
rationale
recession
reconcile
rehabilitate
relentless
render
reprisal
retaliate
revulsion
rigor
rupture
sanctuary
saturate
scrutiny
sinister
speculate
squander
succumb
suffice
syndrome
taint
tangible
terminate
transcend
transient
traumatic
turmoil
venture
vile
vindictive
virile
vulnerable
waive

List of the 200 Words in
ADVANCING VOCABULARY SKILLS, SHORT VERSION

abrasive
adept
admonish
ambiguous
analogy
annihilate
antithesis
attrition
atrophy
auspicious
austere
berate
bolster
circumvent
clandestine
cohesive
collaborate
complement
connoisseur
conspiracy
contingency
contrite
criterion
culmination
decorum
deplore
depreciate
deprivation
deride
derogatory
despondent
detriment
dexterous
discreet
discretion
disparity
dissident
distraught
docile
egocentric

emanate
embellish
emulate
encompass
entrepreneur
equivocate
eradicate
esoteric
espouse
estrange
euphoric
exacerbate
exhilaration
exhort
exonerate
exorbitant
expedite
extenuating
extricate
fabricate
facetious
facilitate
facsimile
fastidious
flamboyant
flout
foible
forestall
fortuitous
fraudulent
fritter
germane
gregarious
grievous
grotesque
heinous
hierarchy
holistic
homogeneous
impeccable

impending
imperative
impetuous
implement
impromptu
inadvertent
inane
incapacitate
incongruous
indigenous
indiscriminate
infallible
inference
innocuous
innuendo
inquisitive
insidious
insinuate
instigate
interrogate
intuition
inundate
juxtapose
lethargy
liability
liaison
lucid
macabre
magnanimous
masochist
maudlin
mesmerize
metamorphosis
meticulous
misconstrue
mitigate
nebulous
notorious
objective
oblivious

obsequious
obtrusive
omnipotent
opportune
optimum
orthodox
ostentatious
panacea
paramount
perfunctory
permeate
placebo
plight
predisposed
presumptuous
proficient
prognosis
prolific
propensity
provocative
quandary
rancor
rebuke
recrimination
redeem
regress
reinstate
rejuvenate
relegate
relinquish
replete
reprehensible
repugnant
resilient
reticent
retribution
retrospect
robust
rudimentary
sanction

scoff
scrupulous
sedentary
sensory
sham
solace
solicitous
sordid
sporadic
squelch
standardize
staunch
stint
stringent
subordinate
subsidize
subversive
superficially
superfluous
symmetrical
synchronize
tenet
tenuous
terse
transgress
travesty
tumult
turbulent
ubiquitous
unprecedented
utilitarian
validate
vehement
venerate
verbose
vicarious
vindicate
vociferous
zealot
zenith

Notes